Transforming Environmentalism

Transforming Environmentalism

Warren County, PCBs, and the Origins of Environmental Justice

EILEEN MCGURTY

RUTGERS UNIVERSITY PRESS
New Brunswick, New Jersey, and London

Library of Congress Cataloging-in-Publication Data

McGurty, Eileen Maura.
    Transforming environmentalism : Warren county, PCBs, and the origins
of environmental justice / Eileen McGurty
        p.   cm.
    Includes bibliographical references and index.
    ISBN-13: 978-0-8135-3966-9 (hardover : alk. paper)
    1. Environmental justice—North Carolina—Warren County.
2. Environmentalism—North Carolina—Warren County.   3. Polychlorinated
biphenyls—Environmental aspects—North Carolina—Warren County—Case
studies.   I. Title.
    GE235.N8M35   2007
    363.7009756'52—dc22   2006010752

A British Cataloging-in-Publication record for this book is available from the
British Library

Manufactured in the United States of America

Contents

List of Tables and Figures

Preface

My first job after graduating from college in 1983 was with the Bronx River Restoration Project, an organization that worked to improve the water quality of the Bronx River, restore and remediate the land adjacent to the river, and develop more opportunities and access to the river for communities in the South Bronx. At the time, I had a belief that the social and economic issues facing these communities related to the environmental quality of their neighborhoods and that the creation of vital communities demanded that both social and environmental problems be addressed in concert. I did not have words to fully explain this view, but it seemed obvious to me that social justice could not be achieved without environmental justice. By the time I returned to graduate school in the early 1990s, an entire new movement dealing with these relationships had emerged. There was a clear articulation of the experiences I had while working in communities in the South Bronx and throughout the New York metropolitan area. The naming of the movement gave me a language to explore the issues and connected my perspective to that of others. I started to ask how, when, and why the naming occurred and kept returning to the Warren County events as a central part of that process.

In this study, I attempt to unpack the formation process of environmental justice and use the Warren County case as a lens into that process. In chapter 1, I describe the salience that Warren County has for the movement identity and also lay out the theoretical framework of social movements that shapes the study. In chapter 2, I explore the complex and rocky regulatory landscape that had emerged to manage toxics and hazardous waste, in response to the environmental movement's framing of the environmental risk from industrial production. Chapter 3 is an explication of the initial collective action in Warren County with a focus on the Not-in-My-Backyard (NIMBY) frame that citizens used. While parochial and limited, the NIMBY activism was essential to the subsequent development of the environmental justice frame. Chapter 4 examines the shift in strategy and identity that occurred in Warren County in 1982 and enabled the articulation of environmental racism. The chapter focuses on availability and construction of political opportunities, social networks, disruptive action, and collective identity. In chapter 5, I trace the influence that the Warren County framing had on the development of the environmental justice movement and argue that its trajectory had contradictory effects on the movement, both expanding and constricting movement opportunities. Chapter 6 illustrates these tensions in the environmental justice movement by returning to Warren County. Ten years after the initial events, the landfill was creating major public health threats and citizens renewed their activism to resolve the crisis. In the epilogue, I try to show that, despite the contradictions in environmental justice, the movement provides many reasons to hope that a new, more sustainable industrial practice can be created.

No book is written by a single individual; the research and writing process is always a group effort. I am indebted to many for ideas, support, and encouragement. First, the citizen activists in Warren County opened their homes and hearts to me, trusted me with their words, and encouraged me to tell their story. I hope that my rendering of their experiences does justice to the gifts that they gave me. In addition to local activists, many others agreed to be interviewed and provided me with necessary documents. The North Carolina Department of Environment and Natural Resources, Division of Waste Management, the Department of Crime Control and Public Safety, and the office for the Warren County PCBs Working Group were particularly patient with all my many, many questions. Several people helped me track down details, especially Tracy Hopkins at the Environmental Protection Agency Superfund program.

The ideas in the book were formed over several years and are the product of many fruitful conversations with colleagues. My dissertation committee at the University of Illinois at Urbana-Champaign, Eliza

Steelwater, Lewis Hopkins, Daniel Schneider, and Geraldo Munck, provided a rich intellectual environment to nurture my nascent ideas and never faltered in their support. At the University of Southern California, Greg Hise, David Sloane, and Martin Kreiger challenged me to extend and develop my arguments. Several scholars have read various parts of the book: Diane Glave, Mark Stoll, Laura Pulido, Carolyn Merchant, Rabel Burge, Tara Clapp, Michael Heiman, and Craig Colten. Arnab Chakraborty produced wonderful maps, and I am grateful to Jenny Labalme for allowing me to use her photos. At Rutgers University Press, Audra Wolfe gave me much needed guidance throughout the entire process of producing the manuscript. Nicole Manganaro, Kendra Boileau, Beth Kressel, and Barbara Glassman provided excellent editorial support.

The completion of this project has required more than just intellectual effort. Antoinette Golding and Mae Thomas opened their home and hearts to me during my many trips to North Carolina. Tina Woiski, Kellie Johnston, Steve Krantz, and my entire family gave me constant support that kept me on the right track. My parents continue to inspire me, through their example, to work for justice. My life partner, Jane Peterson, was unwavering in her faith in me, never tired of reading just one more draft, and helped me keep things in perspective with her wonderful sense of humor.

Transforming Environmentalism

1 | The Significance of Warren County

In the summer of 1978, Robert Burns and his two sons, who operated a waste-hauling company, drove tanker trucks along the state roads in rural North Carolina and remote sections of Fort Bragg Military Reservation. Driving at night to avoid detection, they opened the bottom valve of the tanks and discharged PCB-contaminated liquid, removed from the Ward Transformer Company in Raleigh, onto the soil along the road shoulders. This violation of the Toxic Substance Control Act (TSCA) continued for nearly two weeks until 240 miles of road shoulders were contaminated. Robert Ward had hired the Burnses to illegally dispose of the PCB-contaminated liquid in an attempt to avoid the escalating cost of disposal due to new regulations governing the disposal of PCBs.[1] North Carolina, responsible for remediation of the state-owned road shoulders, quickly devised a plan to construct a landfill in Warren County, a rural area in the northeastern section of the state. A Warren County farmer in the small community of Afton, facing foreclosure and bankruptcy, sold his property to the state to be used to contain the forty thousand cubic yards of contaminated soil from the road shoulders.

The announcement of the disposal site sparked intense resistance from county residents concerned with possible contamination of their groundwater and the potential threat to economic development from the stigma of a hazardous waste facility. Residents in Warren County fought three years of legal battles against North Carolina and

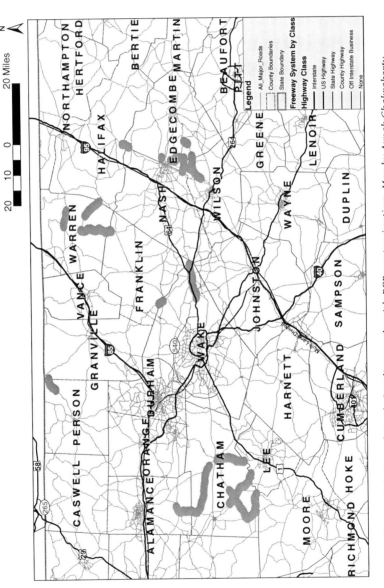

Figure 1.1. Map of North Carolina roads with PCB contamination. *Map by Arnab Chakraborty.*

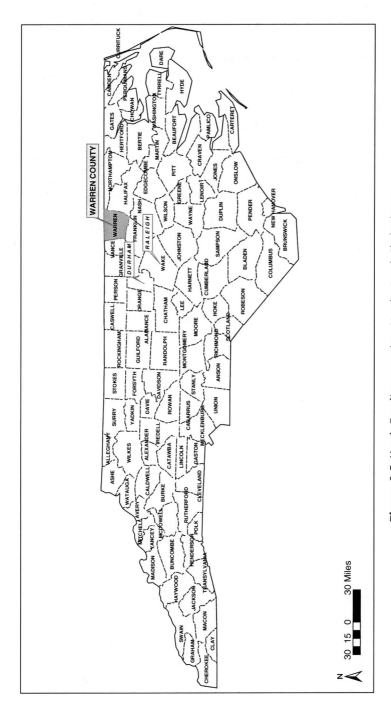

Figure 1.2. North Carolina counties. *Map by Arnab Chakraborty.*

the United States Environmental Protection Agency (EPA) in hopes of stopping the landfill. The resistance was unsuccessful, and in the summer of 1982 the state began construction of the landfill. With all the legal recourses exhausted, Warren County residents decided to mount disruptive collective action at the landfill site. With the start of the demonstrations, the protesters shifted their primary rationale for opposing the landfill site. While threats to groundwater and the local economy were still worries for them, the protesters argued that the site was chosen because the county was predominately African American and poor. As one activist put it, "The community was politically and economically unempowered. That was the reason for the siting. They took advantage of poor people of color."[2] The citizens garnered support from regional and national civil rights leaders and organized protest events daily during the six-week period while soil was delivered to the landfill. The unrelenting protests resulted in a delay and disruption of the landfill project, but they ultimately failed to stop the landfill.

Despite falling short of the immediate objective, protesters in Warren County had wider-reaching impacts. Residents in Warren County, supported by civil rights leaders with authority and power on the national stage, questioned the spatial and social distribution of environmental risks as well as the procedural inequities that perpetuated these risks. When these ideas moved into the public discourse, they resonated deeply with many poor people of color across the country, who were confronted with various forms of environmental risk. The environmental justice movement embodies these concerns, questioning the equitable distribution of environmental costs and benefits, the role of the environmental establishment in creating inequities in environmental risk, asserting the need to ameliorate environmental problems in concert with the alleviation of poverty and oppression, and the potential for eliminating sources of contamination at the point of production as a means of achieving these ends.

The landfill remained in Warren County, and in 1993 the state announced a potential crisis because one million gallons of water was sitting at the bottom of the landfill, threatening its ability to contain the contamination. With the power of the environmental justice movement behind them, citizens demanded to be full participants in the state's decision making about how to handle the crisis and forced the state into action. In 2003, after ten years of citizen-state negotiation, North Carolina began a process to destroy the PCBs in the landfill while avoiding shipment of any contaminated materials to another community. The success in securing their demands demonstrates the impact environmental justice had on environmental decision making. By examining the full story of Warren County, from the initial dumping of PCB contamination in 1978 to the remediation plan implemented in 2003, this study explores the development of environmental justice activism from its early stages to its current expression. This study is an attempt to unpack the meanings about environment and justice that are associated with the Warren County events, demonstrate how and why these ideas were constructed in that particular place and time, and examine how the meanings that emerged from Warren County have influenced the development of the movement and its impact on policy.

Twenty years of the environmental justice movement have deeply impacted environmentalism in all arenas, including traditional environmental organizations, emerging environmental justice groups, and governmental agencies responsible for implementing environmental legislation. In 2000 there were an estimated four hundred environmental justice groups, working on issues from toxic waste to urban sprawl. In addition, numerous regional and national support organizations provide technical and legal assistance to the local actions of the smaller groups.[3] The traditional environmental organizations, criticized for their disregard for unequal distribution of environmental risks and neglect of the impact of environmental issues on the poor and people of color, now boast active environmental justice programs. The Natural Resources Defense Council collaborates with local groups to halt the siting of hazardous waste facilities in poor communities, to increase the number of urban parks, and to secure an adequate supply of drinking water for indigenous people. The Sierra Club, with a legacy of exclusionary membership policies and emphasis on wilderness preservation, works to remove lead paint from houses in Detroit, to test air quality in Memphis, and to halt additional industrial emissions in areas with very poor air quality. Government agencies, also an early target of criticism by environmental justice advocates, are replete with programs: the Office of Environmental Justice at the Environmental Protection Agency oversees the implementation of Executive Order 12898, "Federal Actions to Address Environmental Justice in Minority Populations and Low-Income Populations;" Housing and Urban Development's Office of Community Planning and Development concentrates its environmental justice efforts in lead abatement, brownfield redevelopment, and economic development in Empowerment Zones; and the Department of Transportation's Federal Highway Administration issued guidelines to insure that minority and low-income communities do not experience high-impact and adverse environmental effects from highway projects.

These transformations of American environmental practice emerged directly from the success of the environmental justice movement. Environmental justice, moreover, owes much to the Warren County activists. For movement activists, the events in Warren County were tied to the emergence of the movement itself: "Out of that struggle [in Warren County], a national and international awareness of the disposal of hazardous and toxic waste took place. As a result of that struggle, many communities around this country have been able to successfully organize and stop the disposal of hazardous and toxic waste in their communities."[4] Scholars also argue that the Warren County events contributed to the emergence of environmental justice: "[Warren County] signaled the possibilities for a new kind of environmental protest."[5] Even policy makers see Warren County as a significant place in the formation of environmental justice: "The 1982 demonstration against the siting of a polychlorinated biphenyl (PCB) landfill in Warren County, North Carolina, was a watershed event in the environmental equity movement."[6]

Environmental justice activists often point to Warren County as a formative event for the movement. Whether this is true in a literal sense is less important than the meanings that movement participants and observers attach to the events. As Aldon Morris recognizes in *The Origins of the Civil Rights Movement*, "any attempt to date a social movement is risky."[7] Pinpointing an origin does not imply that a social movement is unrelated to prior events but emphasizes that a radical change in the collective identity and movement strategy occurred. The crystallization of a social movement signifies not a moment in time so much as a transformation in the understanding of the problems and solutions, the empowerment of new social networks, and promotion of disruptive action as a means to bring about those solutions. For Morris, the June 1953 bus boycotts in Baton Rouge, Louisiana, marked the transformative moment for the modern civil rights movement because "it was the first time that large masses of blacks directly confronted and effectively disrupted the normal functioning of groups and institutions thought to be responsible for their oppression."[8] For environmental justice, Warren County was not the first time citizens challenged the equity of an environmental decision, nor was it the first articulation of a relationship between environmental quality and social oppression. The Warren County events, however, were significant in the crystallization of environmental justice in three ways: opponents of a hazardous waste landfill were arrested for civil disobedience, people of color were involved in a disruptive collective action against environmental regulatory agencies, and national-level civil rights activists supported an environmental issue through disruptive collective action. While these issues may seem commonplace twenty years after the Warren County controversy, at the time, the events signaled a transformation in environmental ideas and practice.

The importance of Warren County for the development of the movement cannot be overemphasized. The events, and the meanings that they embody, represent to environmental justice activists what the controversy over the Hetch Hetchy dam in the early twentieth century represents for traditional environmentalists. The fight to save the Hetch Hetchy Valley in the Sierra Nevada did not begin the movement to preserve wild lands from development, nor were the preservationists successful in stopping the dam. The events surrounding Hetch Hetchy, however, gave expression to deeply held beliefs, articulated a problem, provided a clear vision for a solution to that problem, and inspired others to work toward making the vision a reality. The same could be said about significant events in the formation of any social movement. According to Tarrow, social movements are "collective challenges by people with common purposes and solidarity in sustained interaction with elites, opponents and authorities."[9] In order for a movement to crystallize, then, it must articulate the common purpose, create a mechanism for building solidarity among movement participants, and allow for the development of ongoing strategic collective action. This process of defining collective identity, building social networks, and taking action does not occur spontaneously, nor does it emerge fully formed at a particular moment in time but is driven by political, cultural, and economic factors. The Warren County case demonstrates a significant aspect of this dynamic process for environmental justice.

Much of the discussion about the events in Warren County and their importance for the movement can be traced to an article by Geiser and Waneck written in 1983 for *Science for the People*.[10] The purpose of the article was to make complex scientific information about PCBs available to non-experts so that citizens could be a part of creating solutions to toxic contamination. In this way, the authors were participating in the development of the movement by emphasizing a central component of emerging environmental sentiment and activism: knowledge about science was essential to the management of contemporary risks. Armed with the full information about the science of PCBs, citizen action would overcome government ineptitude in implementing regulations, and Warren County was an example of community action forcing the government to protect citizens and the environment. The authors stressed that, although the activists did not stop the landfill, they made major strides in protecting citizens against future hazards by obtaining guarantees that no additional wastes would be put into the landfill, that the ground water would be monitored, and that the state would treat the waste in the landfill once technology became available. Geiser and Waneck told readers that citizens thought Warren County was chosen for the landfill site because the residents were mostly poor, black, and politically powerless, but the success of citizen action had less to do with the power of the environmental racism idea and more to do with citizens compelling government into action.

Geiser and Waneck gave the citizens automatic legitimacy and assumed that they painted an accurate assessment of the situation, reflecting the complex relationship of environmental activism to the role of science in creating change in environmental policies. On the one hand, Geiser and Waneck argued that activists should use science in their organizing because government agencies were not appropriately responding to the real threat from toxic chemicals that science was documenting. Their argument was built on a basic principle of modern environmentalism, built on the approach taken by Rachel Carson. In *Silent Spring*, she used existing scientific data to show that pesticides in general and specifically DDT were hazardous to both wildlife and human health. On the other hand, the authors made no attempt to validate the idea that the state planned to make Warren County into a center for the hazardous waste industry or to understand the process that might lead the state to choose a poor, black community for the landfill. Since the intention was to empower citizen action by showing what could happen when a community came together, armed with appropriate scientific information, to fight against toxic threats, these issues were not of concern. The authors concluded, "United and educated, the citizens of Warren County have developed a true sense of community and a heightened sense of community efficacy."[11] The article downplayed the highly complex social and political factors that led to the activism in Warren County in favor of a narrative that emphasized the power that citizens could wield when knowledgeable and organized.

In *Dumping in Dixie*, Robert Bullard introduces his exploration of black environmental activists with the story of Warren County. Bullard uses the information from the Geiser and Waneck article but emphasizes that the protests occurred in a community of mostly black residents and through the leadership of black activists. For Bullard, the importance of the Warren County events was not just community organizing using science to help their cause, as it was for Geiser and Waneck. The significance of the events emerged from the "[i]ndigenous black institutions, organizations, leaders, and networks . . . coming together against polluting industries and discriminatory environmental policies."[12] Bullard sees Warren County as "the first national protest by blacks on the hazardous waste issue" that "focused national attention on toxics in the black community."[13]

Bullard's rendering of the Warren County story and its importance, built on the article by Geiser and Waneck, became the primary lens for understanding the events and a centerpiece of the historical narrative of the environmental justice movement. As such, this story became critical to activists' understanding of their identity as members of the environmental justice movement. A review of websites and activist publications shows that explanations of environmental justice often begin by recounting a history of the movement, and the story of Warren County figures prominently in these historical narratives.[14] Warren County holds an iconic position in the movement, representing for many members both the essence of environmental justice and its potential. The mythological story of Warren County goes something like this: "PCBs were illegally dumped along the roads in North Carolina. The state decided to build a landfill in Warren County because it had little political clout due to the high percentage of African Americans living there. When faced with the threat to their well-being, African Americans, along with some whites, mounted a powerful protest with over five hundred arrests during the month while the dump trucks brought contaminated soil to the landfill. Civil rights leaders aided the locals in creating meaningful direct action. The protesters put their bodies on the line by lying down in front of the trucks in order to stop the soil delivery. The landfill was not stopped, but the events drew national attention and sparked the movement of people of color fighting against environmental injustices."

Recounting the story in this way serves three functions, each of which are critical to the formation and development of a social movement. First, the narrative constructs an identity of the present by explaining the past. In this way, knowing "who we are" is tied directly to knowing "where we come from." The narrative identifies environmental justice activists as a local group of oppressed citizens fighting against government imposition of an environmental threat. Secondly, the Warren County story creates a unified vision of environmental justice that overcomes any potential fragmentation. Potential participants can see themselves in the common experience of "being dumped on," enabling the necessary social networks and movement-wide structures. Lastly, the narrative uses the past to point to a future. Warren County holds the potential of what the movement can become. It is filled with courageous people, willing to take any risk—being run over by a truck or spending time in jail—in order to create an environmentally just future. The future-orientation of the narrative underscores the need for movements to be engaged in action, not solely focused on construction of meanings. Warren County, as a myth, weaves together identity construction and strategy development, the two central components of social movement practice.

The story of Warren County functions mythologically by providing a communal explanation of the environmental justice movement. The elements of the story are not incorrect, but some details are emphasized while other details are either excluded or not even investigated. It is important to know that local citizens took action; the action was related to their experience of oppression and the environmental threat that deepened that oppression; the events had an impact by causing a major disruption with a large number of arrests and bodies on the road; and civil rights leaders participated in the protests, legitimizing the activists' experience of a connection between marginalization and environmental risks. Additional details of the story have not been fleshed out: How did the organizers mobilize hundreds of people to take such large risks? What motivated civil rights leaders to participate in a local land use conflict? How and when did citizens embrace a relationship between their oppression and the landfill siting? What process led decision makers to site the landfill in Warren County? Exploring some of these details, as I have attempted in this book, can illuminate why the Warren County events carry such significance for the movement and what impact these ideas had on solving the problems the movement named.

Civil Rights and the Critique of Modern Environmentalism

Environmental justice gave a new language to activists working to improve the quality of life of people of color while it also expanded the definition of traditional environmentalism. Minority communities had long been involved in improving the conditions in their neighborhoods. For example, efforts to improve housing, reduce trash, and reclaim vacant lots in poor urban neighborhoods were a significant part of the overall endeavors to improve the quality of life of poor people of color. Rarely, however, were these activities labeled environmental action; they were more often described as community organizing or neighborhood development. With the emergence of the environmental justice movement, community activists had an additional name, "environmental," for the work they had been doing for many years.[15] The new identity did not come easily, however. While the principles of the environmental movement were beginning to permeate public consciousness, creating new cultural understandings of the human-nature relationship, community organizers and civil rights activists had long critiqued environmentalism and environmental policy for its racism, exclusion, and elitism.[16] The potential negative social impacts of both environmental degradation and regulatory policies were part of environmental discussions since the onset of the modern environmental era. Prior to the Warren County events, activists did not envision overcoming these conflicts by demanding to be part of the environmental movement and to participate in creating environmental solutions. After the Warren County events, however, the activists changed their relationship to environmentalism by demanding to be part of it rather than just dismissing it.

Although specific cases vary, evidence indicates that the processes of environmental degradation and social marginalization are interwoven in various cultural and historical contexts.[17] In the United States, discussions about the disproportionate impact of environmental degradation and environmental reform on the poor and people of color occurred in full force in the late 1960s when "environmentalist" became a meaningful identity and part of the public discourse. The ideological clashes between "those who seek environmental quality" and "those who seek social justice" emerged as a concrete conflict over the exclusive membership and staff of major environmental organizations and the regressive impacts of certain environmental policies.[18]

Soon after the 1970 Earth Day euphoria, many claimed that environmentalism had been a fad and was on the way out. To counter this attack, environmentalists tried to demonstrate that environmentalism appealed to a broad constituency. Common speculation held that environmental organizations had an elite membership and staff. This supposition led to one of two conclusions. Either environmental organizations explicitly excluded the poor and people of color or the environmental agenda simply was not relevant to their lives. These suspicions of elitism were confirmed in 1973 when the EPA commissioned the National Center for Voluntary Action (NCVA) to examine environmental volunteerism with the goal of strengthening the movement. The study found that newly formed groups, as well as older "conservation" organizations that had recently changed their priorities and approaches, were staffed primarily by "middle-class, professional, white, married men in their thirties."[19]

The NCVA realized that this narrow base of support was a potential obstacle for the environmental movement. Modern environmentalism introduced several principles that challenged the prevailing views of the natural world and called for a transformation in the way that society viewed nature. One key point that challenged the predominant reductionist and static view emphasized that the different elements of the natural world were linked in a system of synergistic relationships. If this were the case, environmentalists argued, all environmental problems affected everyone, no matter where the problem was initially manifest or who was immediately impacted.[20] In order for the environmental movement to be effective, it had to appeal to a wider range of constituents. The NCVA strongly encouraged organizations to consider the needs of the poor, especially poor minorities in urban areas; however, the report only addressed these concerns in one of its twenty-eight recommendations. The NCVA wanted Volunteers in Service to America (VISTA) to include volunteers for work on environmental issues. Anticipating the argument that such work might divert funds from other social projects, its leaders suggested a separate and independent arm for environmental volunteers. By separating the two programs, the recommendation gave credence to the view that environmental degradation and poverty should be seen as isolated issues with different solutions.

The lack of diversity in the membership of environmental organizations was a concern even before the findings of the NCVA were published. In 1972 Tom Bradley, an African American member of the Los Angeles City Council and future mayor, asked members of the Sierra Club why "to many of our nation's 20 million blacks, the conservation movement has as much appeal as a segregated bus," especially since "the problems of poverty and environmental quality are inextricably interrelated."[21] A few months later, the Sierra Club conducted a survey of its members to determine which general direction the membership wanted the organization to take. In light of the ongoing claims of

elitism, the surveyors also felt compelled to document the socioeconomic backgrounds of their members. The average club member fit
the predicted profile exactly.[22] The club responded with the assertion
that, while all social groups were not represented in the membership,
the actions of the organization were taken on behalf of everyone. The
simpler and less destructive style of outdoor recreation advocated and
practiced by club members enabled more people to enjoy the outdoors.
The issue of access was not addressed. Instead, the club urged members to boost recruitment efforts among minorities and immediately
enroll anyone who thought the Sierra Club had restrictive membership policies. Despite these efforts, when the members were asked,
"Should the Club concern itself with the conservation problems of
such special groups as the urban poor and ethnic minorities?" the majority of members, 58 percent of respondents, did not agree. Posing the
question in terms of "special groups" contradicted the idea that Sierra
Club activities would benefit everyone, regardless of their association
with the organization. While actions to improve outdoor recreation
opportunities or increase wilderness acreage were seen as a benefit to
all, ameliorating urban environmental decay was not identified with
the betterment of all, only select "special groups." The environmental
problems of the "urban poor and ethnic minorities" belonged to them,
not to everyone.

With the survey results seemingly confirming charges of elitism,
the club found a glimmer of hope in younger members, who were more
likely to agree that the organization should be involved in issues of
concern to the urban poor. Another survey supported the club's hope
that attitudes about the relationship between poverty and environmentalism were changing. Eighty-eight percent of black high school seniors
polled in 1971 wanted to see increased federal involvement in controlling pollution. Concern for pollution among these students outranked
"eliminating poverty" (76 percent) or achieving school desegregation
(73 percent). This survey did not indicate decreasing elitism among
conservationists; instead, it indicated that environmental degradation
impacted the daily lives of people of color and that actions to improve
environmental conditions were not adequate.

The Audubon Society also felt compelled to ward off claims of
elitism, but it employed a different strategy. They embraced the underlying principle that environmental action was taken on behalf of
all because environmental issues were everyone's problems. However,
the society acknowledged that environmental activists were elite in

one sense: "Naturally the well-to-do are often best equipped to press these issues because [it] take[s] time, know-how and money. But this does not make the results less applicable to the people as a whole."[23] The suggestion that mainstream environmental organizations would act as a "vanguard" was a controversial proposition at best. Mobilizing resources—technical and political knowledge, time, and money— might be seen as the underlying problem facing social movements, but the solution did not necessarily lie in an elite leadership. Another approach might entail nurturing leadership among the poor and people of color, as well as empowering them to mobilize the necessary resources themselves.

The popular press highlighted the divide between white and black activists. In August 1970, just months after the first Earth Day, *Time* covered "The Rise of Anti-ecology."[24] While the article described a political backlash from both the left and the right, the piece mainly argued that "blacks are the most vocal opponents of all." First, a "black militant" was quoted: "I don't give a good goddam about ecology!" Next, the article quoted two influential black leaders, Carl Stokes, mayor of Cleveland, and Richard Hatcher, mayor of Gary, Indiana. Stokes argued that housing and food for the hungry should be priorities over clean air and water, and Hatcher echoed this sentiment: "The nation's concern with environment has done what George Wallace was unable to do: distract the nation from the human problems of black and brown Americans." This "trade-off" perspective posed economic survival and environmental amelioration as separate problems rather than focusing on the connections between economic deprivation and environmental degradation, as Tom Bradley had proposed to members of the Sierra Club, and it begged a serious question: who would pay for the cost of pollution control and cleanup? In particular, when the Nixon administration estimated that such an operation would require $2.4 billion, public outcries arose against tax increases and higher consumer prices. These impacts from environmental regulation appeared regressive and disproportionately harmful to the poor and people of color.[25] The critique of environmental regulations did not include a demand for more protection nor did it demand a vehicle for inclusion of minorities in environmental decision making.

Environmental justice emerged in the 1980s with a very different critique of environmental protection strategies. Environmentalists' critiques of industrial capital were established in the public consciousness and had led to a major shift in regulatory policies. The movement was successfully challenging the public's blind acceptance of progress, modernization, and industrial development by demonstrating that the by-products of industrial production could cause permanent, irreversible damage to humans and their life-support systems. Twenty years after the publication of Rachel Carson's *Silent Spring* and over a decade of burgeoning environmental protection policies, the principles of environmentalism were beginning to take hold in society.[26] Civil rights leaders, part of the society that was impacted by the environmentalist ideas, embraced an environmental aspect into the civil rights agenda, motivated by the nature of the toxic contamination, the national and local political landscape, and the direct conflict with government agencies responsible for environmentally-related decisions. As civil rights leaders with influence among African Americans and within the established political system integrated the new notion of environmental racism into their programs, the cause gained legitimacy and strength. Although the bulwark between civil rights and environmentalism began to weaken, the conflicts of the period from 1968 to 1975 did not completely disappear with the emergence of the contemporary environmental justice movement. As a result, the "marriage of social justice with environmentalism" remains a rocky union between ambivalent partners.

Environmental Justice
as a Social Movement

The flurry of disruptive collective action in the 1960s transformed the study of social movements from an explanation of the deviance of discontents to investigations that assumed social movement participants had legitimate political claims. The explanations for increased social movement activity, then, took two tacks. One approach, resource mobilization, focused on the "how" of social movements and uncovered their dynamic organizational, recruitment, and mobilizing structures.[27] The other approach asked "why are movements proliferating" and found the answer in the features of what Melucci calls "contemporary complex societies." These so-called "New Social Movements" de-emphasized class issues and attracted middle-class members who were not concerned with their daily bread so much as with the infiltration of modernization into their "life-spaces." As a result of the profile of activists and the shifting focus of their demands, scholars argued that the movements were more fluid in structure and less explicitly political than the "old" class-based movements, with organizations forming and reforming as the need for constructing and reinforcing meaningful life-spaces emerged from the onslaught of modernization.[28]

Upon closer scrutiny, however, the distinction between "old" and "new" movements blurred. While the old Left and its focus on union organizing and material demands was waning in the latter half of the twentieth century, many of the social and political aspects of movements were not new. For example, Calhoun showed that the so-called "new" movement structures and ideas were present in the nineteenth century.[29] Commonalities among movements with divergent ideological focuses can be identified when social movements are distinguished from other collective political actors like interest groups or political parties. Three factors differentiated movements: their level of organization, their relationship to established political systems, and their influence on the policy process. First, social movements are not always organized formally but are fluid, informal groups of challengers.[30] The clearly defined and tangible group is not as important as the continuing interaction between challengers and elites. Second, social movements exist on the margin of institutional politics, walking the line between politics and anti-politics. Movements use the logic of politics to devise strategies while, at the same time, they challenge the established political order in which they are participating.[31] As a disruptive form of politics, movements skirt the edges of the established political system but also can, and must, interact with the established order, even if, in the extreme case, the expressed goal of the movement is the eradication of that system. The power of movements to disrupt social and political norms comes from mass-mobilized protests or their threat. Collective action must create significant uncertainty about the length of the protest activities, the possibility that violence may develop, and the possibility that others may join or construct additional disruptive action.[32] Thirdly, movements influence the policy agenda, or "the list of subjects or problems to which governmental officials and people outside of government closely associated with those officials are paying some serious attention at any given time."[33] Social movements bring new issues into the political arena, and if the movement does not decline because of repression or defeat, those issues become part of the policy agenda. Political integration of new issues could lead to the demise of a successful social movement or the transformation into an interest group.[34] The inevitability of increasing bureaucratization, as predicted by the Weber-Michels theory, is uncertain, but the role of successful movements in transforming the agenda is undeniable.

Many studies about the formation processes of the environmental justice movement are grounded in the resource mobilization/new social movement dichotomy and focus either on organizational structures of environmental justice activism or the contested meanings about environmental identity as the bases of that activism. The resource mobilization approach to environmental justice sees environmental injustice as a resource allocation problem solely. For example, Pellow's study of garbage in Chicago argues that those "who are unable to mobilize resources (political, economic, etc.) will most likely bear the brunt of environmental inequalities."[35] Bullard's *Dumping in Dixie* has been the most influential study in the resource mobilization approach to environmental justice. He argues that as grievances and feelings of alienation of potential participants intensify with worsening conditions, individuals are more motivated to join the movement. Bullard also argues that accessibility for potential constituents is the key to successful organizing. His case studies concentrate on organizations, the memberships, the leadership, the specific actions in which they engage, and the outcomes of these activities. In the cases examined by Bullard, indigenous black institutions, well established prior to the environmental justice activism, initiated and sustained the structural conditions necessary for the development of environmental justice. By focusing on the organizational infrastructure and the struggle to secure necessary resources to mount an effective collective action, the contested meaning of problems is under-emphasized. Even the conflict between traditional environmentalism and environmental justice becomes an organizational problem from this perspective because the large environmental groups do not possess the internal mechanisms to work with people of color and the issues germane to their lives.

An alternative approach focuses on informational and symbolic systems through which grievances and goals are negotiated by members of the movement. The relationship of activists to environmental problems is not defined solely by the environmental issue, or only by a class position. Their environmental identity is shaped by the additional factors of their racial, ethnic, and gender positions. For example, Pulido's study of environmental organizing in the southwest among Latinos shows how both poverty and ethnic heritage heightened the exposure of farm workers to contamination, was the foundation of their rebellion, and informed their strategic choices.[36] In another example, Gottlieb demonstrates how women in anti-toxic activism, from their gendered positions, negotiated an environmental identity in "defense of community," unlike traditional environmentalism.[37] However, once constructed, the new identity, no matter what the origin of its social location, is viewed as an objective, coherent, unitary one rather than as continually negotiated within a social milieu.

If the central task of social movements is, as Tarrow contends, "coordinating, sustaining and giving meaning to collective action," then both constructing identities and mobilizing resources are important to movement formation.[38] The construction of the environmental justice identity, while it blends several social locations, depended on more than just the deterioration of environmental and social conditions in the places people of color lived and worked. The movement that emerged is constantly negotiating access to mobilizing resources while at the same time negotiating the meanings that form the environmental justice identity. Moreover, strategy and identity are tied in a dynamic interaction, not only in the formation of the movement but as it develops and transforms over time. Environmental justice, like all social movements, forms its identity through strategic choices and makes strategic choices based on collective identity.

The Construction and Impact of Environmental Justice

These two approaches to understanding movements, resource mobilization, and new social movements can be synthesized by examining four requirements for the development of movements: political opportunities, social networks, repertoires of action, and cultural frames. First, in order for a social movement to develop, favorable political shifts that improve the chances of success and lower the cost of organizing action are needed. The political system is most vulnerable immediately following the implementation of reforms or when reforms are about to be implemented. Collective action is most possible through partial access to power; full access is not necessary and could be a hindrance. Also, movements need influential allies to interact with institutions and decision makers in order for the movement to avoid repression and to gain an audience. The second requirement for movements is social networks that create organizational structures somewhere between hierarchy and anarchy. They must be flexible, informal, and emerge out of associations of everyday life. As reforms are attained, these mobilizing structures can retreat back to their "organic associations" in occupations, neighborhoods, or families, ready to form again into organizational structures of a social movement, if a renewed opportunity for successful challenge emerges. Third, disruptive action "obstructs the routine activities of opponents, bystanders or authorities" and must be fixed in tactics known and understood by potential constituents.[39] The task of collective action organizers is to create innovations on the recognized forms of action. In this way, potential participants are sufficiently familiar with the action to make participation more likely, but the threat of disorder and uncertainty still prevail. The challenge to movement organizers, then, is to push the norms of convention with disruptive tactics that do not engender militancy. The final requirement for social movements is framing: movements strategically choose symbols from existing cultural beliefs and use them to produce new modes of thinking through collective action. A frame "enables individuals to locate, perceive, identify and label" events.[40] Framing is simultaneously passive and active; social actors construct and maintain meanings for events but social processes establish the potential for meaning construction. A collective action frame shapes meaning for a specific action, and a master frame signifies meanings for an entire movement. Success demands that frames diagnose problems, attribute blame, and construct solutions. Master frames must, additionally, be easily flexible, elaborated and resonant with potential participants.

This study, building on the merging of the two approaches to studying social movements, explores each of these requirements, their interaction with each other, and the shifts in their manifestation over time. Political opportunities were opened through each of the three avenues. Hazardous and toxic waste reforms were in flux, due to the success in the environmental movement in creating emerging risk consciousness; changes in environmental legislation enabled citizens to influence environmental decision making; and shifts in African American politics provided powerful allies. The formation of environmental justice depended on both formal civil rights organizations and informal associations that had receded into the normal activities of daily life only to emerge again as a mobilizing force when the new opportunity arose. The actions in Warren County followed closely the repertoire established by civil rights activism several decades earlier. The routine, tone, and process of these actions were well-known to participants, both black and white, bystanders, and authorities. In order to produce the necessary disorder, the organizers created an innovation on the direct action approach that was honed in the earlier period.

In Warren County, the activists produced the environmental racism frame, an elaborative, potent, and resonant frame that enabled the development of the innovative master frame of environmental justice. The influence of the civil rights master frame on the development of environmental justice is undeniable. The introduction of rights-oriented demands—the right to accurate information, to democratic participation in decisions, right to a clean environment—transformed environmentalism. As the movement developed, however, the rights rhetoric created limitations for environmental justice. Many scholars have argued that the environmental justice master frame "amplif[ied] and extend[ed] mainstream environmental discourses."[41] This study explicates the process of developing that master frame and argues that while its flexibility appealed to a wide range of people, the potency of the frame was challenged by its initial "focus on the environmental inequality of marginalized people."[42]

The narrative I construct about Warren County shows a complicated and contested unfolding of new meanings for a movement that is fraught with fragmentation and disjuncture. While most writing about environmental justice attempts to unify it, Schlosberg argues that the disunity embodied in environmental justice is its strength: the "movement is constructed from difference, revels in that fact, and negates the importance of a singular history, experience, or ideology."[43] The decentralized structures that he studies point to the possibility of a new form of politics, a critical pluralism that can overcome the limitations of traditional liberal pluralism. My study supports Schlosberg's assertion that it is difficult to find a unity for the environmental justice movement. In unpacking the processes of forming the environmental justice identity and creating movement strategies, I hope to point to the full potential embedded in environmental justice: Any hope for a sustainable future must simultaneously address systems of social oppression and systems of environmental degradation. The environmental justice movement has brought us a long way on the path toward this future.

2 | Regulating Toxic Chemicals, PCBs, and Hazardous Waste

The formation of the environmental justice movement was linked to the political challenges waged in the 1960s and 1970s against modern science and technology in the face of seemingly uncontrollable "latent side effects."[1] Although the economy was burgeoning, several incidents of devastating health effects from contamination transformed the general public's understanding of industrial production. Rachel Carson's best-selling *Silent Spring*, published in 1962, was one of the most influential factors in cementing the public's concern about potential widespread, intergenerational damage from rampant and indiscriminant chemical use. Carson's scathing critique of pervasive pesticide use, especially DDT, highlighted not just the immediate health effects but the long-term impacts on wildlife and humans from bioaccumulation and biomagnification, which could lead to future unknown impacts. In addition to showing the evidence of the chemicals' invisible effects, she convincingly argued that authorities ignored available knowledge on adverse effects and did not pursue additional evidence about the human health and ecological problems from pesticides because business interests hindered rigorous and transparent investigation.[2]

Carson's book deeply resonated with many Americans and expressed many of the central tenets of the modern environmental movement. Carson articulated, and environmentalism amplified, the late-twentieth-century understanding of the dangers threatening society. In the past, danger emerged from the whims of an uncontrollable nature. Modern science and technology were supposed to bring order to nature and to provide estimations of the risks from nature so that they could be managed. It seemed, however, that the myriad effects of science created their own set of threats. These dangers—especially nuclear and chemical contamination—remained invisible, unknowable, and incalculable, despite the best efforts of science. The result was a deeply felt anxiety about the promise of modernization. Risks, not as probabilistic outcomes but as unknown future threats, began to define the way that people understood their world and themselves. The concept of risk was constructed when scientific skepticism, a foundational element of modernization, was turned inward to critique science, modernization, and the very idea of progress.[3] In this way, risks were not objective realities but were tied to values and in constant flux. Risks, along with the knowledge and institutions built around them, were never outside society and the construction of meaning. In Lupton's words, risks are "assemblages of meanings, logics, and beliefs cohering around material phenomena, giving these phenomena form and substance."[4]

Paradoxically, science remained an important part of creating solutions to environmental risks, despite its role in their production. The risk society emphasized that scientific knowledge was never neutral but was constructed within a particular social and cultural milieu. The scientized approach to environmental risks, therefore, created new knowledge about risks by asking different questions, by infusing the process of knowledge construction with different values, and by challenging the authority of the established scientific, social, and political institutions as the sole arbiters of truth about risks. The environmental movement was, in part, the creation of a new science, one that made values explicit, challenged the belief systems underlying scientific knowledge, and attempted to infuse the new perspective on risk into the political process. While the movement also legitimized non-expert knowledge about risks, the political dimension of environmentalism embodied debates among experts, using different assumptions and asking different questions about the potential future path of modernity.[5]

The environmental movement was successful in moving risk onto the policy agenda. However, in the process of creating a new environmental policy based on risk, the debate about the "truth" of the potential dangers underscored social and individual anxiety.[6] In addition, the regulatory framework that emerged for controlling environmental risk was fraught with uncertainty. The debates highlighted the fact that the heretofore legitimate social and political institutions had little certainty about how to protect public health and the environment from contamination. Although the public critique intensified, industry and government were reluctant to admit their culpability in creating risks and unwilling to change their practices. Extensive political compromises resulted from the tension between public consciousness of risk and institutional resistance to change, ending in several cumbersome laws. Implementation unfolded in relation to these tensions, as well, with extreme caution by government agencies, and at times, even obstruction of the legislative goals. The regulatory framework that emerged to manage environmental risks was a vulnerable system of complicated policies and incomplete regulations. In 1982, when the environmental justice movement crystallized, it was in the midst of this morass of anxiety, uncertainty, ambiguity, and political compromise.

Three federal environmental laws governed the decisions about the contaminated soil in North Carolina and the landfill in Warren County. The Toxic Substances and Control Act (TSCA) of 1976 controlled the disposal of PCBs and shaped the decisions about the cleanup and the landfill siting. Hazardous waste management, mandated under the Resource Conservation and Recovery Act (RCRA) of 1976, became an indirect but important part of the controversy. According to the regulations, PCB contamination was "chemical waste," subject to TSCA, not "hazardous waste." The technical distinction was unimportant to opponents, who challenged the entire strategy of containing wastes in landfills as a solution to the industrial waste problem. Also, the contaminated road shoulders became one of the first sites to be eligible for Superfund cleanup money after passage of the Comprehensive Environmental Response, Compensation, and Liability Act (CERCLA, also known as Superfund) in 1980. A quick and easy solution for the North Carolina contamination became imperative as the Superfund program was drawn into intense controversy.

The passage of each of these bills illustrates the tensions between growing public criticism of industrial production and the resistance from government and industry to embrace the new understanding of risk. The tensions between these competing views about risk also impacted the implementation of the laws. The dilatory implementation began under Carter, driven in part by the administration's concern about inflationary impacts of increasing environmental regulations and the EPA's emphasis on water and air programs. After the election of Reagan in 1980, the entire hazardous waste and toxics programs nearly came to a halt. When Reagan came to power, very little had been implemented, leaving the toxic substances and hazardous waste programs vulnerable to deep reductions of federal spending and "regulatory relief" for industry. The public supported relaxation of regulations in general but not when it came to regulating toxic industrial pollution. The environmental justice movement formed on this shaky regulatory structure and vulnerable administration.

The Toxic Substances and Control Act

For years, the Ward Transformer Company emptied the fluid from their transformers and flushed the waste into a sewage treatment plant or hired a hauler to take the waste to a landfill that accepted industrial waste. The owner, Robert Ward, might have paid $2 to $5 per ton for disposal. On April 18, 1978, just four months before he hired the Burnses to dump the PCBs on the road, TSCA's final rules for disposal and marking of PCBs became effective and completely transformed waste management of PCB.[7] Under the new rules, the responsibility, liability, and direct costs for Ward, the waste transporter, and the incinerator operator skyrocketed. The removal of dielectric fluid from the transformers was no longer a simple matter but became a major operating expense and management issue. Ward was not the only "midnight dumper" that attempted an easy way around the new regulations. However, as part of the events that led to the Warren County landfill controversy, Ward's attempt to circumvent the TSCA rules contributed to the formation of the environmental justice movement that challenged the underlying principles of those rules. Regulation of PCBs emerged at the end of a five-year debate about the need to control the toxic effects of chemicals in commercial production. The Toxic Substances Control Act of 1976 (TSCA), designed to reorient environmental regulations toward preventing contamination, banned future manufacture of PCBs, severely limited continued use of PCBs, and regulated their disposal.

PCBs are synthetic aromatic compounds consisting of two connected hexagonal rings of carbon (benzene) with up to five chlorine atoms attached to each ring. There are 209 possible structural arrangements, called congeners, depending on the number and position of chlorine, each with distinct chemical properties. In general, PCBs have low flammability, low electrical conductivity, and a high degree of chemical stability, which made them attractive for commercial use in a myriad of industrial applications. PCBs used in industry were complex mixtures composed of up to 50 or 60 congeners, depending on the application. From 1929 to 1977, approximately 700,000 tons of PCB mixtures were manufactured in the United States, almost exclusively by Monsanto under the commercial name of Aroclors. The majority of PCBs were used in electrical applications, primarily in fluids for transformers and capacitors. PCBs also were used in hydraulic and heat transfer systems, lubricants, gasket sealers, paints, plasticizers, adhesives, carbonless copy paper, flame retardants, brake linings, and asphalt.[8] The qualities that made PCBs a commercial success also led to many of the environmental and health hazards associated with their use. Since PCBs are stable compounds, they remain in the environment nearly in perpetuity. They are not water soluble, and once released, they adsorb to the organic components of soils and sediments. They easily accumulate in sediments, which allows for easy entry into the food chain, where they lodge in fatty tissues of organisms. Organisms retain the chemicals through the process of bioaccumulation. These chemicals are also biomagnified, by increasing the concentration at each successive trophic level in the food chain.

The first government attempt to address concerns about potential problems with burgeoning chemical use came in 1971 when a report from the Council on Environmental Quality (CEQ) advocated legislation to manage chemicals prior to their use and production. CEQ argued that the nation "need no longer remain in a purely reactive posture with respect to toxic substances. We should no longer be limited to repairing the damage after it has been done; nor should we continue to allow the entire population be used as a laboratory."[9] The report demonstrated that the cumulative effects of all toxic substances were impossible to quantify and that science knew very little about effects from long-term exposures to the myriad chemicals entering the environment. Scientists were more confident that industrial centers had the highest incidences of cancer and could be linked to "environmental factors." When David Hall, Director of the National Institute for Environmental Health Science, told the Congressional committee reviewing the Toxic Substances Control Act, "This problem constitutes possibly the major health hazard of this decade," he reinforced the idea that something was deeply wrong with the systems that enabled uncontrolled industrial production.[10]

In 1972, 1973, and 1974, Congress attempted unsuccessfully to pass a toxic substance bill. The impasse was attributed to lobbying from the chemical industry. The extent of the industry's influence prompted

Senator Tunney (D-CA) to proclaim, "I have never seen such an effective lobbying effort as was done against this legislation."[11] Cost estimates of the proposed legislation varied: Dow Chemical expected a $2 billion price tag; the Manufacturing Chemists Association thought it would cost $1.3 billion. Government estimates were significantly lower: EPA projected $80–$140 million, and the General Accounting Office (GAO) calculated $100–$200 million. No study included the savings to society from costs offset by avoiding contamination or attempted to determine whether the initial costs for screening chemicals would be greater than the long-term financial benefits.[12] Congress took up the legislation at the next session, a time of heightened public concern about chemical contamination. The tension between a new social understanding of risk and industrial resistance to change did not disappear, but intensified risk consciousness created significant political pressure for action.

Extensive media coverage of the dangers of vinyl chloride was a primary source of the increased anxiety. Vinyl chloride, a gaseous synthetic compound made from petroleum, was used to make polyvinyl chloride, the basis of many plastics. In 1974 doctors linked vinyl chloride to liver cancer in workers in a Goodrich plant in Louisville, Kentucky, and in a Union Carbide plant in West Virginia. The Occupational Safety and Health Administration (OSHA) immediately decreased allowable worker exposure from 500 parts per million to 50 parts per million and eventually lowered it to 1 part per million. Industry opposed the new limits, claiming the rule was "medically unnecessary, technologically unfeasible, and would lead to the loss of 2.2 million jobs."[13] Soon after, scientists found evidence that vinyl chloride was also mutagenic and possibly responsible for miscarriages. Vinyl chloride also put other populations at risk since many consumer products contained the substance, particularly aerosol sprays and food wrap. Under consumer pressure, Clairol voluntarily recalled several hair spray products in April 1974, and a few months later, the Consumer Product Safety Commission banned additional aerosol products, including hair sprays and spray paints. Dow Chemical, the makers of Saran Wrap, took a different approach and denied that consumers would be exposed to vinyl chloride by using their product. Although vinyl chloride was used to manufacture Saran Wrap and workers were exposed to it, the company claimed that it was inert in consumer products, despite the paucity of data about the health effects.

Potential devastating effects of other chemicals also played a significant role in the hearings about TSCA. Committee members introduced newspaper accounts from around the country of at least nineteen chemicals with potential dangers for public health.[14] The House and Senate committees also watched the CBS documentary "The American Way of Cancer," which had initially aired on October 15, 1975. The film examined exposure of average Americans to potentially carcinogenic chemicals and argued that "we have spent millions of dollars in this country looking for cancer cures but evidence now indicates that the way to lick cancer may be to prevent it."[15] The broadcast of the documentary in prime time television underscored for members of Congress that Americans were shifting their attitudes about risk and the need to regulate the chemical industry. President Ford signed TSCA into law on October 11, 1976, and despite opposition from the Office of Management and Budget, he called it "one of the most important pieces of environmental legislation that has been enacted by the Congress."[16]

The compromise resulted in a complicated and cumbersome set of mandates. First, EPA had to publish an inventory of all known chemicals. After publication of the inventory, industry had to notify the EPA of all new chemicals or new uses of chemicals ninety days prior to commercial introduction. The notification process required companies to submit results of any studies about the substance but did not require specific studies to be completed. Only after the notification was submitted could EPA ask for specific testing. The law also mandated the EPA to ask for testing of chemicals already in use, as recommended by the Interagency Testing Committee. EPA was to then determine if the chemical posed an "unreasonable risk" to society. TSCA mandated EPA to determine unreasonable risk by weighing the benefits gained from the new substance against the potential health effects, the risks posed by alternative substances, and the possible health or economic consequences from regulation of the substance. If the EPA determined that a chemical posed an unreasonable risk, the agency could mandate special labeling and handling procedures on products containing the chemical, restrict the use of the chemical to particular types of products or limited amounts, or could ban the chemical outright.

The obstacles in developing a methodology to determine "unreasonable risk" highlighted the value-laden process of scientific investigation and risk management. In attempting to build knowledge to assess risk, scientists tended to make several assumptions that could easily be challenged. They assumed that cancer was the best indicator of health effects, that only a clinical illness was a legitimate manifestation of harm, that all people responded to chemicals in the same way, and that chemicals behaved independently rather than synergistically. In part, these assumptions were dictated by the limitations of the science, but belief systems also played a role in constraining the assessment of risk. Despite the assumptions, experts who quantified risks argued that any understanding outside their calculus was irrational and counter-productive regardless of its own inherent rationality based on different understanding of the world. Not only was knowledge about present and future health and ecological effects limited, but the economic impacts of these latent effects were also unknown. The full economic benefits could not be determined because the full economic costs were incalculable.[17]

When Senator Gaylord Nelson (D-WS) and Representative John Dingell (D-MI) introduced amendments to TSCA to regulate PCBs, these chemicals stood out in the public's view among the 80,000 chemicals in commercial production that warranted immediate action; the amendment faced little opposition. An incident of contamination in Japan demonstrated the damage that PCBs could cause. In 1968 more than 1,600 people ingested rice oil contaminated with PCBs from a leak in a factory pipe. Reported health effects included dermatitis, hyper-pigmentation of the skin, aches and pain, severe headaches, central nervous system and peripheral nerve damage, stomach and liver disorders, and death. By 1975, seven years after the initial incident in Japan and during the time of the TSCA hearings, epidemiologists reported that victims still experienced fatigue, severe headaches, and numbness in limbs. Researchers also found increased incidences of liver cancer, and children born to affected mothers showed decreased birth weight and impaired intellectual development.[18] Despite the growing data about exposure to PCBs, scientists stressed the paucity of information and reinforced the public's anxiety. Not only were the potential health effects from PCBs severe, but by the mid-1970s, PCBs were ubiquitous, showing up in all regions of the globe, including the Artic and Antarctica.[19] In 1975 EPA estimated that 45 percent of the population had PCBs in their tissue. In 1977 the estimate increased to 90 percent of the population. The quick increase in the estimated body burden related to the ability of PCBs to bioaccumulate and biomagnify, indicating that it could take a significant time after the ban went into effect to see a change in exposure risk. The news coverage consistently compared PCBs to DDT, not only because they are related chemically but also because they embodied the same cultural meaning. PCBs symbolized the critique of industrial society that the environmental movement articulated. The miracle chemical that helped electricity fuel a vast expansion of the economy turned out to cause havoc, in unknown proportions, to people and environments.

PCBs entered the environment through various pathways, and several cases of contamination reinforced the severity of the problem. Two of General Electric's (GE) capacitor plants on the Hudson River discharged at least 84,000 pounds of PCBs directly into the river. GE also caused the discharge of 1.3 million pounds of PCBs from bedrock fractures at the GE Hudson Falls plant.[20] PCB-contaminated poultry feed led to the destruction of hundreds of thousands of animals in Texas, North Carolina, West Virginia, and New York. In 1970 PCBs were found in food packaging, apparently from leaks in a cardboard recycling facility that produced packages for noodles and cereals. In 1971 the Food and Drug Administration (FDA) reported finding PCBs in 500 out of 15,000 samples of food. Half of the contaminated samples were fish, but the report solidified the fear that food containers on the shelves of the neighborhood grocery store were contaminated with PCBs. The FDA thought a ban on PCBs was going too far but pressure from consumer groups and Congress led them to eliminate sources of PCBs from food processing and packaging facilities. Monsanto, the sole manufacturer of PCBs in the United States, supported this action as it coincided with their own decision to halt production of PCBs for use in hydraulic fluid and plasticizers. Monsanto continued manufacturing materials containing PCBs for electric transformers, which accounted for nearly 99 percent of all production of PCBs, but support for eliminating PCBs from food processing and packaging facilities made it appear that the company also supported government controls on chemical manufacturing.

Two additional discoveries gave PCBs their final blow. First, contamination of fish in states that depended on the commercial and sports fishery industries caused significant economic disruption. In the Great Lakes, for example, commercial fishing was a $95-million annual industry and $350 million per year was spent on sports fishing.[21] Senator Nelson and Representative Dingell highlighted the economic implications of contamination for Wisconsin and Michigan when they introduced the PCB amendment. Second, the lipophilic quality of PCBs allowed for easy accumulation in breast milk, causing researchers to examine the impact on nursing babies. Scientists found that infant monkeys nursing from mothers with contaminated breast milk developed skin discoloration, loss of eyelashes, and swelling in the eyelids. These symptoms improved for several of the infant monkeys after being weaned from the contaminated milk, but half of the monkeys died from PCB contamination within eight months.[22] The press reported widely on these findings and cemented the view of PCBs as the toxic nightmare. On August 20, 1976, Walter Cronkite reported on the CBS Evening News that PCBs had been found in breast milk of nursing mothers. Two months later, members of Congress voted to include a ban on PCBs as part of TSCA with little vocalized opposition. Who could argue with protecting babies and nursing mothers?

When PCBs were dumped on the roads in North Carolina and throughout the three years of the landfill conflict, EPA made very little progress in implementing TSCA. EPA missed every statutory deadline: The chemical inventory was eighteen months late; the disposal regulations for PCBs were delayed for seven months; and the PCB manufacturing phase-out did not begin until 1982, six years after the legislation calling for the ban was passed. Enforcement proceeded at a snail's pace, indicating that the lack of compliance would have few, if any, consequences for industry. As a result, twelve years into the program, testing had begun for only about 386 chemicals, or less than one percent of the nearly 60,000 chemicals in the initial inventory.[23] As of 1990, a full fourteen years after the passage of the act, EPA had completed regulatory actions to control only five substances, including the mandated control of PCBs. Asbestos, chlorofluorocarbons, dioxins, and chromium were the only four groups of chemicals regulated under the "unreasonable risk" standard set by TSCA.[24] Industry had submitted over 11,000 pre-market notifications by 1988, but EPA banned only thirteen new chemicals outright and subjected 190 to some form of action, mostly requiring workers to wear protective clothing while handling the substance.[25]

Implementation and enforcement of disposal regulations for PCBs was slow and fraught with contradictions. The EPA's strategy relied on high-temperature incineration that burned the PCB liquid at 16,000°C and destroyed at least 99 percent of the PCBs. Landfilling of liquids with PCBs was not allowed, and landfills were only to be used if the PCBs contaminated soils, rags, clothing, or debris. However, the EPA did not permit any incinerators until two and a half years after promulgation of the disposal rules. Generators of PCBs used temporary storage facilities until January 1981, when two commercial incinerators were approved (one in Deer Park, Texas, and one in El Dorado, Arkansas). With no incinerators available, EPA allowed large high- and low-voltage capacitors, containing PCB liquids, in landfills until March 1981, contradicting their policy of avoiding landfill disposal because the integrity of landfills could not be guaranteed in perpetuity.[26] The landfill permit rules, established in 1978, gave regional administrators vast discretion in setting permit requirements. For example, the distance-to-groundwater requirement avoided nationwide criteria. The proposed regulations required that the bottom of the landfill sit at least 50 feet above the groundwater, but public comments pointed out that the geology east of the Mississippi River made it nearly impossible to meet this requirement. Rather than change the rule, EPA allowed regional administrators to grant waivers. The hydrology of the eastern U.S. meant that for all intents and purposes, the distance-to-groundwater requirement was at the full discretion of the regional offices. The slow promulgation of regulations for disposal and marking of PCBs was coupled with inadequate inspection and enforcement due to lack of guidance from headquarters. In 1981 the General Accounting Office (GAO) estimated that 80 percent of the 500,000 facilities that generated PCB wastes could be overlooked through the EPA's inspection strategy. Facilities that were inspected did not receive a notice of violation for seven months after a violation was identified.[27]

The EPA's cavalier attitude towards enforcement of the manufacturing ban demonstrated that the agency was not committed to the legislative goals. The chemical industry continued its attempts to weaken the legislation. The industry pressure, coupled with the administration's concern about inflationary impacts of regulations, led the EPA to reinterpret the law. TSCA states that "effective January 1, 1978, no person may manufacture, process or distribute in commerce or use any PCB in any manner other than a totally enclosed manner." In 1979, two years after the statutory deadline, EPA proposed rules to exclude capacitors as "totally enclosed" PCBs, allowing 99.3 percent of all PCBs in commercial use to be excluded from regulation. In a suit brought by the Environmental Defense Fund, the court ruled against the EPA. Finally, in 1982, the EPA set the requirements for phasing out electrical equipment with PCBs, and in 1985 the final rule for phasing out use of transformers containing PCBs went into effect. EPA took nine years to remove from commercial use the one chemical mandated by the law to be removed. This record did not bode well for moving quickly on any of the tens of thousands of other chemicals manufactured.[28]

The inventory of chemicals in commercial use guided both the requirements for submission of a pre-market notification and the prioritization of currently used chemicals for testing and potential regulation.

Organizational mismanagement and the lack of resources complicated the overwhelming task. EPA proposed an inventory rule in March 1977 that required manufacturers and importers to report only the identity of chemicals in use. Under pressure from environmental groups, EPA expanded the scope in the final rule issued in December 1977 to include production data on each chemical. The rule did not require information on the use of a chemical, a decision that later hampered efforts to implement the pre-market notification regulations.[29] EPA issued the final inventory of 55,103 chemicals on July 28, 1980. The inventory was not comprehensive because the small business exclusions exempted 80 percent of chemical firms from the reporting rules.[30]

The EPA also made little progress in identifying chemicals for testing, issuing test rules, reviewing test data, and determining the health and environmental effects of existing chemicals. TSCA established the Interagency Testing Committee (ITC), consisting of representatives from eight federal agencies, to prioritize chemicals for testing.[31] The paucity of data posed enormous difficulties for the ITC. Gus Speth, chair of the Toxic Substances Strategy Committee of the Council on Environmental Quality and member of the ITC, told the House Subcommittee on Environmental Pollution that "the state of knowledge on how best to assess those [chemicals] that pose an unreasonable risk is imperfect and fraught with questions of scientific and social judgment that are often inextricable."[32] The National Research Council conducted a study in 1984 to determine the state of available information to make a determination about the chemicals on the inventory. The results indicated that toxicity and exposure information were available for only a small fraction of chemicals and that complete health hazard assessment was nearly impossible for the vast majority of chemicals on the inventory.[33] In October 1977 the ITC used the little information available and recommended ten chemicals for testing, but EPA did not initiate testing rules within one year, as mandated in TSCA. The Natural Resources Defense Council (NRDC) prevailed in a suit filed against the EPA and forced action on the ten chemicals in the initial report. The overall approach of the agency, however, did not change: there were no criteria for interpreting tests, nor was there an information system to track the progress of individual chemicals through the testing process. Consequently, after fifteen years of TSCA, EPA initiated testing for only 22 chemicals, completed only 16 of those 22, and took an average of eight years to complete the process for each chemical.[34]

Ambiguous language in TSCA compounded the testing delay. The law mandated the manufacturer to conduct testing if required by EPA. At the same time, TSCA demanded that the agency avoid "unnecessary economic barriers" of regulation and required "substantial evidence" for the issuance of test rules. However, an assessment of risk that met the high standard was impossible without the test data that was being sought. The EPA became even more cautious after several court rulings found that the testing rules did not meet the evidentiary burden.[35] The Reagan EPA further undermined the implementation of the testing rules. The administration wanted to cultivate cooperative relationships with the regulated industries as a way to ease the regulatory burden on industry. The agency attempted to negotiate voluntary test programs with industry, in lieu of issuing test rules. Despite the administration's argument that voluntary agreements could speed up the testing process, the court eventually ruled against voluntary testing agreements because they were not enforceable and not authorized under TSCA.[36]

Congress gave EPA, not manufacturers, the burden to prove unreasonable risk of new chemicals but did not require the pre-market notification (PMN) to include data about the toxicity of a substance. Approximately 50 percent of all PMNs received by the EPA supplied no toxicity data. When data was included, the information was about acute toxicity and of little help to the EPA because the majority of health effects from hazardous substance exposure resulted from chronic, not acute, exposure. Even the data on acute effects did not define a carcinogenic threshold for exposure, and information about synergistic effects from exposure to multiple substances did not exist. The EPA was forced to either conduct its own analysis or provide a more cursory review of the new chemicals. The agency chose the latter since there was no funding for the EPA to take on a large-scale testing program. In the first three years of the program, submissions nearly quadrupled—from 366 in 1980 to 1,272 in 1983—yet during the same time, the budget remained steady at $9.4 million. The agency gave initial reviews and approved the vast majority of new chemicals and only scrutinized about 3 percent of the submissions.[37]

In order to appease the chemical industry and overcome the Congressional opposition to TSCA, the legislation allowed EPA to exempt entire classes of chemicals from the PMN requirement without providing justification for the exemption. Thousands of chemicals received exemptions after the agency was bombarded with requests from the chemical industry. The law also allowed industry to omit information from the PMNs in order to protect trade secrets. Fifty percent of PMNs contained at least one claim of confidentiality related to the chemical formula, the intended uses, amounts to be manufactured, or other information.[38] The omission of information hampered the EPA further in making well-informed judgments about the risk from new chemicals and made outside scrutiny of the claims of the manufacturers impossible. With the overwhelming number of PMNs submitted, it might not have been feasible for environmental organizations to review the PMN claims, but with the limited information contained in the submissions, citizen oversight was a waste of time.

In achieving the passage of TSCA, the environmental movement successfully introduced a formidable critique of industrial production into the policy arena. However, the law and related regulations reflected the burgeoning debate about the nature of risks and the ambivalence toward controlling private production decisions. In this context of tension between competing ideas of the future of modernization, the implementation of the TSCA program faltered. At the time of the dumping of PCB-contaminated liquid on North Carolina roads, EPA had barely developed PCB regulations or attempted to circumvent the intent of the law; testing of new chemicals and chemicals in use had scarcely begun; and regulators and industry evaded any restrictions on toxic substances. Since TSCA set the regulatory framework for both the cleanup of the North Carolina roads and the landfill construction in Warren County, the dilatory approach from EPA gave activists little reason to trust the agency's commitment to protecting public health.

Resource Conservation and Recovery Act

Regulation of PCBs piggybacked on legislation to control the introduction of chemicals into commerce, but hazardous waste regulation was the hidden stepchild of the management of common household and business trash. In the 1960s growing piles of trash began to overwhelm local governments.[39] In 1970 Congress mandated EPA to study methods to encourage reuse and recycling of materials as a way to reduce wastes. The results emphasized the practicality of burning wastes for energy production over the complexities of materials recycling and the need for legislation to encourage federal leadership of solid waste management.[40] Following the lead of the new federal controls of air and water pollution, the framers of the Resource Conservation and Recovery Act (RCRA) envisioned a future of a centralized approach and strict pollution standards for garbage, the "third pollution." The Nixon administration did not want federal involvement in regulation of garbage but advocated a stronger hazardous waste program in RCRA in exchange for a decrease in federal involvement in solid waste.[41]

The RCRA regulatory framework was very straightforward. Hazardous waste would be separated from conventional solid wastes and tracked from "cradle to grave," existing commercial hazardous waste facilities would be regulated, and safer facilities would be built. Anxiety over risks would be assuaged with labeling wastes and hiring permitted disposal companies while interference in production decisions would be avoided. Chemical companies viewed the regulation of hazardous wastes as a mild and acceptable form of government oversight in comparison to the potential constraints of TSCA, which addressed the public's anxiety about risks by aiming directly at the heart of production. Industry lobbied intensely for years to prevent TSCA, but a few provisos were all that was needed to gain acceptance of RCRA. The law required EPA to promulgate rules to define the full scope of the wastes to be regulated and also allowed EPA to grant exemption for wastes, allowing more time to influence the full scope of the law. Industry demanded that the generator of hazardous waste be released from liability after the disposition of the waste. RCRA also allowed existing facilities to apply for interim permits while EPA developed the regulations for formal permits. The interim permits had no technical standards and were easily received but gave the impression that facilities were operating safely because they had federally issued permits.

Congress had little understanding of the extent of hazardous waste generation, treatment, or disposal and depended on an EPA report, issued in 1973, for information to design the hazardous waste sections of RCRA. The report estimated that industry generated 10 million metric tons (mmt) of hazardous waste annually. The agency claimed that the technical ability for environmentally sound treatment of hazardous waste existed, but industry continued to use the cheaper and less desirable landfills. If the regulatory program would force industry to internalize the full costs of managing hazardous waste, a switch to better technology was likely. New treatment facilities would be built by the private sector in response to the demand created by regulation. EPA envisioned five large facilities, each capable of handling approximately 1.2 million metric tons per year, for the five major industrial regions in the United States, and fifteen medium-size facilities to each process

145,000 metric tons, built in various locations around the country to provide reasonable access from other waste generation points. After treatment at one of these twenty facilities, a small portion of residues, containing about 5 percent of the total annual waste generated (204,000 metric tons), would require disposal in special, secure landfills. EPA presented a straightforward system for assessing and managing risks of hazardous wastes with little impact on industrial production. EPA estimated that the total costs, while significant, were equal to about one percent of the value of products that generated wastes, an amount that could painlessly be incorporated into the price of commodities. The price change would be small, but the benefit to society in avoidance of hazardous contamination would be large.[42]

Without full knowledge of the extent of the problem, the law established a highly complex and unwieldy framework for managing hazardous wastes. In its report, the EPA acknowledged that the amount of hazardous waste generated each year was increasing at a rate of 5 to 10 percent due to increasing production and consumption rates and controls on air and water pollution that created hazardous wastes by removing contaminants from pipes and stacks.[43] By 1976, just after RCRA's passage, the initial estimate of 10 mmt of hazardous waste soared to an unexpected 46 mmt by 1977 and 52 mmt by 1983.[44] Future studies eclipsed the early estimates. By 1981 EPA estimated 264 mmt with a possible range of 135 to 402 mmt annually. In the same year, the Office of Technology Assessment (OTA) concluded that 255 to 275 mmt would be generated each year, and in 1983 the Congressional Budget Office (CBO) estimated an annual generation of 266 mmt with a range of 223 to 308 mmt. Although these reports in the early 1980s produced similar estimates, each was based on different methodologies with unique assumptions and limitations. There was no consensus, even years after the passage of RCRA, on the volume of hazardous waste generated and even less certainty about the future.[45]

Congress gave EPA one year to inventory hazardous waste disposal sites, eighteen months to develop regulations for safe operation, and until 1983 to bring sites into compliance. None of these could be accomplished without a definition of hazardous waste. The process of defining waste was presented in seemingly objective scientific language but was infused with beliefs about the extent of risk from industrial production and the role of the public in regulating industry. Disembodied facts cannot determine what is and what is not a hazardous waste; only people, informed by a particular historical moment and a set of values, can decide how the categorization should proceed. In the process of creating the definition, the tensions between growing concern about risks and a desire to nurture unencumbered progress were manifest. The final definition, issued in 1980, two years after the April 1978 deadline, was substantially different from the March 1978 draft definition. Under intense pressure from industry, EPA focused on a limited list of specific wastes and eliminated most testing protocols except a revised and limited toxic characteristic. Wastes treated on-site were not subject to review. In addition, companies generating less than 1,000 kg per month of hazardous wastes were exempt from the cradle-to-grave system. The result was a circumscribed definition and an abbreviated list of wastes subject to RCRA regulations.

Initial implementation was slowed by a small budget and low priority in the EPA.[46] In an effort to pass some of the financial burden onto the states, RCRA allowed states to apply to operate their own hazardous waste programs. Yet none of the states had a system set up to operate the RCRA program. The states did not know how much waste was generated within their boundaries, how it was treated, or the location of its final disposal.[47] The states also lacked knowledgeable personnel to implement the law. RCRA provided limited funding but not enough for states to build and oversee secure landfills and treatment facilities. Identifying and managing so-called hazardous waste was an entirely new enterprise with no predetermined, objective methodology awaiting implementation. The entire infrastructure—physical and administrative—needed to be constructed. EPA had incentive, however, to push responsibility for waste management onto states quickly even if the state program was inadequate.[48] It was in this context of uncertainty about the adequacy of the burgeoning infrastructure that North Carolina took responsibility to design and operate a landfill for the PCB wastes in Warren County.

In 1980 EPA issued rules for interim permits for existing facilities, enabling them to operate until EPA reviewed a final permit application. RCRA depended on the availability of enough disposal capacity, so it was imperative for facilities to easily obtain the interim permits.[49] From 1980 to 1982, the critical time in the Warren County landfill controversy, the EPA liberally issued RCRA interim permits to myriad hazardous waste landfills. The distinction between a chemical waste landfill for PCBs, governed by the TSCA regulations, and hazardous waste landfills, coming under RCRA's jurisdiction, was meaningless to the general public. The only issue that mattered to the public was that the EPA granted permits to landfills that would be deemed inferior, even by the standards of experts at the agency. It seemed to residents in Warren County that the agency was not fulfilling its mission of protecting public health by knowingly allowing contamination, based on their own definitions, to continue. Even after promulgating final regulations for landfills, the agency had allowed operators to submit insufficient data, so the design of appropriate groundwater monitoring requirements and corrective action was nearly impossible. EPA knew the limitations but did not revise the regulations until 1986, and only 34 percent of the landfills had received permit review by 1988.[50]

While experts disagreed about many aspects of assessing and managing contamination, all the experts agreed that landfills eventually leak. An EPA report in 1977 concluded, "Few hydrogeologic environments are suitable for land disposal of hazardous waste without some risk of groundwater contamination."[51] The study examined older landfills, designed without liners, but the hope that clay liners would solve the problem of leaking landfills was quickly challenged. Another study showed that the impermeability results of clay liners in the lab could not be duplicated in the field.[52] Worse news came in 1981 with the "Princeton Report" that showed newly built landfills with clay and plastic liners leaked in a matter of months, resulting in groundwater contamination.[53] On February 5, 1981, the Federal Register declared, "There is a good theoretical and empirical evidence that the hazardous constituents which are placed in land disposal facilities very likely will migrate from the facility into the broader environment. This may occur several years, even many decades after placement of the waste in the facility, but data and scientific prediction indicate that, in most cases, even with the application of best available land disposal technology, it will occur eventually."

Despite the agreement among experts about the inadequacy of landfills to protect groundwater, in December 1982 Rita Lavelle, the EPA's assistant administrator for solid waste and emergency response, testified that landfills offered a viable technology for waste management and that they could be constructed, operated, and closed safely. Her testimony directly contradicted the evidence and highlighted the notion that environmental protection decisions were deeply infused with values. The EPA said that "any liner will begin to leak eventually," but under Lavelle, the agency required only thirty years of monitoring, lowering the costs for disposal while also increasing the risks from exposure.[54] Lavelle also suspended the ban on liquids in landfills.

During the eighteen days when liquids were allowed, a waste company in Colorado dumped thousands of barrels of liquid waste into landfills. When news broke that another assistant administrator at the EPA had recently served as a consultant to the same company, it cemented the idea that the institutions developed to manage the risks from industrial production were culpable in the perpetuation of those risks, in the service of industry. As a result, Congress demanded the ban of liquids be reinstated.

The RCRA vision of treating wastes required public acceptance of new facilities. A survey in 1973 by EPA found that people did not oppose the idea of a hazardous waste facility near their home. While the EPA was not certain these results would stand when the same people were faced with a real facility, the agency used the findings to argue that siting of the necessary facilities would be smooth. The resistance to facilities, however, began soon after RCRA's passage and led to a shortage of supply early in the program's implementation. EPA told Congress that resistance to siting was the primary reason for difficulty in implementing RCRA and argued that a federal role in siting was required. The siting problem was hindering some aspects of RCRA implementation but was eclipsed by a myriad of other challenges. Congress left siting decisions to local governments, and the problem expanded in the 1980s as the possibility of toxic contamination became more real to Americans around the country.

The purpose of RCRA was to move waste management—garbage and hazardous waste—away from reliance on landfills and toward treatment and recovery. The failures to implement RCRA were many, but none was as far-reaching as the failure to institute a waste management system based on treatment rather than land disposal. Treatment technology for many wastes was readily available, as the EPA stated in its 1973 report, but private industry steered clear of developing these facilities. The interim permits allowed landfills to operate for years at very low costs. New treatment facilities would be subject to the stricter, more costly regulations and could not compete with the landfills. The increase in liability made investors wary, and even large companies with vast on-site treatment facilities had no interest in moving into the commercial waste treatment business. The treatment industry failed to flourish as a direct result of the failed regulatory program.

The RCRA implementation problems led to unprecedented legislative oversight into program administration. The intensity of oversight increased after 1980, and when EPA administrator Anne Gorsuch

resigned in 1983, under scandalous accusations of broad mismanagement of the toxics and waste programs, Congress had the political
clout to demand sweeping changes to RCRA. In the Hazardous and
Solid Waste Amendments (HSWA) of 1984, Congress tried to circumvent attempts by Reagan to squash hazardous waste regulation. The
law included seventy-six statutory deadline provisions. Many of these
had "hammer provisions," which stipulated that more stringent actions, as detailed in HSWA, would take effect automatically if the
deadlines were not met. The paltry inspection record at EPA motivated
Congress to demand an enforcement strategy from EPA with the goal
of insuring 90 percent compliance.[55] According to GAO, the strategy
did little to improve the inspection and enforcement actions against
hazardous waste facilities.[56] HSWA also included a "waste hierarchy,"
stating that the preferred management option was reduction of waste
at the source, followed by recycling, treatment, and, lastly, landfilling.
The law avoided mandating waste reduction, assuming that economic
incentives induced by regulations would be enough for industry to
see the long-term financial benefits of reducing wastes. The vision of
reduced dependency on landfills did not come to pass. By 1992, just
as the Warren County landfill controversy was heating up again, few
treatment facilities had been built and landfill disposal was still the
primary form of management.[57] In addition, the overwhelming majority of landfills operating had not completed the corrective actions that
were stipulated in the permits, and most closed landfills did not comply with closure and post-closure regulations.[58]

Superfund

Two years after the passage of TSCA and RCRA,
Love Canal solidified the risk-society mindset and produced what Andrew Szasz calls "the toxic construct," with its deep-seated anxiety
about toxic contamination and loss of faith in social and political institutions to address the source of the problem.[59] On 2 August 1978, the
network evening news broadcasted that New York State had ordered
the evacuation of 240 families from Love Canal, a small working-class
community in Niagara Falls, New York. Toxic contamination from an
abandoned industrial chemical waste dump had seeped through the
soil into basements of homes, creating a public health emergency. For
nearly a decade prior to Love Canal, Americans heard many stories of
toxic contamination, but the Love Canal tragedy transformed the toxic issue. After 2 August 1978, toxic contamination became a tangible,

silent killer that made children sick, caused women to give birth to deformed children, and seeped into basements and backyards. Television viewers learned that toxic contamination alone had not destroyed families in Love Canal. The debacle demonstrated that the government was culpable in contamination from disposal of industrial waste and that the response was inadequate and inept. As the drama unfolded before the television audience, empathy for the Love Canal residents transformed the entire landscape of toxic policy.[60]

William Love built the canal in 1880 in hopes of cashing in on industrial development at Niagara Falls. His dream did not materialize, and Hooker Chemical Company took possession of the property. Between 1947 and 1952 Hooker disposed of over 43 million pounds of industrial wastes into the sixteen-acre canal. In 1953 the Niagara Falls school board purchased the canal from Hooker with a provision in the deed to absolve Hooker of any future liability. The board built a school and sold the area surrounding the canal for residential development. By the early 1970s black sludge was seeping into basements. In August 1977 the city confirmed that the sludge came from leaking drums containing Hooker's waste. Several children at the school suffered from asthma, lethargy, and cancer, and several women had miscarried or had children born with birth defects. In May 1978 the school board denied a request made by Lois Gibbs to transfer her son from the school because of his health problems. In response to the denial, she circulated a petition to parents in the neighborhood, trying to close the school, initiating citizen action that eventually spurred the state to conduct a health survey of the neighborhood. By August the state decided to evacuate 240 families. The families who were left behind demanded to be relocated. In 1979 the state agreed to temporarily relocate 100 additional families in hotels. In 1980 an EPA-sponsored pilot study showed chromosomal damage to residents and recommended further study. The report leaked before the EPA could determine what to do about the situation, highlighting that the government had no systematic way to evaluate the potential health impacts from hazardous wastes. News of the study forced the Carter administration to declare a state of emergency and to relocate the remaining families.[61]

Just seven days after the first network news story about Love Canal, farmers in North Carolina reported an oily odor coming from the road shoulder. Six days later, within two weeks of the Love Canal story, North Carolina confirmed PCB contamination of over two hundred miles of roads. Love Canal, and the understanding of toxic contamination that permeated the American consciousness as a result, shaped the response to the contamination on the roads and to the Warren County landfill. On August 9 CBS and NBC reported the North Carolina contamination as part of a long segment that included an update on Love Canal.[62] In the years leading to the passage of TSCA, citizens had learned that PCBs were highly toxic, so toxic, in fact, that they were the only substance specifically banned by Congress. For residents, the contaminated soil had the potential of creating worse public health problems and economic disaster than the debacle in Love Canal.

Love Canal was not the first incident of uncontrolled toxic waste that impacted the health of communities. RCRA was, in part, an attempt to avoid future Love Canals. However, the unprecedented media coverage of Love Canal created an iconic symbol of industrial pollution ruining American families; Congress had to respond. The Comprehensive Environmental Response, Compensation, and Liability Act of 1980 (CERCLA), commonly known as Superfund, gave statutory authority and financial means to the federal government for cleanup of abandoned contaminated sites. The powerful public response to Love Canal meant that no member of Congress could oppose legislation for cleanup, nor would industry dare to suggest that there was no problem. The toxic construct had partly decreased the ambivalence about risk, strengthening the view that progress came with a high price. Instead of debating the need for action, Congress focused on the size of the fund needed, the source of the funding, the liability of responsible parties, and victim compensation. Advocates for a powerful bill gained strength during the spring of 1980. On the eve of Earth Day, Chemical Control Corporation in Elizabeth, New Jersey, exploded, causing a major chemical fire and the evacuation of a vast area of the city. The company had refused to remove nearly 40,000 drums of industrial waste, highlighting the need for funds to start emergency cleanup when a company refused to comply.[63] A month later, in May 1980, EPA released the findings of the pilot study of thirty-six individuals in Love Canal that indicated chromosomal abnormalities in eleven of those studied. The EPA insisted that the results of the limited study did not lead to a conclusion that the chromosomal damage had been caused by the contamination. Despite the caveats offered by the EPA, it was the worst possible scenario for abandoned toxic waste, and the public mood pressured Congress into action.

With this unprecedented level of support, only extremely conservative members argued that the bill was "wasteful and unnecessary" and likely to hamper progress. The House passed a bill on the eve of the 1980 elections, but the Senate delayed action. After the elections, with economic worries among the electorate giving the Republicans both the White House and the majority in the Senate, it appeared that they had the full advantage to squash any action. With toxic waste, however, the political situation was complicated. A survey conducted by the Louis Harris Organization and ABC News found that 93 percent of Americans wanted stricter federal standards for toxic waste, and 83 percent were in favor of federal investigations into contaminated sites, even if these investigations led to over $10 billion in expenditures by the government. The chemical industry did their own research and found similar trends in public attitudes.[64] The public perception of the risk meant that Republicans could not dismiss the bill outright but could force Democrats to grant major concessions. On the last day of his presidency, Carter signed CERCLA to create a $1.6-billion fund, 80 percent to come from taxes on chemical feedstocks and the remainder from general funds, for emergency response and permanent cleanup of abandoned toxic sites. The fund was much smaller than Democrats wanted, and the compromise forced the exclusion of strict and joint and several liability, but federal court rulings concluded that Congress intended the courts to develop a common law of joint and several liability.[65] Many supporters of the bill were particularly unhappy with the elimination of victim compensation. Senator George Mitchell (D-ME) commented, "In effect, under the legislation, it's okay to hurt people but not trees."[66]

Despite the strong support for federal cleanup and the "polluter pays" approach of Superfund, the new administration was grounded in the ideology of regulatory reform and hindered the implementation of every aspect of the new law. The lack of cleanup standards in the National Contingency Plan, the arbitrary choice of sites for inclusion on the National Priority List, the refusal to use the fund to initiate cleanup, and the use of negotiations rather than enforcement contributed to a near complete breakdown of Superfund. From 1981 to 1983 the entire Superfund program was in disarray, causing the EPA to lose all legitimacy. As a result of the abysmal Superfund implementation, confidence in the EPA was replaced by "anger, fear, confusion, apprehension and a deep sense of betrayal by business and by government."[67]

Anne Gorsuch, Reagan's appointee as EPA administrator, and David Stockman, the newly appointed head of the Office of Management and Budget (OMB), headed the administration's assault on Superfund.

Prior to heading the EPA, Gorsuch was a Colorado state legislator with no experience in either environmental issues or administration of a large organization. She was good friends with many of Reagan's supporters from the conservative West: James Watt, Reagan's choice to run the Department of Interior; businessman Joseph Coors; and Bob Burford, a Coloradan appointed to lead the Bureau of Land Management. These leaders in the so-called Sagebrush Rebellion wanted to wrench public lands away from the federal government and put them into the hands of private landowners.[68] Gorsuch came to the EPA with the purpose of imposing the same ideas on pollution control: her primary qualification was a vigorous opposition to regulating hazardous waste disposal while she was a state legislator. As director of the OMB, David Stockman's primary mission was to "deter, revise, or rescind existing and pending regulations where clear legal authority exists."[69] Executive Order 12291 gave him the power to accomplish this goal by requiring all federal agencies to conduct a cost-benefit analysis on all regulations, to be reviewed by OMB. Stockman targeted all federal agencies but specifically wanted to curtail the "no-growth, zero-discharge ideology" at the EPA. Intense scrutiny of EPA fit with Stockman's ideas about the environmental laws that had passed while he was a member of Congress from New York. To his mind, RCRA and Superfund stood out as "regulatory overkill." Stockman was one of the very few members of Congress who dared to proclaim that toxic contamination in abandoned sites was not a serious problem. He told the House, "[T]here never existed, especially in recent times, a regulatory or legal vacuum that permitted widespread gross irresponsibility and negligence in disposal and storage, nor are we consequently faced today with a national landscape thickly littered with industrial time bombs."[70] Despite the growing sense that the full costs from contamination were incalculable, Stockman hoped to use the seemingly objective language of cost-benefit analysis to show that waste regulation was an inefficient use of resources and an undue burden on industry.

In the time between Reagan's inauguration and Gorsuch's nomination in May 1981, the Carter EPA staff prepared the National Contingency Plan (NCP), as mandated in CERCLA, stipulating that cleanups make use of existing standards for drinking water, ambient water, and air quality. When Gorsuch took office, she rejected this approach and ordered the NCP rewritten several times. In July 1982, after a lawsuit by the Environmental Defense Fund, the EPA published the Gorsuch NCP. In the new plan, the level of cleanup was to be decided on a case-by-case basis. While most experts agreed that each site was unique, commonalities across sites could be identified and a wide range of contaminants had existing standards.[71] By rejecting the use of existing standards, Gorsuch damned Superfund to an endless debate of "how clean is clean" that contributed to the glacial pace of remedial actions.

CERCLA mandated EPA to identify at least 400 sites for federal cleanup. However, a preliminary list of only 115 sites appeared in October 1981, and under intense pressure EPA issued a final "National Priority List" of 418 sites in December 1982. The law stipulated the minimum number of sites to be listed but did not specify the criteria to be used for selecting the sites. EPA developed the hazard ranking system for site selection that scored sites, on a scale of 1 to 100, based on the possibility of contamination release, the characteristics of the wastes on the site, and people and environments potentially impacted by the wastes. Gorsuch decided to use a score of 28.5 as a cut-off for listing. There was little scientific basis for choosing any score as a cut-off, but 28.5 produced a list that just met the minimum. It was clear that Gorsuch was implementing the letter of the law, not its spirit. In the long run, the arbitrary cut-off led to a much more extensive list. By 1988, with 29,000 potential sites, 1,200 sites were on the NPL.[72]

Gorsuch ignored the intent of the law to use the fund to initiate cleanup, followed by enforcement actions against responsible parties to replenish the fund. Approval for funds was granted only when no responsible party would take action. Since one responsible party at each site could usually be found, the agency focused on motivating that responsible party to take action rather than initiating cleanup with the fund. In the first two years of the program, the EPA appropriated only $311 million, a mere one-third of the $960 million approved by Congress.[73] If the five-year program had continued along these lines, the surplus would have supported the argument that the fund did not need renewal. The refusal to use the fund as Congress intended was coupled with a nonconfrontational approach to enforcement. While a nominee for the EPA post, Gorsuch told Congress that she preferred "workable compromises" to confrontations and that "the emphasis has to be on voluntary participation."[74] Yet her unwillingness to use enforcement as leverage in negotiations meant that there was no incentive for responsible parties to settle and that very little was actually accomplished. Gorsuch reorganized enforcement five times, settling on a scheme that separated the legal and technical enforcement activities and centralized all enforcement decisions in Washington.

The Congressional Oversight Committee began to suspect political meddling and sweetheart deals for companies with ties to EPA officials. Many appointees at EPA were from large regulated corporations, lawyers representing these firms, or Washington lobbyists. The general counsel, for example, was a former Exxon lawyer. The assistant administrator overseeing Superfund and RCRA was Rita Lavelle, the same official who insisted hazardous waste landfills could be built safely, despite the scientific evidence to the contrary. Lavelle had been the public relations director for a subsidiary of Aerojet General Corporation, a California company with the third worst pollution record in the state. When the oversight committee subpoenaed 700,000 EPA documents related to Superfund enforcement, Gorsuch acted under the advice of the Department of Justice and refused to hand them over, claiming they contained sensitive enforcement information and were subject to executive privilege. The issue led to a major confrontation between Congress and the executive branch. Even conservative members of Congress who supported Reagan were uncomfortable with Gorsuch usurping their power. After Gorsuch refused to turn over the documents, she was cited with contempt of Congress, but the Justice Department, who had counseled her to make the refusal, would not prosecute and appealed to the federal court to void the contempt charge. The federal court in the District of Columbia dismissed the suit and ordered the two sides to work out an agreement. Congress sensed its upper hand and pushed relentlessly in their investigation. Several EPA officials were accused of perjury, destruction of records, and manipulating the Superfund process to benefit companies. The deputy administrator was forced to resign for his alleged role in altering a report to exclude reference to Dow Chemical as a major source of dioxin contamination. Rita Lavelle was found guilty of perjury in her testimony before Congress about ordering an investigation of an EPA employee who had been critical of the administration's handling of the Superfund program. She was also accused of delaying a Superfund grant to clean up the Stingfellow Acid Pits in California in an attempt to hurt Jerry Brown's gubernatorial campaign. A later investigation emphasized that she often dined with executives of companies under investigation for hazardous waste violations, insinuating that she helped them avoid enforcement action.[75] Lavelle became a political liability when surveys showed the majority of the public thought that Reagan cared more about the companies that were polluting than he did about enforcing environmental protection laws. Reagan fired Lavelle on 4 February 1983, and in December 1983 she was sentenced to six months in prison for perjury. The press coverage was unrelenting, and the president risked complete loss of support for his entire approach to regulation if the image of Superfund did not improve.[76] Gorsuch had to go. She resigned amid scandal in December 1983 and left a completely demoralized and gutted EPA in a shambles. Abatement and control staff declined by 21 percent and enforcement staff by 33 percent. The overall budget for the agency had been slashed by one-third. For hazardous waste programs, the cuts were 39 percent.

Reagan appointed William Ruckelshaus as EPA administrator in an attempt to calm the political storm over toxic waste. Ruckelshaus, who had been the first head of EPA under Nixon, had a proven record among Washington power brokers, environmentalists, and industry. As a condition of accepting the position, he demanded that the agency be freed from the grip of OMB oversight. With this shift, Ruckelshaus was able to make some significant changes, including a 343 percent increase in appropriations to Superfund. He ended the negotiation approach and began to use the fund to begin cleanups. Despite these changes, Superfund remained bogged down in delays and very little progress was made on specific sites. The agency was still subject to the case-by-case standard setting of the NCP. The requirement to use the most cost-effective approach meant that containment was nearly always the preferred method of remediation. Use of containment for Superfund wastes compounded the RCRA problem of discouraging research and development of alternative strategies and technologies. While landfilling was cheaper in the short run, many observers thought "carting toxics from site to site" would be more expensive in the long run. The myopia was particularly pronounced in light of the EPA proclamation that all landfills eventually leak. Ruckelshaus was also constrained by a requirement to balance the fund among sites. Spending at any one site could not be so large as to limit the ability to clean up other sites. The result was that little funding was released for actual cleanup.

By the time Superfund came up for reauthorization, the entire context had shifted. In 1985 everyone agreed that the full extent of the problem was significant and that the NPL was a conservative estimate. When the Superfund Amendments and Reauthorization Act (SARA) of 1986 passed, Congress raised the fund to $8.5 billion, expecting additional funding to come from the required state contributions and payments by responsible parties. SARA spread the tax burden over a wider range of entities, including taxes on petroleum and chemical feedstocks and a general corporate environmental tax. The reauthorization was a substantial increase in funding, but even this amount was probably too little. Estimates for cleanup of NPL sites ranged from $106 to $302 billion, with the lower amount for containment and the upper amount for treatment. The funding situation was even worse because SARA also extended Superfund responsibility to include leaking underground storage tanks. SARA, like HSWA, moved Congress into the role of "reluctant regulator" in an attempt to stop the Reagan administration's evisceration of the regulations.[77] The inclusion of schedules to start cleanups forced EPA into action. The omission of completion goals meant that the debate over "how clean is clean" was not resolved. As a result, the pace of cleanup increased but was nowhere near the needed rate. In 1991 only 63 sites of the 1200 on the NPL were considered fully cleaned. It took an average of 13 to 15 years for a site to move from proposed listing on the NPL to completion of the principle cleanup work. But some sites could take as long as 30 years before construction began.[78]

The EPA listed the contaminated roads in North Carolina on the preliminary NPL and provided funding for cleanup of the site. The cleanup was logistically and technically difficult, but the perpetrators were identified so that funds used on the site would most likely be recouped from the responsible parties. The circumstances of the contamination—midnight dumping at the same time as the Love Canal debacle—gave the case a very high profile. A quick and successful completion of the cleanup would help the EPA demonstrate that the Superfund program was functioning well, despite the attacks on Gorsuch, Lavelle, and the EPA in general. Once the NPL and Superfund became part of the solution for the roadside contamination, it was even more imperative to move quickly on completing the landfill and cleaning up the site. After the soil was removed, the roadside PCB contamination was determined to be clean and was then one of the first sites deleted from the final NPL.[79] With this accomplishment, the EPA could claim that all three of its toxic programs were achieving their goals: TSCA was managing PCB wastes, RCRA was developing safe disposal for wastes, and Superfund was cleaning up abandoned wastes.

When the landfill was built in Warren County, the toxic construct was embedded in the general public through both the incidence of ill effects from pollution and the public debates about appropriate action to address these impacts. The new risk consciousness, as expressed in the environmental movement, critiqued the social and political institutions that served the modernization project and faced resistance. The ambivalence that emerged between public anxiety over environmental risks and a desire to continue on the path of economic prosperity opened a new political space. The government was politically vulnerable to challenges because of the incomplete implementation of toxic reform. With each delay in promulgating regulations and each new incident of toxic contamination, trust that the federal government would protect public health and ecological integrity deteriorated. The political opportunity enabled a burgeoning environmental justice movement to challenge the toxic policies, initially by pointing out the inequitable outcomes of the policy framework and then by attempting to bring policy back to the primary goal of TSCA: prevention of contamination by transforming production.

3

The Collective Action Frame of "Not in My Backyard"

On 4 January 1979 the EPA held a public hearing on whether the agency should approve the permit to construct a landfill in Warren County. One by one, citizens took the microphone to present every conceivable argument as to why the landfill should not be allowed. Some made technical arguments, suggesting that the design or the characteristics of the clay soils made it a particularly dangerous place to locate a waste facility. Others were more concerned with the process that led to the decision to site in Warren County. Still others leveled deeply emotional appeals. No matter what tack each resident took when presenting arguments to the panel, the united theme was clear: the landfill would harm the county and its citizens irreparably through contamination and negative economic effects.

The only conclusion that these residents could draw was that treatment of the contaminated soil should not involve their county. Citizens pressed for any number of alternative approaches, including the possibility of multiple landfills in each of the affected counties and in-place treatment of the soil. The most attractive alternative, however, was shipment to a federally approved hazardous waste landfill in Emelle, Alabama. From the perspective of Warren County, this was the ideal solution. The Alabama site had been approved by the EPA, already existed, and, as far as they knew, had been operating successfully. Ken Ferruccio, one of the most vocal leaders in the citizen opposition, articulated the position at the first public hearing, "PCB on the shoulders and PCB in temporary storage [should] be sent to Alabama, one of the three legal national dumping sites where I understand every precaution has been taken, unlike the situation here in Warren County."[1] Residents of Warren County even traveled to the site, just after the hearing, to see if it was an acceptable place for the contaminated soil. They found it suitable. According to one resident who went, "They buried this stuff 70 feet deep with 630 feet of clay under that."[2]

The residents' insistence on alternatives did not go unnoticed by state officials. The day after the hearing, Governor Hunt directed Herbert Hyde, appointed Secretary of Crime Control and Pubic Safety (CCPS) just two days earlier, to reassess the entire situation in hopes of avoiding a political debacle. Hyde considered two alternatives: in-place treatment and shipment to Emelle, Alabama. While in-place treatment would not be possible because of federal regulations, shipment to Emelle was a different story. Secretary Hyde and his assistant, David Kelly, met with five representatives of Chemical Waste Management (CWM), owners of the Emelle landfill, who estimated a cost of $8.8 million for shipment and disposal in Alabama.[3] By the time the environmental impact assessment was complete in 1980, the price tag for disposing of the material in Alabama had ballooned to $12 million, while the Warren County landfill was estimated to cost only $1.7 million.[4] Residents were convinced that the state was basing its decision on cost and were outraged that the state would jeopardize their health, the health of future generations, and their shaky economy in order to save money. How could the state put a price tag on the value of lives in Warren County?

Shipment to Alabama, no matter what the cost, was the official position of the local opposition. Both the county government, who filed suit against the state to stop the landfill, and the "Warren County Citizens Concerned about PCBs" (Concerned Citizens), the local citizen group that formed to fight the landfill, pushed for this route. Ironically, neither the local citizens nor the county commissioners thought to ask about the community of Emelle or how the landfill might impact its residents. As it turned out, the small community of Emelle in Sumter County, Alabama, where one-third of the residents lived below the federal poverty level and over 65 percent of the residents were black, also did not want a waste landfill in their community. Organized opposition in Emelle began in 1978, just as soon as CWM (a subsidiary of one of the largest waste management multinational corporations, Waste

Management, Inc.) began construction of the site. It was intended to be one of the first hazardous waste landfills under the new RCRA regulations.[5] After a group of workers had walked off the site because of unsafe working conditions, activists insisted on rigorous monitoring and accountability of the facility. Eventually, citizens in Emelle demanded the closure of the entire operation.[6]

The citizen activists of Warren County and Emelle were part of a larger movement of communities who resisted the implementation of the new "cradle-to-grave" system of waste management initiated through the RCRA regulations. Local resistance to the siting of these facilities was becoming a major obstacle to the implementation of the new waste policy. By the 1980s less than one percent of the proposed hazardous waste facilities had become operational due, in large part, to local opposition to siting.[7] Authorities used the pejorative title "Not in My Backyard" (NIMBY) to signal that the parochial view was a self-interested tactic by those who wanted the benefit of the processes and products responsible for the generation of waste but did not want to bear the costs. Experts believed they could calculate the risk and anything outside this quantified view of risk was irrational. By attaching the additional label "syndrome" to the phenomenon, critics of the local resisters further discredited groups that objected to waste facilities. The "NIMBY syndrome," reminiscent of medical conditions like Down syndrome or Tourette syndrome, pathologized the local opposition groups as part of a social malady that would lead to devastating outcomes.

The initial resistance to the Warren County landfill was a NIMBY response that embraced the idea that risks are real not because of the probability but because of their incalculability. Estimates of chance did not assuage the anxiety of NIMBYs, not because they were irrational, as decision makers portrayed them, but because they used different criteria to weigh risk. Their rationality was based on the idea that the harm could happen at some unknown future time to any member of their community, as yet unidentifiable, without their having any control over the outcome.[8] NIMBY was also a manifestation of another aspect of risk society. Since the modernization process itself was implicated, the social and political institutions that supported the process were challenged. During the nearly four years that the landfill was disputed in the courts and eventually redesigned, Warren County residents, county government leaders, and networks of other local communities dealing with waste facility proposals actively engaged in various forms of collective action. These actions were characterized by the three attributes of the classic NIMBY response: risk aversion, distrust of government, and feelings of disempowerment.[9] Collective actors engaged in framing, one of the essential ingredients for collective action formation, by strategically choosing cultural symbols to produce new cultural meanings. The resulting NIMBY frame had limited ability to solve the specific crisis of PCB-contaminated soil but wielded significant power in mobilizing and sustaining local collective action. The NIMBY frame motivated residents to fight the landfill for four years and cemented their commitment to opposing the landfill even in the face of highly improbable odds. Despite its narrow scope and limited solution, it named a problem and those responsible in a way that opened the possibility for joining with civil rights leaders, as they would do in the fall of 1982. The NIMBY collective action frame, as produced in Warren County, laid the groundwork for a later transformation into the environmental racism frame that would, in turn, give rise to the environmental justice movement. NIMBY can be disparaged as parochial and self-centered, but without it the environmental racism frame might not have been as rich and potent.

The NIMBY label imposed by the authorities implied that the landfill opponents' parochialism was harmful because the landfill was a societal necessity. In the early stages of the opposition, the locals had no way of countering this claim. They had not fully understood that one implication of their risk aversion was to challenge the underlying assumption of the regulatory structure that attempted to manage risk from industrial production without changing production processes. Since their focus was on the immediate objective of stopping the landfill, however, their central task was to convince people that this was a legitimate and potentially worthwhile endeavor. The collective action frame—naming the problem, attributing blame, and proposing a solution—was constructed to demonstrate that the landfill was unjust and immoral and was caused by an external force that could be successfully challenged. The NIMBY frame in Warren County possessed the three qualities necessary for effective mobilization: empirical credibility, experiential commensurability, and narrative fidelity.[10] Although citizens of Warren County had difficulties building networks and coalitions beyond a narrow geographical context, the NIMBY frame remained a powerful organizing force for the locals. The parochial view of the problem ultimately undermined the objective of stopping the landfill but was able to sustain collective action for four years and prepare the county for a new and more expansive collective action frame of environmental racism.

The framing work in Warren County faced the same difficulty of any collective action mobilization effort. The mobilization faced the complex challenge of selectively producing new meanings from existing cultural symbols within a contested environment between the activists and the authorities.[11] The Warren County mobilization against the landfill in the period 1979–82 constructed a collective action frame that was credible, resonated with the experience of residents, and spoke to their deeply held cultural beliefs. First, while the residents needed to show that their interpretation of the situation had empirical credibility, they did not need absolute verification of the facts. It was only necessary to achieve the appearance of validity, demonstrating a real problem caused by an external force that was subject to intervention.[12] The credibility emerged from the scientific uncertainty about contamination and the shifting nature of the regulations. Activists had an ambivalence about the role of science. On the one hand, they often critiqued the regulators for relying solely on scientific knowledge and argued that their experience gave them different, more embodied knowledge. On the other hand, citizens began to see that the scientific process veiled the values that it embodied. As a result, activists did not eschew science completely, but used the disembodied, objective language of science strategically to bring new beliefs into the debates.[13]

Secondly, the collective action frame could not focus solely on abstract facts but also needed to speak to the lived experiences of people who were being asked to take action. In order to create a frame that was action-oriented, leaders situated the diagnosis, attribution of blame, and proposed remedy within the everyday lives of the residents. Experiential commensurability moved the problems away from the realm of scientific evidence and into the day-to-day reality of potential constituents. Continued economic decline in Warren County in the 1970s created an environment where the potential for negative economic impacts from the landfill resonated with the residents' lived experience. The collective action frame was closely aligned with the belief systems embedded within the culture of the rural South, yet was able to escape wholesale adoption of existing cultural meanings. Lastly, narrative fidelity was secured by finding the intersection between the inherited myths of the sacredness of local land use decisions and the goals of the collective action.

Contamination and Building Credibility

In the summer of 1994 Florence Somerville, who lived just down the road from the landfill, recalled that she and her husband, Ed, became involved because "we were scared. It could cause cancer. We use well water here. Many people had cancer at the time. . . . Some people who didn't live near to the landfill didn't think they needed to be involved, but they didn't realize that if it got in the water, it was everyone's problem." According to Ed, those who eventually became involved did so because "they knew the damage it could do to your body."[14] Nine years later, both Ed and Florence had died of cancer. According to their neighbor, Massenberg Kearny, whose land abutted the landfill site and was across the road from the Somervilles,' their deaths must have been tied to the contamination from the landfill. Despite the fact that the Somervilles used a special filter on their well, as did the Kearnys, Massenberg felt that the illness came from water contaminated by the landfill. "Normally, people live longer. My parents were in their nineties." A tear came to his eye as he thought about the ordeal they had endured. "I hope our children and grandchildren will be able to live on the land."[15] Luther Brown, the pastor of Coley Springs Baptist Church, where both the Kearnys and the Somervilles were members, concurred that the threat of contamination was paramount to motivating participation. "The fear was the thing that drew people out, especially fear of the water becoming poisoned. No one could give us a guarantee that it wouldn't happen. . . . People were scared to death."[16]

Nothing was more worrisome to the residents of Warren County's Afton community, where the landfill was to be built, than its position over the drinking water supply. Citizens feared the worst could happen—that the hazardous materials from the landfill might enter the aquifer and contaminate their water supply. Risk of contamination to the nearby Richneck Creek and Fishing Creek, used for subsistence fishing by Native Americans, was also a worry, but the aquifer and residents' well water stood out as the primary threat. This concern was immediate as well as intergenerational. Citizens put it clearly at the first public hearing in January 1979. "We have children. We have grandchildren living in Warren County. We Warren County people do think something of our children and grandchildren. We don't want this PCB in Warren County at all. We must look out for our children."[17] Another citizen at the meeting put it this way, "The children of the future coming on in eastern North Carolina will have to drink what you destroy."[18]

Warren County residents were carving out, unbeknownst to them or regulators, a subsequent standard path of NIMBYs, whose primary objection to unwanted land uses, especially waste facilities, was the perceived threats to public health from water supply contamination. It should not be surprising, however, that contaminated water supplies would be a primary motivator for citizens to resist the remnants of industrial processes. Long before the waste facility siting controversies of the 1970s, fear of contaminating water supplies from industrial production had deep cultural resonance When Henrik Ibsen wrote *An Enemy of the People* in 1882, it was not by accident that he chose contamination of water supply as the device to explore the relationship of the individual to authority in the modern, industrial world. In the play, the protagonist's efforts to voice the truth about contaminated water led to the ultimate destruction of his entire life by the powerful forces of industrial capital and the state. Ibsen knew, perhaps, that audiences throughout the industrial world accepted some pollution as necessary for progress but that destruction of a community's access to clean water stepped over the line.

The task of the collective actors in creating a successful frame was to construct evidence that showed the threat of contamination to drinking water was significant no matter how negligible the estimations from authorities. However, residents came to understand that a declaration of low risk did not indicate fact but rather a judgment grounded in myriad assumptions and interpretation of data. The veil of objectivity covering the state's claims of negligible risk was removed to reveal the subjectivity in the production of scientific knowledge. Residents used this vulnerability as an opportunity to build credibility for their own assessment of evidence about the way PCBs behaved in the environment, the health threats they posed, and the safety of the landfill design.

Despite the value-driven risk assessment, citizens faced a particularly difficult challenge in portraying the PCBs as a danger to the water supply. PCBs are hydrophobic compounds that bind to solids, are attracted to the soil, and pull away from water. As a result, any PCBs that came in contact with water, either below ground or on the surface, would probably not stay in solution; rather they would cling to suspended solids and fall out of the water with settling. This significantly limited the ability of PCBs to move through the environment if they entered it. In other words, if contamination of water occurred, it could easily be contained. State officials took advantage of this same characteristic of PCBs when they stabilized the soils on the road shoulders by first applying activated charcoal, mixing it into the soil column and then remolding the road shoulders and covering the area with asphalt. This was also the theory behind the various suggestions for treating the soil in place rather than digging it up and building a landfill. The state ran a test of in-place treatment in February and March of 1979, but the EPA found that the level of adsorption to the activated charcoal was not sufficient. On the one hand, this meant that the EPA would not approve the state's request for an exemption to the rule that PCB–laden soil had to be landfilled; but on the other hand, it gave credence to the residents' claims that a PCB-contaminated landfill threatened their environment and their health.

The second argument that state officials used to assuage citizens' fears was that the health consequences of exposure to PCBs might not be as devastating as earlier studies suggested.[19] Since the passage of TSCA and the ban on the manufacture of PCBs, a flurry of research had questioned whether PCBs were the menace that they had been portrayed to be. The epidemiological work that the state conducted in Warren County highlighted the uncertainty about the toxicity of PCBs. The state's environmental epidemiologist, Dr. C. Gregory Smith, argued that the potential for exposure to PCBs from the landfill was highly unlikely and that this exposure would pose minimal risk. The exposure necessary to increase the body burden beyond the average twenty milligrams was so significant, according to Smith, that even an earthquake that completely ruptured the landfill would probably not create that level of exposure. "What is hard for people to understand is that carcinogenic risk is determined from lifetime exposure for seventy years. One week or so wouldn't change the risk."[20]

When the state presented its position that exposure to PCBs carried little or no health risks, residents were outraged. Evidence was amassing by the late 1970s that PCB exposure could lead to myriad health problems, including skin abnormalities, liver cancer, developmental disabilities, and birth defects. Moreover, residents knew that scientists had significant uncertainty about the threshold level that would induce any of these effects. The epidemiological estimation of probability was beside the point, so when Dr. Sarah Morrow was speaking at a public meeting about the low cancer risks from short exposures, residents, through a preplanned organized effort, walked out en masse in the midst of her presentation.[21]

The largest opening for the NIMBY collective action frame to develop empirical credibility came from the authorities' claim that the

state could engineer a landfill that would successfully contain any remaining risks. According to the state, even if the PCBs did move more
easily through the environment than believed, and even if the health
consequences of exposure would be as devastating as imagined, there
was no need to worry about these issues because the PCBs would not
enter the air or water in the community in the first place. Warren County would have the "Cadillac of landfills," a facility so secure that it
almost eliminated the possibility of contamination. As articulated by a
science advisor for the EPA's Office of Environmental Justice in 1994,
"There were specific requirements for the landfill, designed to prevent
the PCBs from getting into a surface water environment, which is the
only potentially significant route of exposure. The design was filled
with an overabundance of safety features. The landfill created a situation with zero risk. No one wanted it, [but they] had very little understanding about the likelihood of risk."[22]

The emphasis of the state on the technical merits of the landfill
enabled opponents to gain credibility because no one was willing to
say that there were no risks, just that the best judgments of officials led
them to conclude that the risks were minimal. Citizens came to realize
that the evidence leveled to support this claim was steeped in interpretation of scientific data that was influenced by political and economic
considerations. The landfill design debates enabled residents to bolster
the credibility of their own evidence because the technical discussion
was infused with uncertainty, interpretation, and judgment.

The state's original application for a permit to construct the landfill
strengthened the empirical validity of the opposition claims because it
leant itself to serious criticism from technical experts. Activists used
the language and practice of science in order to challenge the assumptions underlying the decision to build the landfill in Warren County. A
landfill is simply a container for waste, engineered to enclose the contaminated material so that nothing moves into the environment through
the air, surface run-off, or into the groundwater. The basic premise of
building a sound landfill is to design several methods for insuring that
the contamination is contained in the landfill space and that it has no
negative impact if it does move out. This design approach uses four
components: an appropriate site selection, impermeable liners, a leachate collection system, and a monitoring system. The characteristics of
each one of these components in the Warren County landfill design
were open to technical criticism; each technical challenge bolstered
the credibility of the opposition.

In the 1970s appropriate landfill site selection criteria focused on geologic features as well as nearby land use factors. A good landfill had geological conditions that would slow the movement of contaminants off site if the landfill were breached and contamination escaped. This meant, at the least, that there must be no seismic activity, the gradient must not encourage movement outside of the site, and the hydrologic conditions must separate the landfill from the groundwater. When the interim regulations were written in February 1978, the EPA required a 50-foot distance between the waste in the landfill and the groundwater. Since the Warren County site was only 13 feet above groundwater, the state was forced to request a waiver of this regulation. In May 1979, just before the Afton permit was granted, however, the EPA had proposed changes to the groundwater distance regulation from 50 feet to 10 feet, so North Carolina would no longer need an exemption. Many residents speculated that the EPA wanted to change the regulation in order to make the Afton site more acceptable; however, this seems unlikely because the federal regulations had already been under review before the Afton site was proposed. Apparently, while the 50-foot requirement may have been scientifically sound, the geology in the eastern United States made it nearly impossible to site a landfill with this requirement, and the EPA contended that the change to a 10-foot distance was necessary in order to implement the cradle-to-grave framework for waste management. Although the proposed change was withdrawn at the last minute, no waiver was granted for the North Carolina site, despite its only 13-foot clearance.[23]

From the state's perspective, the site needed to meet the federal requirements so that a permit would be granted, despite the fact that they knew a site with a 50-foot groundwater distance could never be identified in North Carolina. The state's selection process therefore emphasized a site that would enable an expeditious solution to the problem of the contaminated roadways. Concern about a potential public health disaster, the possibility of severe economic impacts on the agriculturally dependent communities near the contaminated sites, and the impending public relations disaster made the need for expediency foremost in the minds of the state officials involved in the site selection process. Within a week of the discovery of the illegal dumping, the state issued a plea for private landowners to come forth with possible sites while they also examined all state-owned property in areas with low population densities. The state was determined to keep the landfill out of population centers, as one of their methods in managing the risks. Ninety sites in all were examined and eventually whittled to two sites. One of these was publicly owned: a section of the Chatham County solid waste landfill. At a public hearing in Chatham County on 11 December 1978, citizens voiced strong opposition to the county's plan to sell part of the landfill to the state for the PCB waste disposal. The following day, the county withdrew its offer, and the state submitted its request to the EPA for a permit to construct the landfill on the only remaining property: a farm owned by Linda and Carter Pope in the Afton community in Warren County.

The Division of State Property began negations with the Popes in September 1978 and signed an option to buy on 1 December 1978. The Popes' land was available, relatively inexpensive, and the sale was not subject to public review. Purchase of the property also helped the state avoid the sticky problem of using eminent domain. While it was important to state officials that the landfill be located in a sparsely populated area, finding a location with little potential for resistance did not enter the deliberations. At the time, waste facilities had not faced major obstacles from local residents.[24] Given the economic situation in the county in the 1970s, it was not surprising that a farmer in Warren County was willing to sell his property to the state in an effort to regain financial security.

The Popes' property was convenient, but it was not necessarily the best place to put a chemical waste landfill. Its suitability was part of the uncertainty that fueled the residents' credibility. Yet, according to state and EPA officials, this did not necessarily rule out the possibility of constructing a safe landfill at the site. For the EPA, the science of landfill design, while in its infancy in the 1970s, would ensure that no contamination left the containment.[25] The uncertainties associated with engineering a safe landfill, coupled with the implementation debacles, bolstered the credibility of the residents. Activists emphasized the role that uncertainty played in buttressing their cause. "The position was that engineering principles can transform an unsafe site to a safe site. . . . They (EPA) could change the regs to be closer to groundwater. It gave us a lot of ammunition because all waste management is based on a unsubstantiated hypothesis. Scientific opposition was strong because the data was not in."[26]

The central component to this engineering feat is the double-liner system. One liner was supposed to be built from compacting the clay soil extracted at the site, and the other liner was to be made from plastic. The clay liner had several regulatory specifications, but permeability, the speed at which water could move through the soil, was of the most concern to regulators. Clay liners are best made from soils with low permeability, so that any water passing through the clay would move very slowly. The tests indicated that the clay at the Afton site had extremely low permeability, suggesting that the engineers could construct an effective barrier between the waste and the groundwater. At the same time that the state was seeking approval for the landfill design, the EPA had proclaimed that all landfills would eventually leak. However, North Carolina was so confident in the ability of the clay to do the job that they used these data to back up their request for two additional waivers from the EPA. The EPA requirement for permeability was 1×10^{-7} cm/second, and the state estimated the clay in Afton at a permeability of 1×10^{-10} m/second. If the clay was as good as they thought, then a plastic liner and a leachate collection system were unnecessary. In hindsight, their requests (which the EPA luckily denied) would have created a very high-risk situation even by the most conservative engineering standards.

The language that decision makers used to discuss the landfill was technical, and citizens embraced it as part of their NIMBY resistance. The technical criticisms of the state's plan to engineer the Afton site into a safe landfill were primarily articulated by the consultant hired by the county commissioners. Charles Mulchi, a soils scientist at the University of Maryland, was also a relative of a Warren County resident. His evidence, however, focused on the mineralogy of the clay rather than its permeability. The type of clay impacted the structure of the particles, which in turn impacted the cation exchange capacity (CEC), the adsorption ability of the soil. If the clay had a high CEC, cations moving through the soil would be sorbed to the clay. From this perspective, even if the clay liner would meet the EPA requirements for permeability, the high percentage of kaolinite in the soil at the site made it unsuitable as an effective liner because this type of clay has a very low capacity to sorb particles. Even if the water did move slowly, the contaminated materials would move through the clay rather than stick to it. Mulchi first presented this information at the public hearing on 4 January 1979, and his testimony prompted the EPA to ask the state to conduct additional soil tests to support its application to build the landfill from the clay at the site.[27] Despite these additional tests and the continued testimony of Mulchi through the long court proceedings from the county lawsuit, the regulatory framework offered no recourse because the TSCA regulations lacked standards for the type of clay and mineralogical content.[28] This disagreement among the experts about which measure was more appropriate for determining the safety of a liner highlighted the role of values in science-based decisions and empowered the NIMBY frame with empirical credibility.

Mulchi strengthened the potency of the clay debate for the NIMBY frame when he argued that the area surrounding the Chatham County landfill, which had been the first choice of the state, had soils with clay that was more appropriate for the construction of a clay liner for a chemical waste landfill. Further, if the state could not have obtained the Chatham County site itself, even by eminent domain, then surely another site with the superior properties could have been located. Mulchi commented that a quick look at a good soils map of North Carolina would have led the state to several options in other counties.[29] Mulchi's analysis, originally developed as expert testimony for the county's case, became the basis for the technical arguments of Concerned Citizens. Leaders of the group used his work to give them the technical credibility they needed to argue against the state's ability to engineer a safe landfill. Deborah Ferruccio remarked, "We immediately hired Charles Mulchi, a relative of a county resident. His contributions were significant." For Ferruccio, Mulchi was invaluable, "His point was that the site was intrinsically unsuitable and could not be made suitable by engineering principles. . . . He discouraged the use of plastic liners to make a suitable site because he saw that it would only be temporary."[30]

Leaders of the opposition also believed that Mulchi's testimony had not been considered in the lawsuits, and this fueled their conviction that the landfill should be placed elsewhere. Despite the belief that Mulchi's opinion was not examined, however, it was entered into evidence and became a significant part of the county's case. After the state agreed to conduct an environmental impact assessment as specified in the North Carolina Environmental Policy Act, the county continued to rely on Mulchi for a technical response to the draft environmental impact statement (EIS). His testimony was allowed, contrary to the belief of residents, but his concerns were dismissed in the issued opinion. Using the Addendum to the Final Environmental Impact Statement prepared by the state, the court concluded that North Carolina was not required to consider clay type in the liner design because "[t]here is no standard for percentage of clay, type of clay and mineralogical content in the . . . regulations."[31] On the substantive questions, the court relied on the regulations developed under the expertise of the EPA.

The second component in the double-liner system was to be made from plastic. Different types of polymers had various strengths and predicted usable lives, but none were guaranteed to last in perpetuity. The initial permit granted by the EPA on 4 June 1979 allowed the state to build the landfill without a plastic liner. Within a few years, this type of waiver would be unheard of because new data indicated that plastic liners would be absolutely necessary to slow the eventual movement of contamination out of the landfill. The waiver request allowed activists to argue that the state was more concerned with saving money than with safeguarding the citizens of Warren County. The scientific language of engineering design became suspect as the activists succeeded in showing that economic considerations drove the state's decisions. The citizens' alternative interpretation of the scientific data, then, gained in credibility. The state acquiesced by including a thirty-millimeter plastic liner in the revised design scheme created to fulfill the environmental impact assessment requirement imposed by the courts.

Two additional safeguards were supposed to be added to the landfill design in case the double-liner system failed. First, a leachate collection system would collect any water that happened to move through the barriers before the water entered the aquifer. The collected water would be tested for contamination before being pumped to a holding pond adjacent to the landfill. Secondly, monitoring wells would be installed down gradient from the landfill, both on the site and immediately off-site, to detect any contamination that may have slipped through the double liners and avoided early detection in the leachate collection system. By testing water from the monitoring wells on a regular basis, contamination would be discovered early enough to avoid complete adulteration of the water supply. The original permit application included a request to waive the leachate collection system, but the EPA declined to grant the waiver. However, distrust of the government and their motives was deep, and the inclusion of the leachate collection requirement in the EPA approval did not eliminate the citizens' anxiety about the potential for contamination and their conviction that the government was willing to sacrifice the health of Warren County residents in order to save some money on the design and construction costs.

Eventually, through negotiations emanating from the court case and the required state environmental impact statement, the landfill design was modified to include a plastic liner and a double leachate collection system, one above the liner and one below. Most importantly, the landfill was redesigned to include a plastic and clay liner on the sides and top, as well as the original liner system on the bottom of the landfill. In this way, the landfill was supposed to create a totally enclosed tomb for the waste.

The opposition had built empirical credibility quickly, using the tactic of an alternative science. The first sign of success in this area came when the EPA decided to delay their decision on the state permit application so that additional information could be gathered and analyzed. Several organizing efforts by Warren County activists, maximizing the opportunity to challenge the validity of the state's evidence, contributed to this delay. At the first meeting of nearby residents after the announcement of the Afton site, the group set an initial goal of getting a large turnout to the January 4 public hearing held by the EPA concerning the state's permit application to build a chemical waste landfill.[32] The strategy worked. Although the group placed an ad in the local paper to encourage participation, personal conversations with friends and neighbors about the public health threat brought more people to the meeting. From that first meeting, Ken and Deborah Ferruccio had taken a lead role in the organizing. Ken explained how the organizing happened. "We met personally with civil leaders . . . simply stated our case that the burden of proof was on the state that they could do this safely. . . . In a small town you just have to call a few people and you can get to nearly everyone." Deborah emphasized the point that the rural culture facilitated their organizing efforts. "It is an interwoven net." The fledgling group convinced nearly a thousand people to attend.[33]

Although this was significant for any public hearing, it was especially impressive in a county with only fifteen thousand residents. Riding on the success of the public meeting, the group decided to demand a direct meeting with the governor. They had obviously gained enough power from the public hearing to be able to have their demand met. On 19 January 1979 a group of nine members of Concerned Citizens headed to Raleigh, where the governor tried, in vain, to convince the group that the landfill would be constructed safely. The citizens felt that he "wouldn't listen to us" and asked the governor, "What is the state going to do when this problem has magnified itself to the point of civil disobedience?"[34]

Despite the confidence of authorities that the risks were minimal, the citizens underscored the scientific uncertainty about risks associated with industrial wastes and landfills. Citizens knew that scientific knowledge was always expanding, which meant that a full understanding of the potential risks was impossible. As one resident articulated it, "[N]ew statistics and methods are making (EPA standards) obsolete. Who provides the new statistics? The families of New York and Maryland, the victims of Virginia who were told that it was safe, the radiation victims of Utah and Arizona who were told nuclear testing was safe? Are the people of Warren County to become tomorrow's statistics . . . statistics tell us human error is inevitable. I am frightened with these possibilities."[35]

When Governor Hunt acknowledged the scientific uncertainty about hazardous wastes in the letter to the citizens of Warren County that he wrote in October 1982, as the landfill was being capped, he played right into the hands of the mobilizing efforts. Ten years later, activists repeated his words as a testimony that their concerns about risks had been warranted, not because the data infallibly supported their claims, but because the data did not infallibly support the claims of the authorities. The governor's letter stated, "The state is convinced, on the basis of the best scientific evidence that is available to us that the landfill is safe and will remain safe in the future. But you and I have seen that scientists can disagree and their disagreements concern us. That is why I intend to see that the State of North Carolina keeps its commitment to you, your children and your grandchildren to continue to press for detoxification of the site, to closely monitor it and to guarantee its safety for generations to come."[36]

When the illegal roadside contamination first occurred, citizens from all over the state heard warnings of danger. The state told citizens not to eat produce grown near the contaminated soil or to walk in the vicinity. The media were filled with the potential health hazards of PCB contamination.[37] Since Warren County had over twenty-six miles of road shoulders contaminated, they were particularly attuned to the warnings. However, as the time passed and the PCB-contaminated soil stayed along the road, the state introduced several amendments to the initial warnings. For example, the Department of Agriculture changed the advice about agricultural products, and the Division of Health Services issued conflicting recommendations. It seemed that the concept of acceptable risk was uncertain and debatable. "I have not been able to find one expert that can tell us that 'x' number of parts per million is safe or dangerous," said one Warren County resident who lived near a contaminated road.[38] These uncertainties and varying interpretations of scientific data continued to provide credibility to the claims of the opposition that the risks were higher than the state was acknowledging.

Economic Decline and Experiential Commensurability

Activists built the credibility of their collective action frame by demonstrating that the science and regulations related to chemical wastes and landfills were fraught with uncertainty. The experiential commensurability of the NIMBY frame was built on the economic issues that faced residents on a daily basis. While risks from contamination evoked a deep uneasiness in residents, the reality of public health problems from exposure to PCBs was not a daily part of their lives. Residents did, however, struggle every day with the impacts of ongoing economic decline. The national recession, along with the drop in the agricultural sector, was particularly severe in Warren County. The regional disparities in the state added to the resentments of county residents who thought the landfill was one more example of the state ignoring their needs.

The economic issues of concern for residents had less to do with a potential decrease in property values than would be expected. Perhaps this is reflective of the already very low land values in Warren County. Also, most residents of Warren County had no plans to sell their land and move out; rather, they envisioned their family living off the land for generations. The economic concerns of the NIMBY frame in Warren County reflected the particular economic situation of rural North Carolina in the late 1970s; the landfill would create problems for the economic development plans of the county. Hosting the landfill would either deter industry completely from Warren County, or the county would become extremely attractive to one type of business enterprise only: the waste industry.

The recession of the late 1970s hit hard in Warren County. The per capita income in Warren County at the time of the protests was 39 percent below the per capita income for the nation overall. In 1980 Warren County was nearly the poorest county in North Carolina: ninety-third in household income out of a total of one hundred counties. To make matters worse, by 1982 the unemployment rate for the county had reached its highest point of 13.3 percent.[39] As the poverty in Warren County increased, and farming proved less and less profitable, the county pushed for increased industrial development. However, the economic development plans for Warren did not bear fruit. By the time the landfill controversy began, only a few small industries were established in the county, accounting for a few hundred jobs. With an unemployment rate of over 13 percent, and 45 percent of workers leaving the area to find jobs, the outlook was rather grim. For residents, any action that might possibly limit their economic development options was to be resisted at all costs because survival depended on expanding the possibilities. Expansion, however, was nowhere in sight. No new companies with significant employment opportunities had established businesses in Warren County since the Cochrane Furniture Company opened in 1970. The furniture industry had become part of the rural North Carolina economy by taking advantage of the agricultural demise that had created a large labor pool wiling to work for low wages and to remain nonunionized.[40]

The economic situation in the late 1970s in Warren County was in stark contrast with the major metropolitan areas in North Carolina. The triangle area of Raleigh/Durham/Chapel Hill and Charlotte was booming. The regional disparities in North Carolina had long been vast, but by the 1970s the income inequalities mushroomed. Between 1945 and the 1970s, the state had recruited industries successfully to both urban and rural areas. In fact, North Carolina had one of the fastest growing rural manufacturing labor forces in the country, where small firms in the textile, furniture, and apparel industries found a large labor pool willing to accept lower wages. As rural North Carolina became less competitive with the lower wages in Latin America and Asia, however, factories closed and the flow of new industry slowed. Even those that stayed in the state found it important to the bottom line to move closer to urban areas to be near airports and interstates.

Despite the decrease in manufacturing jobs, the state's economy continued to expand, resulting in a 60 percent increase in the employed labor market in the 1980s. The surge was centered in the six-county metro areas of Raleigh-Durham and Charlotte, where information and financial industries dominated employment rather than the manufacturing sector. The gaps between those living in the metro areas and those in the rural areas grew deeper and at faster rates. The Research Triangle area, just fifty miles south of Warren County, was a significant part of the state's recovery from the recession in the mid-1970s and consistently had one of the lowest unemployment rates in the country during that time. The industries in the growing areas provided plenty of jobs paying good wages and attracted labor from outside North Carolina. The rural counties, with a large pool of lower-skilled labor, did not benefit from the boom.[41]

Since Warren County was in such dire economic need, the threat of destroying any potential for appropriate economic development in the county created a strong sense of outrage. The landfill, seen as a stigma that would scare off potential companies, was a danger to the county because it threatened to completely undermine any hope Warren had of attracting businesses to the area. Blacks in Warren County were particularly sensitive to this issue. As Henry Pitchford pointed out at the first public hearing, "I represent the Warren County chapter of the NAACP . . . we feel that PCB pose a great threat on our health and safety and hampers our efforts to demand new and involved industry which is so badly needed in Warren County."[42]

The potential impact of the landfill on local economic development was of utmost concern to the county commissioners, as well. On 5 January 1979, the day after the first public hearing, the county manager wrote to the EPA Region IV administrator, John White, expressing in writing the reasons for the county's opposition to the plan. He thanked the administrator for "indulg(ing) some very emotional statements made by the residents" but also argued that "some relevant points were made."[43] The most relevant point from the county's perspective was the potential destruction of their last hope for an economic upswing. The county manager explained to administrator White that Warren County had just completed the necessary infrastructure improvements in the proposed industrial corridor in the county. However, the landfill would discourage most industries from locating in Warren, leaving the county in debt from their investments and without potential tax revenues to meet their financial obligations. These sentiments were repeated in letters from residents to the EPA and to the state, as well as in the local paper in editorials, articles, and letters to the editor. The landfill would stigmatize Warren County and halt any development of industry in the county. For example, "Is this what the officials in the state offices want? A county that is already struggling for industry? A county that has an economy at a low level because there is no industry? A county that already has a low educational level because there is no industry to keep the educated people in the county? A county that has very little political power because those qualified for such power move away to better jobs than is [sic] available in Warren County?"[44]

The concerns of black residents that the landfill would cause economic disaster to the county were intensified by the vestiges of an all-black community, Soul City, on the western edge of the county. Soul City was the brainchild of Floyd McKissick, former president of the

Congress of Racial Equality and a lawyer in Durham. Under the auspices of Housing and Urban Development's (HUD) New Town program, Soul City was envisioned as a city of 45,000 black residents with enough industrial development to provide employment for the entire town. However, the project faced enormous obstacles from the start, especially intense resistance from newly elected Senator Jesse Helms of North Carolina. Although McKissick had successfully received $18 million from HUD and had helped HUD to develop the New Town Program, the Soul City project finally died when funding was removed from HUD's New Town program. McKissick had not been successful in attracting residents (only about 400 lived there in 1994) nor had industry chosen to locate in the vicinity.

As the original plans crumbled, the project was reoriented toward developing an industrial park on approximately 1700 acres of unincorporated land. In order to make the idea a reality, significant infrastructure development was needed. In 1978 HUD granted the county over $900,000 to construct a water line connecting Soul City to the towns of Norlina and Warrenton. Warren County had access to two million gallons of water per day through a contract with Kerr Lake Regional Water System. The county only used one-quarter of their allotment, leaving a significant surplus for new industries. Also, the sewer lines were connected to the newly constructed Warren County Regional Wastewater Treatment Facility. Using classical locational analysis, it was hoped that these infrastructure improvements, coupled with a major airport and metropolitan area just fifty miles away and deepwater ports and prime recreational facilities in fairly close proximity, would turn around the local economy. Additionally, the county attempted to improve the marketable skills of the local labor force through the area community colleges. Despite these efforts, the skilled labor force remained low while the illiteracy rate was high. Warren County had the lowest percentage of high school graduates of any county in the area.

It was about the same time as the landfill controversy began that one economic development project was about to come to fruition. In 1979 Perdue, one of the largest processors of poultry in the nation, planned to locate a $20-million facility in Warren County, adjacent to Soul City. The corporation purchased five hundred acres of prime industrial property, but then Perdue delayed its expansion plans. The state's EIS had claimed that Perdue's desire to site a new facility in Warren was proof that worries about detrimental economic impacts were unwarranted. However, the company never did open the Warren facility; instead, it opened a much smaller plant than the one planned for Warren in a nearby county. The loss of the estimated one hundred jobs was devastating to the county's hopes for economic stability, and local residents claimed that the corporation, a large player in the food industry, had been frightened away by the landfill proposal. Perdue denied that the landfill had anything to do with the decision to delay the project, but the company's assurances that the landfill was not a factor did not satisfy those in Warren County worried about the drying up of employment opportunities and deteriorating economic conditions in rural areas.[45]

The threat of scaring away local industrial development opened up another possible economic impact. Residents worried that Warren County could be destined to become the center of a waste industry. The county wanted to attract industry and had gone to extensive lengths to that end but was not willing to become a waste capital of the east coast. Some industries were acceptable, for example, the Perdue poultry plant, but the hazardous waste industry was clearly not the type of economic development that the county had imagined. Fear of the waste industry grabbing hold was most clearly articulated in a letter written by Ken Ferruccio, the leader of the Concerned Citizens organization, to the *Warren Record*, the local newspaper. According to Ferruccio, the industrial sewage system that was supposed to launch the economic development plans for the county was paid for, in part, by the EPA, the same agency that approved the PCB landfill. To make matters worse, the HUD grant to build the sewage system required that the state take control of portions of Soul City. If the state owned the land at Soul City and the 140 acres of property in Afton, then the state would have significant input into industries coming into the county. If the state only needed 20 acres for the landfill, why were they purchasing over 140 acres? Would the extra land be used in the future to either expand the landfill or to build an additional hazardous waste facility? The situation was more complicated when the citizens attributed blame for this part of the problem to local government as well as the state and federal agencies. From this perspective, the Warren County Industrial Commission was also implicated because of their involvement in infrastructure improvement.

The fear of the state, and specifically Governor Hunt, having a vested interest in expanding the waste industry in Warren County was deepened by the involvement of Monroe Gardner, a resident of Warren County and campaign manager for Hunt. In the autumn of 1978 the state decided to run a test of removing the PCB-contaminated soil from a stretch of roadway along Highway 58 in Warren County. They needed a place to put the soil once it was removed from the side of the road and proposed the Department of Transportation (DOT) maintenance yard on the outskirts of Warrenton. The town, however, was successful in gaining an injunction against the temporary storage, arguing that it was too close to a population center and the water supply for the town. Gardner, then, volunteered to lease a piece of his six-hundred-acre property to the state for temporary storage of the soil. His ties to the governor made citizens wary of the underlying intent: Were Gardner and Hunt going to entice waste-related companies to the county by establishing this precedent-setting land use on Gardner's property? For landfill activists, the state's goal of developing a waste industry in Warren County was real: "The Governor had targeted Warren County to be developed into a waste center." They concluded this was the goal because, a few years before the landfill controversy, "he made a big speech about industrial development in Warren County, highlighting its rural, sparsely populated characteristics as attributes for development. It made sense after the fact that Hunt was talking about development of waste facilities."[46] In fact, the low population density in Warren County was one of the most important characteristics for choosing the Afton site for the landfill.

Although the Gardners did not renew the lease, due to pressure from the county commission and the residents, the contaminated soil from the removal test remained on their property for the duration of the landfill controversy. This illegal action on behalf of the state only fueled residents' conviction that Warren County was destined to become the hazardous waste center of the Southeast. As late as 15 September 1982, the first day the DOT trucks brought the contaminated soil to the landfill in Afton, the threat of expanding the waste industry in the county was still a primary issue for residents. On that now infamous first day, the Secretary of Crime Control and Public Safety, Herman Clark, wrote to residents of Warren County addressing their concerns about the landfill. He began his letter with a comment that devalued their anxiety, claiming that the citizens' worries were "based on incomplete, misinformed or misinterpreted information." He then outlined four specific issues "that have been raised time and time again by the citizens of Warren County." Two of the four were related to the threat of the waste industry grabbing hold in Warren County. First, Clark explained that the landfill was only designed to hold the forty thousand cubic yards of contaminated soil to be removed from the road shoulders and then would be capped. Federal law prohibited removal of the landfill cap. He emphasized that the deeding back of the extra 120 acres of land to the county, a concession the state made as part of the court settlement with the county commissioners, guaranteed that the state would not expand the landfill beyond its current borders.

The second issue was slightly more of a problem for the secretary: "Will the location of the PCB landfill in Warren County open the door to other landfills?" Of course, Clark could not make any guarantees. Private companies could look at Warren County to locate a waste management facility. Nothing could be done to stop them from proposing a facility, but the state and the federal EPA would have to approve the permit applications. Warren County residents did not take much comfort in his assurances. Another success of the landfill opposition, however, was the passage in the next legislative session of a law that prohibited a hazardous waste facility within twenty-five miles of any other hazardous waste facility. Warren County residents could be assured, then, that no additional waste-related industry would put roots down in their county.[47]

Although these economic threats were highly probable outcomes from the perspective of county residents, there was no expertise upon which they could draw to present evidence in support of their claims. Research into the economic effects of hazardous waste facilities was certainly in its infancy and focused primarily on the property value impacts that might occur from noxious land uses like waste facilities. No one had thought about how to measure the impact that the facilities might have on economic activity. This boded well for residents because the authorities could not amass evidence to show that their fears were unwarranted, but it also limited the ability of residents to use science and quantitative data to support their claims in this area. Even if there had been studies that showed negative economic impacts from hosting a hazardous waste facility, the agencies that administered the siting process were not required to consider the economic impacts of these facilities. As far as regulators were concerned, the economic impacts of the landfill did not impact the site selection and approval. While there were no official channels available to address these concerns, the mobilizing potential of the economic issues were a significant aspect of the NIMBY frame because even the slightest chance that the landfill would impact the local economy resonated deeply with residents' lived experience of struggling through decades of decline from the fall in agricultural income and inability to attract alternative employment. After the landfill was constructed in Warren County, the county fell from the 97th poorest to the 100th poorest county (out of 100) in North Carolina, yet the triangle area, fifty miles down the road, continued its economic boom. While scholars might debate the validity of claiming that the landfill caused the continued decline, residents were absolutely convinced that the stigma from the landfill was the reason for hitting bottom.

Local Control and Narrative Fidelity

The collective action frame that dominated the early resistance by Warren County residents connected with the strong bonds to the land held by citizens in the rural South. The landfill could only be sited, according to local opponents, by the government usurping local control over a land use decision. The land used for the landfill had been privately owned, was purchased legally by the state, and had no restrictions on its use at the time of the proposed siting in December 1978. However, the state's insistence on moving ahead with the siting, despite the opposition of local residents, convinced them that the government had taken over their right to control the land in their community. It was this perceived loss of control over land use decisions that resonated so deeply with residents in Warren County, whose identity was tied to farming and family land. While making a living off the land in Warren County was never easy and was becoming more difficult each year, it was still an agricultural community. The ties to the land were strong, and the belief that local residents should decide how that land was used was even stronger.

Initially, residents focused their intense resentments toward government on the state and federal levels for forcing a perceived risky enterprise on Warren County without input from the residents. It seemed to the citizens that the government had "already made up their minds" by the time they asked for citizens' thoughts at the first public meeting. When citizens met with Governor Hunt on 19 January 1979, he tried to convince the group that the landfill did not present an unreasonable risk. Residents who attended the meeting asked, "What is a reasonable risk?" and "Who should determine what constituted reasonable?"[48] Citizens came to understand that policy decisions, while perhaps based on science, were fraught with uncertainty and were not value-free. If there was a judgment to be made that intimately affected their daily lives, citizens in Warren County wanted more input into the decision.

While the risks of contamination and economic decline could have been debated with the language of calculations and probabilities, the deeper issue was determining who made decisions about what level of risk residents in Warren County should accept. The NIMBY frame motivated citizens who felt they were losing control over their land and their lives to take it back.

The first event that signaled to opponents that the county had lost control over a local decision was when the county officials learned of the state's plan from reading the announcement in the newspaper on 20 December 1978.[49] Time and again, the state and federal governments neglected to even inform the local government of the decisions being made about county land. When the EPA approved the state's permit application in June 1979, news reporters contacted the chair of the county commissioners for a comment before he even knew the approval was granted.[50] The animosity of the county board was intensified by the unwillingness of the state to communicate directly with them. Residents, who saw the county board as their representatives, also felt slighted and disrespected by the lack of direct communication: "They never let us know until the very last minute. That was the strategy. Keep Warren County unaware."[51] The lack of communication also fueled the county's worries that the state had a hidden agenda, including the establishment of a waste industry in Warren County.

The public involvement process in the siting decision exacerbated the tensions between government and citizens, reinforcing the notion that citizens had lost control over their land. Siting decisions for PCB facilities fell under the jurisdiction of the Toxic Substances Control Act and were not subject to public review, unlike the hazardous waste facilities mandated under the Resource Conservation and Recovery Act. Despite this loophole, the EPA decided to hold a meeting, just two weeks after the state filed for the EPA permit to construct the landfill. That first meeting occurred long before government and industry had developed mediation techniques, compensation packages, and other methods designed to diminish local opposition. Moreover, the conveners of the meeting thought of it as an opportunity to distribute information to the community, to help them see that the facility would be safe. While their motivation may have been sincere, the approach backfired. EPA Region 4 administrator John White, in opening remarks at the meeting, indicated that they had "no provision to deny the issuance of the permit because of public dislike for a site located in a particular geographical area."[52] As one activist described her reaction to the EPA meeting, "They tried to explain the hazards of PCB. The EPA testing of the situation didn't mean anything. I know the EPA is not reliable. It is the government."[53]

When the January 4 meeting was announced in the local newspaper, concerned citizens had only two weeks—during Christmas time—to organize. Despite the short time frame, the fledgling Concerned Citizens organization maximized the qualities of their rural community to recruit residents to attend. A letter to the editor of the *Warren Record* was not nearly as important as the personal contacts members of the group made. The strategy was ideal for the rural community, according to Ken Ferruccio: "In a small town you have to call a few people and you get to nearly everyone." They also met with civil rights leaders, especially the board of education and the local chapter of the NAACP. Local churches were particularly important because "that is the main source of information in the county."[54]

At the meeting, the EPA and the state bombarded citizens with massive amounts of highly technical material without even an attempt to make the information accessible to the average citizen sitting in the armory. One attendee noted, "The things that Mr. Meyer said were mostly impossible for me to understand. They were highly technical. And I doubt that there are five people in here who understand a thing that he said."[55] An outside observer, Professor Robert Kreiger, a toxicologist from the University of California at Davis, validated these observations. He was on sabbatical in Raleigh and attended the hearing to learn more about the situation. "I am very disappointed in [the hearing]. We have had invisible visual aids. We have had technical language, very inappropriate for a public hearing. And I am uncertain what the take-home message was supposed to be. I don't think the simple fact sheets that you take home is [*sic*] sufficient."[56]

The conveners of that initial public hearing in January 1979 hoped to gain the support of county residents, but the meeting galvanized the opposition against the state instead. For many citizens, it appeared that the state and the EPA had already decided what to do. Four years later, on 27 October 1982, the armory was the site of another public hearing held by state officials. At one point in the meeting, one activist gave a signal, and the entire group of several hundred residents attending the meeting stood up, walked out, and held a rally outside. By this time, the landfill had been constructed and the contaminated soil was on its way to the site. Activists did not want to hear about how safe the situation was and how all the appropriate precautions had been taken. They felt that the meetings had not been designed genuinely to consider their concerns and opinions. These feelings of alienation from the government were translated into a thorough distrust of those who worked for government. Even if government officials were working in appropriate and competent ways during this episode, the feelings of distrust were rampant because the residents believed the state had taken control of the land away from them.[57] The government was out of touch with what was happening in real people's lives on a daily basis. When Linda Carter of the Afton Ladies Auxiliary asked at the public hearing, "How long has it been since Governor Hunt was in Afton? How long has it been since any government official was in Afton?" she was expressing this deep sense of distrust.[58] Another resident suggested that government officials should be let go for neglecting to do their job. She began her claims by focusing on the importance of land in the lives of the local residents. "When people's interest and land we love . . . becomes undermined by private interests and political games of a few behind closed doors, it is time to demand change. So-called public servants should be replaced with others who can insure that the industry being considered for Warren County will be for the public good."[59]

The distrust of government that had been cemented through the NIMBY frame became central to the resistance when the state attempted to conduct epidemiological studies of residents living near the landfill. The state decided to draw blood samples of residents living near the landfill to establish a baseline of PCB levels in case it was needed to compare with levels after the unlikely exposure scenario. The state's epidemiologist, Dr. Greg Smith, was very reluctant to do this sampling because he believed it unnecessarily reinforced the emotional and irrational response of the activists. Despite his reluctance, the serum sampling was conducted—just as the soil was being trucked to the landfill in the autumn of 1982—at the insistence of others working on the project. Smith maintained that the usefulness of these data was questionable, particularly because of the paucity of data on the demographic and physiologic variation in concentrations of PCBs. Moreover, he maintained that there was no "data on the biologic and clinicopathologic importance of various concentrations of PCBs in human tissue." On the outside chance that an exposure event would occur and the state decided to draw additional "after" samples for comparison, it would be very difficult to draw conclusions about the impact of the exposure.

The state epidemiologist contacted residents living within a 1.5-mile radius of the landfill site between the ages of twelve and sixty about providing a blood sample. After several attempts by the county health department, blood samples were obtained from only forty-five residents, only three of whom were African American. The state froze the samples for later analysis, if needed. However, the small sample size would hinder appropriate statistical analyses. Residents resisted the blood sampling because they believed that the government would "fix" the tests to prove that the landfill was not a public health threat.[60] For blacks, the issues were more problematic. The legacy of racism in the name of biology made for deep distrust of government-sponsored research. Just a few years earlier, in 1975, the federal government had settled a suit with the NAACP on behalf of the Tuskegee Syphilis Study victims. In the government-sponsored Tuskegee study, researchers had selected black men with syphilis, solely because of their race, to study the effects of the disease. The men were never told that they had syphilis nor were they given treatment, even after penicillin was found to be effective. Some speculated that the men had been deliberately infected with syphilis, like human guinea pigs, although this was never proven. Given the past history of government health studies, blacks in Warren County were not willing to allow a government worker to put a needle into their arms for fear that they might become another scientific experiment.

Usurping local decision making became epitomized in the reported comments of David Kelly, special assistant to the secretary of CCPS in charge of the state's remediation efforts. Citizens were distraught over his comment that "public sentiment won't deter the state's plan to buy the site in Warren County."[61] As interpreted by the residents, this symbolized the major problem with a government out of control. Kelly's words frightened and angered the local residents. Ten years after the incident, residents could not remember exactly where they heard Kelly utter the offensive words. It did not matter what exactly was said or the context. The important issue was that residents heard his words to mean a disregard for their opinions about the situation. As far as the state government was concerned, the local residents did not count. Kelly had discounted their feelings and, as a result, took away the citizens' control over the destiny of their land.

The NIMBY frame cultivated the cultural value of land by blaming the state and federal governments for seizing the right of residents to make choices about the land in the county. Eventually, citizens extended culpability to the county commissioners. The county board filed suit in federal court against the state on 16 August 1979 and requested a preliminary injunction against the purchase of the Popes' property and the construction of the landfill. The court granted the injunction against construction but allowed the state to continue the property purchase. It took one and a half years to hear the case, during which time no remedial action could be taken. The PCB-contaminated soil remained on the road shoulders, covered with activated charcoal and asphalt. The county's arguments presumed that a suitable site did exist someplace. The unacceptable properties of the Afton site were often compared to the properties of other sites, both real and hypothetical.

In May 1982 the county commissioners withdrew the lawsuit they had filed against the state after the state had made several concessions. The environmental impact assessment was forced by the court proceedings, which gave the county opportunities to impact the design and operation plan of the landfill. Not only had the state redesigned the landfill to include the plastic liner, a double leachate collection system, and liners on the sides and top, it also agreed to give 120 acres of the Pope property back to the county. The landfill itself and the necessary buffer land required only 20 acres, so the transfer of the property gave assurance to the county that the landfill would not be expanded. Also, this gave the county control over the land again. As a result, a major victory was won as far as the county commissioners were concerned.[62] The county was satisfied after gaining control of the land and voluntarily withdrew the suit on 26 May 1982.

When the county commissioners settled the suit against the state and accepted the landfill in Afton, the county government also became part of the problem. As far as the residents of the county were concerned, they still did not have the ability to make decisions about the land in their county because their representatives made a decision to which the majority of residents objected. The sentiment among the residents was that "the Commission sold us out." It was unfathomable that the commissioners could have agreed to the landfill, and the only explanation that residents could conceive was that the commission must have had something to gain. Perhaps they, too, would benefit from the development of a waste industry in the county.

Conclusion

The NIMBY frame constructed the siting problem as a threat to local health, environment, and economy that had been forced upon the citizens by an uncaring and too powerful government in collaboration with industrial capital. The rickety regulatory foundation opened up an opportunity for citizens to use science in developing credible alternative interpretations of data and information. The activists demonstrated that experts disagree about the extent of the risks to public health. The notion that the Warren County economy would worsen resonated with residents, who experienced on a daily basis the national recession and disparate regional economic development. The loss of local control over a land use decision was experienced by citizens as a grave injustice.

The mobilizing potency in the NIMBY problem definition and assignment of responsibility was successful in organizing an ongoing four-year opposition but did not make up for the major limitation of the NIMBY frame in Warren County. The "anywhere but here" solution meant that the residents did not want the landfill in their community, no matter what the state and EPA told them about its safety. The solution offered by the local opponents provided no viable alternative because it moved the problem spatially but did not address the underlying issues. If the risky land uses were placed in other locations, then those communities would be facing similar threats from the risks, bearing the full costs of providing the social benefits for everyone. Regulators argued that NIMBY hinders environmental progress and leads to irrational outcomes for society because of its parochial view. However, both citizens embracing the NIMBY frame and the regulators fighting against it were caught in the regulatory framework that puts the responsibility for waste onto the public, rather than private enterprise that generates the waste.[63] From this perspective, NIMBY was a perfectly reasonable response to the uneven distribution of social costs from the existing waste policy system. The NIMBY frame, while not irrational and purely self-serving, restricted the development of a significant offensive against the waste policy system. NIMBY had limited capacity to amplify or extend the collective action frame outside the local context. As a movement frame, NIMBY failed because it did not have an elaborative and universal structure. This limitation hindered NIMBY and stopped the Warren County citizens from successfully blocking the landfill because they could not build alliances and coalitions, thereby eliminating an entire array of approaches to attaining their goal.

Despite the limitations, the NIMBY frame was necessary for the new collective action frame, environmental racism, that developed in Warren County. The environmental racism frame used many of the same diagnoses that had been established with NIMBY. Contamination of water supply, economic stagnation, and loss of local control to a distant government bureaucracy were all part of the new frame. The major shift occurred when the attribution of blame and the proposed solutions changed, enabling a more flexible, elaborative, and resonant frame to emerge. NIMBY was a necessary precursor to environmental racism. After the standard approaches to challenging government decisions were exhausted—lawsuits, public meetings, letter writing, meeting with officials, the collective action in Warren County was ready to move into contentious politics and made this shift by joining forces with civil rights leaders. Transforming the three issues—contamination, economic inequality, and citizen control of public decisions—into the environmental racism frame occurred as the NIMBY frame met the master frame of civil rights and encountered open, ripe political opportunities for a new form of contentious politics.

4 | Constructing Environmental Racism

Political Opportunities, Social Networks, and Collective Action

On 15 September 1982 trucks filled with soil from the contaminated road shoulders began rolling toward the landfill in Afton. At 9:15 that morning, over two hundred people began a mile-long march from Coley Springs Baptist Church toward the same destination. An hour later, the protesters blocked the entrance to the arriving trucks. Nearly one hundred officers from the State Highway Patrol, a battalion from the North Carolina National Guard, and a helicopter were waiting for the protesters, poised to remove and arrest anyone who tried to halt the delivery of the soil. The day ended with sixty-seven arrests and forty-six truckloads of soil. For the next seven weeks, while trucks continued to bring the contaminated soil to the landfill, citizens protested, marched, blocked the road, and were arrested. At the end of the nearly two months, protests had been staged on twenty-five separate days, 523 arrests were made, and 7,097 truckloads of contaminated soil, approximately 40,000 tons, were brought to the landfill.

The protests could be viewed as just another demonstration against a landfill, part of the growing opposition to RCRA and TSCA sitings, but the Warren County protests stood out among the burgeoning anti-toxic movement.[1] Several prominent civil rights leaders were among those arrested, and the protesters argued that the government chose the Afton

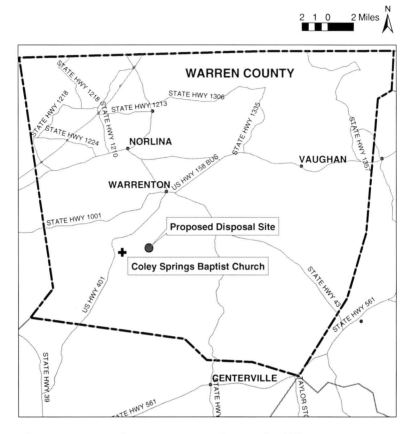

Figure 4.1. Map of Warren County showing landfill site. *Map by Arnab Chakraborty.*

site because of environmental racism—the majority black population in Warren County made it a place of least resistance to the politically charged decision of siting the chemical waste landfill. The protests underscored the conviction that social and political issues, based in particular belief systems, would influence environmental decisions. At the time of the siting, the county was nearly 60 percent black and 3 percent Native American (see table 4.1). Activists who promoted the environmental racism frame argued that the state thought residents in Warren County either would not be as upset about the landfill as a majority white population, or if concerned would not have the power to change the decision. The protests were designed to prove that assumption wrong.

Table 4.1. *Population of Warren County, North Carolina, 1970–2000.*

	1970		1980		1990		2000	
	Total	Percent	Total	Percent	Total	Percent	Total	Percent
White Population	5,909	37	5,827	36	6,600	38	7,769	39
Black Population	9,467	60	9,653	59	9,870	57	10,882	54
Native American Population	434	3	752	5	795	5	1,321	7
Total Minority Population	9,901	63	10,405	64	10,665	62	12,203	61
Total Population	15,810	100	16,232	100	17,265	17,265	19,972	100

Source: U.S. Census.

The environmental racism frame was an extension of NIMBY that had developed through the years of organizing against the landfill. During the protests in Warren County in 1982, the problems of groundwater contamination and continued economic decline in the county remained the central concerns for the protesters but were transformed as the diagnosis changed to political powerlessness, blame was attributed to racism, and the solution focused on halting any additional environmental risks borne by people of color. The environmental racism frame, as articulated in Warren County, transformed the self-interest position of NIMBY to a broader critique of hazardous waste policy by challenging one of the fundamental principles of the hazardous waste management system. Since the entire system was predicated on siting sufficient landfills to contain an ever-expanding pile of waste, the problem of imposing a land use decision on a local community was fundamental to implementing the policy. Environmental racism highlighted the possibility that the entire waste management framework could result in an inequitable distribution of risk where communities with resources, knowledge, and political power would not be host to waste facilities but communities that were poor and lacked political clout would be unduly burdened.

The environmental racism frame expanded the critique of waste policy that had started with the NIMBY frame and enabled the formation of a more robust movement. NIMBY limited the potential scale of influence because a specific situation, per se, could not be widely diffused. However, the scale of impact broadened beyond the local NIMBYs with the linkage to another cause.[2] The Warren County situation brokered the link between the local, mostly white residents working against the specific land use and the black civil rights activists and established organizations with national-level impact. The resulting multiracial coalition did not just change the scale of the conflict to the national level; it also transformed the meaning of the conflict for everyone involved—the local participants, the civil rights participants, the government opponents, and bystanders and observers.

In many ways, the Concerned Citizens group in Warren County in the early 1980s seemed an unlikely organization to stage such a successful series of demonstrations and give rise to an innovative social movement. Members of the group did not have any experience in organizing a direct action nor was it a part of the cultural experience of the mostly white Concerned Citizens. In fact, demonstrations in the South were associated with black activism leveled, in many cases, against local whites. Some of the white members of Concerned Citizens were directly impacted by that earlier activism. The fight to end Jim Crow did not escape the small community of Warren County, where many confrontations between black residents and white residents occurred in the middle of Warrenton on Main Street. During the civil rights movement of the 1950s, blacks had blocked entrances to businesses and marched in the streets to end segregation in services and in education. During the years of fighting the landfill, Concerned Citizens had reached out to both Ronald Reagan and Jesse Helms. The willingness of Concerned Citizens to ally with Reagan and Helms, two major opponents of civil rights activists, demonstrated that the majority white group did not automatically or easily engage in an analysis of racial discrimination. Further, not all of the white participants in the protests claimed environmental racism as the cause of the problem but instead emphasized the political powerlessness of the rural poor.

Environmental justice activists claim that the disruptive action in Warren County occurred because citizens felt the injustice of a landfill siting decision based on the race of the community, not on the inherent assets of the site. Grievances against the perceived injustice were part of the motivation, but as with other social movements, environmental justice did not spontaneously materialize just because conditions reached a crisis level. If the depth of injustice was the primary reason for the appearance of a social movement, why didn't the civil rights movement form during the early twentieth century, when Jim Crow repression was all-pervasive in the South, or the Solidarity movement crystallize long before the 1980s as conditions in Poland were deplorable for decades? Grievances alone do not account for successful organizing of collective action in Warren County or the social movement that it sparked.

Three mechanisms supported the Warren County mobilization: broadening political opportunities, existing social networks and structures for mobilizing, and innovative action bathed in uncertainty. The production of an innovative disruptive action and eventual emergence of a social movement benefited from each individual mechanism as well as the interaction among them. First, political opportunities centered on the election of Ronald Reagan. Rather than constricting political opportunities for disruptive action in the national arena, it led to a realignment of black political power. Second, informal social networks had been established twenty years earlier during the civil rights movement and were ready to reemerge from their "organic associations of everyday life" as soon as the political opportunities were ripe.[3] Third, the disruptive actions in Warren County were based on the established repertoire from the civil rights movement but included innovative and dramatic actions to create significant disruption of the status quo. The innovative actions at the landfill led to deep uncertainty among officials about the level of disruption and the possibility of violence. The fight against the landfill enabled civil rights activists to continue their efforts to increase political power among blacks in the South

Political Opportunities

Why would the group of citizens in Warren County think they could be successful in staging a protest at the landfill? It is possible that they may not have had much hope that their protests would stop the landfill but only acted because they felt so unjustly treated by the siting process. The group was certainly resource-poor compared to the all-powerful state and federal environmental agencies that had been working to get the landfill sited. The likelihood of success increased, however, when the group collaborated with activists well versed in tactics of social protest. Concerned Citizens rallied the support of very influential civil rights personalities and organizations from the national and regional stage. While it seemed unlikely that the local Concerned Citizens organization would reach out to civil rights organizations, it was also improbable that civil rights leaders would choose Warren County as a site for a major effort for black liberation. Several important shifts in the political landscape enabled this situation to develop. The shifts included a conservative, but not totalitarian, regime change with the election of Reagan, a policy opening with the Voting Rights Act (VRA) reauthorization, and local elections as a manifestation of the VRA issue. The renewal of the VRA in 1981 and 1982 energized black activism. Formal civil rights organizations launched a major campaign that highlighted the continued weak political position of blacks in the South, despite the initial successes of the VRA. They prevailed in defining the VRA renewal as an opportunity for increased activism, as Reagan was forced by public opinion to support the renewal despite his initial reluctance.

It might seem that the election of Ronald Reagan and the national shift toward a conservative social agenda would have closed the opportunities for any collective action on behalf of civil rights. However, the mixed political environment, not completely open but not completely repressive, created the ideal circumstances.[4] Reagan's appeal included two positions that were a threat to gains made by blacks in the previous two decades. First, he was a vocal opponent of several civil rights practices, particularly mandatory busing for school desegregation and quota systems to overcome employment discrimination. Secondly, Reagan blamed inflation and the entire recession on the increasing federal budget and based his economic program on significantly decreasing funding for federal social programs. Cuts to environmental regulation were matched by proposed cuts to enforcement of civil rights programs through the Civil Rights Division of the Department of Justice. In 1982 Reagan asserted, "Blacks would be appreciably better off today if the Great Society had never been inaugurated."[5] Civil rights activists were not surprised by this declaration; it only served to reinforce the notion that Reagan would dismantle everything they had achieved. Coretta Scott King, wife of slain civil rights leader Martin Luther King Jr., declared Reaganomics "the most negative and even irrational elements of our society."[6]

The Carter administration had failed to meet the high expectations of blacks who overwhelmingly voted for him in 1976, and by the 1978 midterm election there was a significant decrease in black voter turnout, which continued with the 1980 presidential race. The low black voter turnout in the South contributed significantly to Reagan's sweep of the Electoral College. These were the voters who had been vital to Carter's victory in 1976 but were discouraged by the unfulfilled promises of his campaign.[7] Although some blacks made the Republican turn to support Reagan, the majority of blacks who voted in the 1980 presidential election supported Carter. A burst of civil rights activism immediately followed the election in response to the political attacks from the Reagan administration as well as the increasing number of physical attacks against blacks. The election of Reagan created fear and anxiety among blacks, which reinvigorated their political activism on specific policy issues. In North Carolina, black activists credited Reagan with reenergizing civil rights activities because of the fear that the gains of the 1960s would be lost. The head of the state's Black Leadership Caucus said, "With the onset of Reaganism, many who thought that things have progressively gotten better have been shocked into the realization that many gains may disappear overnight." The head of the state NAACP put it more succinctly: "We can credit Ronald Reagan with the change. . . . He got our act together."[8]

The election of Reagan had a similar impact on environmentalism, revitalizing the movement. Trends in memberships in the large Washington-based environmental lobbying organizations illustrate how the Reagan administration significantly increased activity. Between 1972 and 1979, growth rates in memberships had leveled off from the burst during the three-year period (1969–72) surrounding Earth Day. Then, between 1980 and 1983, membership surged in the environmental lobbying organizations.[9] Part of this increase was related to successfully introducing direct mail solicitation, but under the strong deregulation approach of the Reagan administration and the deepening scandals in the waste programs at the EPA, deep distrust of the government created a reinvigorated environmental movement under Reagan.[10]

There were several civil rights policy battles to wage under the new administration. Civil rights activists tried to bring attention to waning support for civil rights legislation, challenged appointments to major civil rights positions, and joined with other Democrats to halt the cuts to federal social programs. In fact, the Congressional Black Caucus was a major force behind the Constructive Alternative Budget, an attempt to create a unified front against the Reagan budget cuts. However, the major emphasis of the civil rights community in the first two years of the Reagan administration focused on the reauthorization of the VRA of 1965. The original VRA was viewed as one of the most important reforms of the civil rights movement because it drastically changed the

political landscape by removing the obstacles to black voter registration and voting. The general provisions of the act eliminated any prerequisites to voting or registering to vote, like a poll tax or literacy test.
In addition, there were special provisions that applied if a jurisdiction
previously had a preconditional test or device for voting or registering
and less than 50 percent of the total voting-age population was registered or voted in the 1964 presidential election. Jurisdictions that met
these conditions were required to submit all proposed changes to electoral rules and procedures to the Department of Justice (DOJ) for review
of their impact on minority voters. The so-called "preclearance" provisions of the VRA were an attempt to halt communities from taking other measures to stop blacks from voting. The possibilities were many:
"inconvenient location and hours of registration, dual registration for
county and city elections, refusal to appoint minority registration and
election officials, intimidation and harassment, frequent and unnecessary purging and burdensome re-registration requirements, and failure
to provide or abusive manipulation of assistance to illiterates."[11] Between 1965 and 1980, 35,000 requests for changes were submitted, and
the Attorney General only challenged 850 of them. There was some
evidence to suggest that many jurisdictions made changes without the
preclearance.[12]

The VRA immediately led to major political changes, especially
in the South, and by 1980 many jurisdictions covered by the preclearance reported voter registration for more than 50 percent of the minority population.[13] Despite the increase, minority registrations lagged
behind white registrations in all the jurisdictions covered by the 1965
law. In North Carolina, for example, 72 percent of whites were registered to vote but only 55 percent of blacks.[14] The election of black
officials throughout the South was another important measure of the
effect of the VRA. Prior to the VRA, the initial states covered had an
average of 0.47 percent of elected offices held by blacks. By 1980 an
average of 5.6 percent of the elected offices were held by blacks, mostly
local officials in either all-black or nearly all-black jurisdictions. Over
40 percent of the counties in which blacks constituted at least 20 percent of the population still did not have a single black in a county
office.[15] As Joseph Lowery, president of the Southern Christian Leadership Conference (SCLC), explained to the House Subcommittee in
1981, "There are no black Governors, few county commissioners, almost no school superintendents, very few sheriffs, practically no pros-
ecuting attorneys, extremely few judges. There are few minority city

council members and mayors in communities where white majorities exist, although there may be substantial black population. The Voting Rights Act must be extended. It must be strengthened not only to establish equality but equity."[16]

Civil rights leaders felt that any more progress, no matter how modest, was precarious with the conservative turn in the country. The preclearance provision was scheduled to expire in August 1982, and in the midst of the political climate of the Reagan years, the conservative wing of the legislature was empowered to try to roll back civil rights gains. At the start of the hearings in April 1981, it was uncertain if there were even enough votes in the Democratic-controlled House to extend the law, let alone enough in the Senate, with its newly empowered Republican leadership. If the legislative hurdle was overcome, there was uncertainty about a presidential veto and even more uncertainty about getting enough votes for an override.[17]

The two senators from North Carolina, Jesse Helms and John East, both denounced the legislation as a "slap in the face to the South."[18] In fact, the North Carolina delegation led the Senate opposition, with Helms staging a filibuster that ended only after he was promised a full Senate debate on a constitutional amendment to balance the budget and anti-abortion legislation. The role of federalism was central to the opponents of renewal, who argued that the imposition of DOJ review infringed on states' rights. In 1981 Reagan's DOJ reviewed the act and came out in support of the states' rights argument and strongly recommended the bail-out option. Civil rights leaders were horrified by the rhetoric of states' rights since this had been a prominent part of the Jim Crow justification. Jesse Jackson responded by saying, "For black people, states' rights has mainly been states' wrongs."[19]

The renewal of the VRA became the priority for civil rights organizations, resulting in an extensive and intense campaign that took two approaches. First, civil rights groups staged several large demonstrations, hoping to bring attention to the issue. On the eve of the first House hearings in April 1981, the SCLC organized a reenactment of the 1965 Selma-to-Montgomery march, led by Martin Luther King, an important symbol of the power of the civil rights movement in achieving the initial VRA. By the time the Senate took up the debate in early 1982, activists had organized a larger and even more dramatic event in Alabama to emphasize the need for VRA extension. In February thousands of marchers left the Selma Bridge, where seventeen years earlier police attacks had caused the death of protesters. Before heading to the state capital, demonstrators knelt and prayed at the spot of the violent clash between peaceful protesters and law enforcement. A four-day march to Montgomery ensued. In April 1982, as the Senate was preparing to vote on the bill, the march headed from Montgomery to Washington, DC, where protesters built a "tent city," much as they had done in 1965.[20] In addition to dramatic demonstrations to bring attention to the issue, civil rights advocates embarked on an extensive lobbying effort and turned out en masse to the congressional hearings.[21]

Conservatives argued that a results test might create proportional representation, or electoral quotas. The compromise, crafted by Robert Dole (R-KS), won wide support in both the House and the Senate. It retained the stringent bail-out provisions, included a results test that explicitly rejected proportional representation, extended the preclearance for twenty-five years (the House had passed a permanent extension), and extended the language provision for a decade. Even Strom Thurmond (R-SC), a staunch segregationist, supported the bill, but both Senators from North Carolina voted against it. Reagan had changed his position on extension several times since coming to office and, at the urging of Attorney General William French Smith, had come out strongly against the results test. But the Dole compromise assuaged him, if not Smith, and Reagan vowed to support the Senate version. The political pressure to improve the Republican image forced Reagan to acquiesce. In part, this demonstrated that the initial VRA had been successful because the minority vote had become a powerful force in national politics.

Civil rights leaders also accepted the compromise but were not convinced that Reagan's support of the final bill meant that he had become a friend of minorities. Benjamin Hooks, executive director of the NAACP, attended the signing ceremony at the White House on 29 June 1982 along with several other leaders of civil rights organizations. He commented, "Blacks have no confidence that the Civil Rights Division of the Justice Department will enforce the law." Given that Attorney General Smith had been the most vocal opponent in the administration of extending the preclearance, keeping the bail-out, and including the results test, civil rights leaders were warranted in their deep concerns that passage of the bill would only be a symbolic victory. If there were to be any real impact, they would need to keep active with constant vigilance to ensure a full implementation under the Smith DOJ.

Equal representation was strongly influenced by district boundaries, and the VRA was designed to insure that redistricting did not dilute the hard-won votes of minorities. North Carolina, subject to the preclearance review of any election rule changes, passed a redistricting plan based on the 1980 census that was rejected by DOJ review. A second attempt by the state created a congressional district in the northeastern part of the state with 40 percent black population that divided four counties but included Warren County in its entirety. In the past, court rulings did not support congressional redistricting that split local jurisdictions, but the DOJ gave preclearance to the new plan for North Carolina on 11 March 1982.[22] It was the first time in the twentieth century that the state had a real chance to elect a black member of congress. The opportunity was not lost on civil rights leaders. In 1982 North Carolina became central to the organizing strategy of civil rights activists. Registration of blacks was imperative, as was the need to energize the black voters to go to the polling booths on election day.[23]

Under the original formula in the VRA, changes affecting the entire state of North Carolina needed preclearance, but not all counties came under the special provisions. In Warren County, prior to 1965, there had been severe restrictions on voting registration, including requirements to read and interpret the Constitution. However, the number of registrants exceeded the threshold set by the VRA. As a result, any voting changes made in the county were not subject to federal review, nor did federal observers watch the polling places in the county. Although Warren County did not qualify for the special provisions, the issue of extending the VRA was still relevant to county politics. The VRA reauthorization was particularly important in Warren County because the number of blacks registered to vote was close to a level that could make a difference in the outcome of the election. Elections in the South were still determined by racial lines: blacks voted for blacks, and whites did not. In this political atmosphere, it was appalling to African Americans that prior to 1978 there were no black elected officials in Warren County. Although the county had slipped by the special provisions, the majority of the county, 64 percent, was unable to elect a black representative. All this could change with a small increase in registrants and voter turnout. African American residents in Warren County took advantage of their newly won access to the political system through the general provisions of the act. After the initial VRA was passed in 1965 and the prerequisites for registering and voting were removed, there was a significant increase in the numbers of blacks registered to vote. By 1976 an equal number of blacks and whites were registered. However, it was not until 1978 that there were enough blacks registered who also voted to elect the first African American, George Shearin, to the county board.

Civil rights leaders participated in the Warren County landfill protests in 1982 as a part of their commitment to increasing black voting power and black political representation. North Carolina was important to this effort because both Senators had been vocal opponents of the VRA extensions; the state had the lowest percentage of blacks registered in the states originally covered; and the new congressional district created an important opportunity for increased black representation on the national level. African Americans in Warren County, through connections with civil rights leaders, took advantage of the renewed commitment to voting rights in 1982. The subsequent voter registration drive intensified in the spring of 1982 with door-to-door registration campaigns throughout the county as well as registration booths set up in black churches. These same key individuals in the 1982 voter registration push were involved in the protests during the autumn of the same year. Not only did the renewed commitment to voting rights result in increased numbers of registered black voters and black elected officials, the voter registration gave blacks throughout the county a sense of political power, which extended into their participation in the landfill opposition.

Intensified voter registration drives and "turn out the vote" efforts expanded during the 1982 election season in the late summer and fall of that year. As a result, the entire political landscape changed in November 1982. The overall number of voters registered in Warren County increased by 30 percent; 76 percent of the overall increase was from nonwhite registrants, resulting in 27 percent more nonwhite registrants than whites. The chair of the county board, a white man who lost reelection in 1982, declared: "Starting in 1982, some blacks—much more radical than they are now—really pushed the voter registration. They had the majority and in the 1982 election, blacks beat the whites."[24] African Americans won major positions at the polls in Warren County, including the majority of seats on the county board, the sheriff, the registrar of deeds, and a state assembly representative. Warren County became the first county in North Carolina to have a majority African American membership on the board of commissioners. On 8 December 1982 the *Durham Herald* declared the county "Free at Last" because they had elected representatives more reflective of the constituency.

The success of African Americans in the elections was tied to the intense political action against the landfill during the fall. This activity, with the support of civil rights leaders and extensive participation by black residents of the county, led to continued politicization of blacks at the voting booth. According to the pastor of Coley Springs, "Whites were not going to help blacks into politics. The PCB woke everybody up. The political avenue opened up. Blacks started to register and to vote."[25] Dollie Burwell, who won the Registrar of Deeds position in 1982 and continued in that position until 1996, played a significant role in the black voter registration drive. Her efforts were directly tied to the larger agenda of the national civil rights organizations, especially through her involvement with the United Church of Christ Commission on Racial Justice (UCC) and the SCLC.

According to leaders of the protests, the political empowerment of blacks in the county was one of the major successes of the landfill opposition. The collective action was not successful in achieving its goal of stopping the disposal of PCB-contaminated soil in the landfill at the Afton site. The long-standing animosity between black residents and the white board was intensified when the board settled the case with the state. They were seen as "selling out" the blacks in the county, fueling the heated political atmosphere, and gave black residents another reason to vote against the majority white political establishment. The landfill protests became part of the attack against that establishment as well as part of the motivation to keep the attacks going—right into the election booths. The involvement of hundreds of blacks in disruptive collective action for the first time in over a decade was part of the political organizing for black voting rights and led to increased voting by and for African Americans.

Social Networks

In the summer of 1982 all other options were exhausted, the soil delivery was looming, and Concerned Citizens decided to "exercise their right of free assembly through non-violent direct action."[26] It was not the first time that the group had discussed the possibility of demonstrating. At the first public hearing in January 1979, several Warren county residents told the EPA that a direct action against the site was a real possibility. Later that same month, when nine residents from the county met with Governor Hunt, they also leveled a threat of direct action, if due process did not yield the results they wanted. These threats were repeated during the subsequent three years, yet the group delayed action, supporting the county commissioners and believing their cause would triumph in the judicial system.

Given the long history of racial discrimination and tension, it was most astonishing that the majority white opposition in a rural southern county reached out to black protest leaders for help and advice to revive their movement. It was even more astonishing that many whites (although not all) stayed and participated in the meetings, marches, and acts of civil disobedience. However, everyone—leaders, participants, and bystanders—attributed the success of the coalition building to Ken and Deborah Ferruccio. The couple was highly respected because of their unceasing work to halt the landfill. By 1982, several years into the conflict, their judgment was trusted by the Concerned Citizens. Even twenty years later and after a major rift developed between the Ferruccios and the other Concerned Citizens, their leadership and tenacity were admired. Ken and Deborah Ferruccio moved to North Carolina from Ohio in 1975, looking for a quiet rural setting to raise a family. Since they were not from the South, they were often dismissed as outsiders. However, the tradition of successful collaboration between black southerners and white northerners from the earlier civil rights actions opened up an opportunity for the necessary connection. Not all civil rights organizers felt comfortable with the past collaborations, but those who worked closely with Concerned Citizens believed that multiracial coalitions were a necessary ingredient for success. According to Golden Frinks, a long-time organizer with the SCLC who was responsible for guiding the organizing on a day-to-day basis in Warren County: "We were talking about brotherhood, white and black. Preserve all of us together."[27] The collaborative approach was important to the eventual development of the environmental justice identity. However, these sentiments did not embrace the ideas of conventional modern environmentalism that understood pollution as an equalizing factor in modern society. Environmentalism might argue that social divisions had become less important because, eventually, the risks from modernization impact everyone, even the producers of the risks and those who profit from them. The collaborative efforts in Warren County did not emphasize the equalizing process of risk but highlighted the differential impacts. The sentiments were strategic organizing ideas, not a proclamation of an even playing field.[28]

When these northern whites were able to gain the respect of both the local white landowners and the local and national black civil rights activists, it was a catalyst for the unlikely coalition between blacks and whites in this southern county. Neither Ken nor Deborah had any direct ties to the black leaders. They needed someone to broker a connection between their group and civil rights activists. The pastor of the near-by black Baptist church, just a little over a mile from the landfill site, knew the Ferruccios through his parishioners who were involved with Concerned Citizens. Reverend Luther Brown of Coley Springs Baptist Church was not a politically active pastor; he did not believe that the spiritual well-being of his congregation depended on fundamental po-litical and social change. In fact, he felt that it was inappropriate for a pastor to expand into political activism and preferred to keep focused on spirituality. But toxic waste was unlike other political issues, and in early 1979, after reading Ken Ferruccio's letter to the editor of the *Warren Record*, Brown became deeply concerned for the health of his parishioners. He eagerly met with Ken, Deborah, and a few of the oth-er Concerned Citizens and eventually moved into the political work he had eschewed. In 1982, when the group began to seriously discuss direct action, Reverend Brown and Ken Ferruccio met with Reverend Leon White, a politically active minister of the local UCC, at the west-ern edge of Warren County, and a member of the UCC's Commission for Racial Justice. Brown did not know Reverend White well, just in passing and by reputation. However, Brown's position as a black pastor was essential to the bridge between Concerned Citizens and the civil rights community.

Many participants in the Warren County protests believed that White and the Commission had courted Concerned Citizens. The Com-mission could not have been oblivious to the intense opposition and the discussion of possible civil disobedience. Since they had been involved in disruptive action in the county and throughout the state since the 1960s, they would not easily let go of an opportunity. Further-more, at the same time as the landfill organizing, in the summer and fall of 1982, the Commission was at the center of the voter registration in Warren County that was linked to the congressional debates about renewal of the VRA. When environmental justice advocates tell the story of the origins of their movement, they quickly point to the cen-tral role of the UCC in the Warren County protests and the subsequent landmark study, *Toxic Waste and Race*, conducted in 1987 by the UCC Commission on Racial Justice.[29] Advocates highlight the importance of civil rights leaders in linking environmental issues to social concerns. They downplay the role of Concerned Citizens, with its white leader-ship and predominately white membership. However, both players and the bridge created between them were equally central to the actions that led to environmental justice. Reverend White had vast experience

in organizing disruptive collective actions and was willing and ready
to work with Concerned Citizens because he needed to discredit the
claim of being an outside agitator.[30] The work was mutually beneficial
to both groups, and each developed a deep respect for the other.

Increasing black political power was a primary goal of the organizing efforts, but the development of a multiracial coalition was also
a central tenet. Black civil rights organizers took primary leadership
for the demonstrations, marches, and acts of civil disobedience. Civil
rights leaders supported the local leadership, in part, to avoid a dis-
missal of the protests as the work of "outside agitators" and also to cultivate multiracial organizing. Since most of the leaders of Concerned
Citizen were white, the collaboration between the local group and the
national civil rights leaders meant building racial bridges. The coalition shared a common interpretation of the central problem of the landfill siting: the state had imposed a land use decision with potentially
dire consequences on politically powerless citizens. It was common to
see civil rights leaders and white citizens of Warren County leading the
protests arm in arm (see fig. 4.2).

Figure 4.2. Black and white activists in Warren County protests. *Photo by
Jenny LaBalme.*

The white citizens active in the opposition welcomed the "spiritual, religious and moral leadership" of the civil rights organizations.[31] Henry Rooker, a resident near the landfill and active Concerned Citizen member, was not used to multiracial work and felt "a little uneasy at first" but came to value the collaboration. Ferruccio, also, felt deeply indebted to the civil rights leaders but always insisted that "the leadership is the citizens of Warren County."[32] The importance of the multiracial focus was highlighted at the September 17 protests. During the event, two teenagers, one black and one white, stood arm in arm before the crowd of over one hundred people. The black teenager proclaimed, "Some people are beginning to feel this is a racial issue. It's not a racial issue. It's a people issue." His friend concurred, "We've got to [do] this as people. We've got to be together on this."[33]

The brokerage of the UCC and Concerned Citizens broadened the networks available to the landfill opponents. The local networks expanded to include regional and national activist leaders and many activists who had not previously dealt with environmental issues. Benjamin Chavis was one of the most prominent of those involved in the Warren County organizing as a result of the UCC and Concerned Citizens collaboration. Later, he became a leading spokesperson for the movement and was given credit for coining the term "environmental racism" while director of the UCC's Commission for Racial Justice at the time when they produced the influential *Toxic Wastes and Race* report. Ben Chavis, born and raised in Oxford, North Carolina, about twenty miles from Warren County, had been recruited for the Commission while attending the University of North Carolina at Chapel Hill by Leon White, then the director of the North Carolina field office for the Commission. In 1971, through his work with the Commission, Chavis became the leader of the infamous Wilmington Ten by organizing a boycott by black high school students in Wilmington, North Carolina, after their request for the school to observe Martin Luther King's birthday was denied. During the several weeks of protests in Wilmington, the group was continually harassed. During one evening's events, a grocery store owned by a white man was fire-bombed and burned to the ground. The activists were wrongfully accused, arrested, convicted, and sentenced for terms from seven to twenty-nine years. In 1978, the same year the PCB contamination was illegally dumped along the road shoulders, Governor Hunt shortened the term for Chavis. He was finally released in 1980, after four years (1976 to 1980) in prison for a crime he had not committed. His release came when a federal court reversed the conviction because the investigators and prosecutors had framed the ten activists. They had hired the witnesses to perjure themselves by claiming to have seen Chavis and the others at the scene. Even after the witnesses stated that they had lied in court, the federal courts were slow to review the case.[34] Finally, after nearly ten years of legal battles, Chavis was released.

In the interim, he had become a hero for blacks and the civil rights cause. Nowhere was this truer than in his home in the northeastern section of North Carolina, where Chavis had helped organize blacks for civil rights actions. As a previous member of the United Church of Christ located in Warren County, he was a part of the local community. Through contact with White and the Commission, he became an important symbolic leader for the local blacks in the protests. He delivered a motivational speech to the group, and on the third day of the protests, Chavis was arrested while leading a group of protesters in blocking the DOT trucks. Residents viewed his willingness to be arrested as a great sacrifice for them in light of his previous experiences with law enforcement in North Carolina. Chavis's participation increased the visibility of the activism, but he was careful to share center stage with residents of Warren County. On September 17, the same day that the two teenagers proclaimed their unity, Ken Ferruccio and Ben Chavis led the marchers walking arm in arm on the road from Coley Springs.[35]

Renowned as the leader of the Wilmington Ten, Chavis evoked respect from African Americans, caution from law enforcement, and intense interest from the media. Chavis was connected to his roots in northeastern North Carolina, but his national reputation gave meaning to the local struggle and created the uncertainty necessary for successful disruptive action.[36] Although law enforcement officials were not surprised by his participation nor taken off guard by it, Chavis gave the action a serious connotation, not to be taken lightly. Though nonviolent, the potential was always present. The outcome was unpredictable and was dependent upon the reaction of others—participants, bystanders, the state, and other elites. Chavis did not participate in every local action for civil rights. The fact that he did in Warren County, even if only for a few days of the seven-week ordeal, was cause to stand up and take notice. The vast media presence due to the participation of Chavis heightened the uncertainty about the potential for extreme social disorder and kept the State Highway Patrol anxious about a possible violent confrontation being broadcast across the nation.[37]

The other leader brought into the fold by the UCC's involvement was Dollie Burwell, a member of Leon White's church who began her political career as Warren County Registrar of Deeds. Burwell had not been involved in any of the activities related to the landfill in the long and arduous years prior to 1982.[38] However, she became a leading spokesperson in the county against the landfill as soon as the UCC and Concerned Citizens joined forces. Her participation in the landfill protests was directly tied to the voting registration campaign and her own political campaign, which had heated up at the same time as the soil was placed into the landfill. Immediately following the protests, she was one of the blacks elected to county office in the November 1982 elections. Burwell was a leading force behind the efforts in the county to register black voters. She also was responsible for motivating blacks in the county to turn out for the protests. The Ferruccios may have had the initial idea and the civil rights leaders may have created a viable strategy, but Burwell was pivotal in her ability to turn out the masses. She became a symbol for the environmental justice movement, as an average black woman who stood up and made a difference.

In addition to the expertise from the UCC, the local opponents received the support of the Southern Christian Leadership Conference (SCLC), the organization associated with Martin Luther King and the nonviolent civil rights actions of the 1950s and 1960s. The initial involvement of the SCLC led to the arrest of a congressional representative and chair of the Congressional Black Caucus, Walter Fauntroy, and the increased media attention associated with this unusual occurrence. The involvement of a powerful political ally was possible because of another national leader in the civil rights movement and a key figure in Warren County, Floyd McKissick.

McKissick, a lawyer in Durham, North Carolina, was named national chair of the Congress on Racial Equality (CORE) in 1963 and was a featured speaker at the March on Washington that same summer. Black residents in Warren County were very active in sit-ins organized by CORE and were quite loyal to McKissick. Many of these same black residents were active in the landfill opposition.[39] McKissick became director of CORE three years later and tried to focus CORE's activities on promoting programs to improve the economic situation of blacks and move CORE away from civil disobedience. However, other black members of CORE wanted to take a more radical stance and eventually the "black power" faction of CORE gained leadership of the organization, leading to the creation of a black-only membership.[40] McKissick then took two steps that set him apart from other civil rights leaders. First, in 1972 he switched his party affiliation from Democratic to Republican and supported President Nixon's bid for reelection. McKissick was not the only black leader to take the conservative turn; most notable, Ralph Abernathy, King's successor at SCLC, also endorsed Nixon. Next, McKissick focused on building an all-black community under the new town development program of the Department of Housing and Urban Development (HUD). The result of his efforts was Soul City, on the edge of Warren County, which was struggling to survive at the time of the landfill controversy.

McKissick's concern about the impact of the landfill on Warren County was directly tied to his investment and commitment to Soul City. The landfill threatened to intensify the deteriorating economic conditions in the county. The stigma of hosting a hazardous waste landfill could cause further economic hardships and lead to the demise of Soul City's last hope for even the slightest success. McKissick participated in the first two days of demonstrations and was arrested on the second, along with six others. Given that McKissick had long ago abandoned the civil disobedience approach for the more conservative entrepreneurial strategy, this uncharacteristic move demonstrated the degree to which he saw the landfill as a threat to the economic well-being of the county. For McKissick, Warren County was a place to prove his idea that economic development was the key to gaining equity for African Americans. Although some of McKissick's public statements focused on permanent health effects on children and future generations, the landfill also threatened Soul City's last chance to attract industrial development and pushed McKissick to participate in the disruptive action.

In another significant turning point, McKissick also brought his old friend Golden Frinks, an experienced organizer, to the Warren County demonstrations. Frinks and McKissick knew each other from their work together in labor unions in the 1940s, the NAACP in the 1950s, and sit-ins in the early 1960s. Frinks, also a native of North Carolina, worked for SCLC from 1962 to 1977. Much of his organizing occurred in North Carolina, especially in Edenton, on the northern coast of the state, also in a predominately African American county. He was well known in North Carolina as a skilled civil rights organizer.[41] McKissick knew that Frinks would bring years of experience in organizing disruptive collective action to Warren County. Frinks joined the group within the first week and stayed for the duration of the demonstrations as the key organizer in the field on a daily basis.

As a professional organizer, he was very familiar to activists and law enforcement officers throughout the Southeast, especially in North Carolina. The presence of Golden Frinks was sufficient to warrant over two hundred State Highway Patrol (SHP) officers, the largest show of law enforcement at any protest in North Carolina. During the entire six weeks, the SHP clocked a total of 35,892 person hours to enforce order on what was seen as a very volatile situation. The SHP kept a high level of security throughout the episode, despite the fact that no violence had occurred for several weeks. The number of personnel working at the landfill remained between fifty and a hundred each day until near the end of October, when it dropped to about a dozen for the last week.[42] Although the law enforcement officers had some disdain for the civil rights actions of the 1960s, referring to them as the "Martin Luther King riots," they also had some respect for Frinks as a professional. His presence in the demonstrations had a paradoxical effect on the patrol. On one hand, Frinks had enough trust and respect for the patrol officer in charge to talk over much of the daily plan with him so there were very few surprises. On the other hand, the professional civil rights organizers attracted both the media and a large audience to the demonstration. Frinks, seen by many as a colorful character with a commanding presence and voice, was particularly attractive to the media. The presence of the media, according to the SHP, was the fuel that blew the demonstrations out of proportion and kept them going for weeks. For the SHP, the media were a major part of the problem, but for the organizers increased media attention was a sign of successful organizing. The media would have disappeared, or never materialized in the first place, had it not been for Frinks and the civil rights leaders with national reputations that he brought to Warren County.

At the request of Frinks, Joseph Lowery, the president of the SCLC since 1977, arrived in Afton, North Carolina, on 20 September along with his wife, Evelyn, and a colleague, Reverend Fred Taylor. As a founding member of the organization in 1957 along with King, Shuttlesworth, and Abernathy, Lowery was critical to many major civil rights demonstrations throughout the South in the 1960s.[43] Taylor and Lowery were both arrested on their first day in Afton, prompting Andrew Young, then mayor of Atlanta, where the SCLC is headquartered, to request that Governor Hunt release Lowery and that disposal of soil at the landfill be stopped, making the landfill an even more complicated political liability. The three participated extensively over the next few weeks in several capacities. Reverend Lowery commanded great respect because of his reputation and because of the rapport he built with many local white activists. As a gifted speaker, he gave many motivational speeches to the group and led them in prayer. Most importantly, Lowery's experience helped the group avoid potential disasters, especially eruptions of violence. His professional leadership style also steered the SCLC and other leaders from usurping all control from the locals. Locals were particularly impressed with his ability to keep a low profile, respect the locals, and encourage their leadership, while also keeping a tight rein on the entire action.

At the request of Lowery and the SCLC, Walter Fauntroy, a nonvoting member of Congress from the District of Columbia, went to Warren County, gave a motivating speech to the group, participated in the demonstration, and, much to Congressman Fauntroy's surprise, was arrested on 27 September 1982. It was the first time a member of Congress was arrested in a protest. He hit the headlines; the State Highway Patrol received a call from the governor, and Fauntroy was released immediately. Fauntroy remembers clearly why he went to Warren County: "One of the problems with groups in towns like Warrenton is that they fail to make the media and get public attention. If you don't have the public attention, you can't raise the consciousness of the body politic. SCLC and Lowery show up, some people from AP, UPI, ABC, and CBS might show up and show it on the six o'clock news. Dr Lowery and the staff went to Warrenton and then came a time when they had to raise visibility even higher. We know a member of Congress. If a member of Congress gets arrested, it might raise public consciousness even higher."[44] Fauntroy had long been involved in Washington politics. In the early 1960s he was the District of Columbia liaison for the SCLC and worked as a key organizer for both the March on Washington in 1963 and the Selma-to-Montgomery march in 1965.[45] When Fauntroy became a nonvoting member of Congress, representing the District of Columbia, he was involved in forming the Congressional Black Caucus (CBC) in 1972.[46] As an active member of the CBC, Fauntroy worked to halt Reagan's attacks on social programs. He obtained support from white representatives of districts with at least 25 percent black voters by urging black voters in these districts to put pressure on their representatives.

Fauntroy held highly visible and powerful positions at the time of the Warren County demonstrations and was able to successfully bring the environmental justice issue to a government agenda, albeit in a small way, by persuading the General Accounting Office (GAO) to investigate the demographic characteristics of communities near commercial hazardous waste landfills. The GAO responds to requests from congressional members according to their rank, giving requests from committee and subcommittee chairs priority. Since Fauntroy was not even a member of a committee that dealt with environmental matters, he had to secure the support of a colleague in Congress who could successfully request GAO action on the matter. Fauntroy approached Jim Florio (D-NJ), who was deeply engaged in the congressional oversight of EPA's waste programs. The EPA debacles of implementation had reached crisis level in 1982, eradicating all legitimacy. The GAO report was very limited in its scope and rigor but started the spate of investigations about equity and the distribution of environmental risk that became the heart of the environmental justice movement. It was possible because the civil rights networks enabled a brokerage with the larger investigation into regulatory failure.[47]

Despite connecting the Warren County situation and the likelihood of environmental racism with the broad attack on the Reagan EPA, the civil rights framing did not involve the established environmental movement nor did the African Americans expect or desire their involvement. With no attempt to broker connections between civil rights organizations and environmental organizations, networking was limited to civil rights activists and local opponents, who did not identify as environmentalists. The collective action in Warren County created new meanings for civil rights and broadened the understanding of environmentalism, but the lack of coalition building with environmentalists also constrained its identity. The participants thought the only environmental organizations that could possibly be interested in the issue were the agencies responsible for environmental protection because the environmental identity embraced by activists in Warren County was constructed as an opposition to these agencies and differed sharply from what participants perceived of as traditional environmentalism. Activists involved in the Warren County action understood an environmentalist to be someone who either was a member of large, Washington-based environmental organizations or ascribed to the positions of an environmental organization, just like a civil rights advocate was understood as either a member of a well-known civil rights organization (i.e., SCLC or NAACP) or one who ascribed to the positions of these organizations. One of the central ideas of modern environmentalism—that unbridled industrial production created untenable risks and undermined the goal of modernization itself—deeply influenced the residents' perspective on the landfill. The risk-based critique also carried an intense distrust of the ability of institutions to mitigate the risks. As a result, Warren County activists built their environmental identity without solidarity with environmentalism, per se, but in opposition to governmental institutions responsible for environmental protection.[48] No attempt was made once the civil rights organizations entered the fray to contact the large environmental organizations with national-level influence in the policy arenas. Despite the fact that civil rights organizations also enjoyed the power and prestige of influencing Washington, a brokerage between the two movements did not occur. The protesters did depend on the information provided by the anti-toxic organizers. Lois Gibbs, Love Canal activist and founder of the fledgling Citizen's Clearinghouse for Hazardous Waste, spoke to the protesters in Warren County, supporting their efforts to defend the health and well-being of the community and to challenge government agencies that were not living up to their responsibilities to protect the public from environmental risks. Lois Gibbs had sway because of her role in Love Canal but in 1982 the anti-toxics activist was just beginning to build power, authority, and credibility enjoyed by the environmental organizations.

The absence of substantial participation by traditional environmental organizations in the Warren County controversy was due, in part, to the avenue taken by civil rights organizations to incorporate an environmental identity. In addition, the difficulty that environmental organizations faced in embracing a civil rights agenda kept them on the periphery of the activism. Despite the many attempts through the 1970s at incorporating both urban and minority concerns into their agenda, the idea of "environmental racism" did not come easily to environmental organizations. According to activists fighting environmental racism, the obstacles were due to the focus of traditional environmentalism on the protection and conservation of nonhumans. As Dollie Burwell put it, "African Americans are not concerned with endangered species because we are an endangered species."[49] Although a significant amount of effort of the environmental movement focused on preservation of the natural world and conservation of natural resources, many of the major successes of the movement could be characterized as "people protection," not "nature protection." Traditional environmental organizations were deeply engaged in pushing for passage of toxic laws (TSCA, RCRA, and Superfund). They also fought tenaciously to protect human health though appropriate and timely implementation of these laws. The challenge for large, national-level environmental organizations was not a proclivity toward protecting nature over people or a neglect of protecting public health. The conceptual obstacle came from an inability to understand why concern for legal, social, and economic equality should impact their analysis of an environmental issue. People, no matter what social space they occupied, would benefit from environmental protection. An environmentalist, then, helped everyone by fighting for strong regulation and enforcement to protect human health and the environment from contaminated air, water, and land. For the established environmental organizations, equality had little to do with environmental protection because the regulations were designed to reduce risk. According to this line of reasoning, as long as these regulations were implemented and enforced, risks for everyone would decrease.

Two influential environmental organizations, the North Carolina chapter of the Sierra Club and the Conservation Council of North Carolina, participated in the landfill controversy prior to the involvement of civil rights organizations. Both the Sierra Club and the Conservation Council, concerned about the potential threats from the contaminated soil, were involved in the technical review concerning the landfill. Neither participated in the protests; nor did the civil rights organizers ask for an alliance with them, despite their earlier input. While both of these groups were dedicated to ensuring protection of human health, neither could overcome the dichotomous analysis that bifurcated equality and environment. David Levy, the Conservation Chair of the Sierra Club chapter, wanted first and foremost to "get the stuff up and out of the immediate environment" and lobbied the state to take immediate action after the illegal dumping in 1979. The club had faith in the cradle-to-grave system and regulatory structure designed to ensure safe containment of chemical waste. They took two approaches to advocating for a sound and quick solution to the debacle of the PCB dumping. Working with a soil scientist, Levy submitted comments on the permit application and landfill design, arguing that the exemptions should not be granted and the double liner should be constructed to surround the entire landfill. Also, Levy attended the public hearing in January 1979 and was dismayed by the ineffective public participation process. The Sierra Club advocated for a full environmental impact assessment process with the appropriate public involvement program. The club offered to design the public participation program, but the state did not take advantage of their expertise. The court forced an EIA, but the state's public participation process was barely adequate. Once the permit was granted and construction began, the club's work was finished.[50] Neither the club nor the civil rights organizations had reason to construct an alliance since the club could not undermine the permit process nor challenge the principles of the cradle-to-grave system.

The Conservation Council, like the Sierra Club, fit the profile of the traditional environmental organization with an exclusively white and middle-class membership. In 1969 a group of concerned scientists, lawyers, and academics organized the council in an effort to halt development on Bell Head Island, a unique barrier reef island off the southern coast of North Carolina. The council quickly broadened its focus beyond resource protection to include air, water, and waste issues and became a significant force in state environmental politics through legislative and rulemaking advocacy and enforcement oversight. Hazardous waste issues were central to the mission of the organization, despite its initial project in preservation, due to the influence of Rachel Carson. According to Jane Sharp, president of the council in 1994, "[Her] book was a kind of bible that told us to watch out for the chemical culture." When the PCB contamination was discovered, the council advocated shipment to the Alabama site because the landfill had been constructed and was operating, as far as anyone could tell, without problems. The landfill paradigm had to work, or the entire regulatory structure for both PCB waste and hazardous waste could topple. Although RCRA and TSCA advocated treatment, residue would always require some containment in landfills. The council sympathized with the local activists and supported their position for shipment out of state, but when the protests began, the support ended, not from lack of concern for human health. The Conservation Council stepped back from the protests not because they didn't care about environmental issues that impacted human health, as many would guess of this traditional environmental organization. The council believed that social dimensions of environmental issues should take a back seat to technical and legal aspects, and they were unwilling to engage in the tactics of direct action. The council thought "social issues are implied in many environmental issues, but. . . . It is better to work in geology and the technical and economic issues—the externalities." The idea of linking discrimination with environmental issues would "only muddy the waters" of both issues, which were already very complicated. The only social aspect of environmental issues of importance was the need for "conserving for future generations," not because conservation only referred to "nature," but because conservation should have benefits for everyone, regardless of social categories. If a technically sound solution were implemented, public health—of everyone—would be secured. Since these issues were very complex, council members felt the need to focus on the details of highly technical questions. They also did not want to risk losing their authority and influence with state decision makers. "We only have so much person power. Our expertise also allows us to concentrate on technical issues. Individual members of the council participated in the meetings and marches, but the organization took a more cautious approach, not wanting to completely antagonize the state government agencies. The Conservation Council uses more conservative tactics. They put out a very good newsletter and included information about what was going on at the landfill. The council did not want to blame the governor for making a bad decision. Lawyers know that if you do something to antagonize someone, they'll do it back to you sooner or later."[51]

Innovative Disruptive Action

The change in tactics that emerged from the collaboration between civil rights leaders and local landfill opponents led to a series of disruptive actions that succeeded in "obstruct[ing] the routine activities of opponents, bystanders and authorities."[52] The protest events continued for seven weeks and attracted crowds from as small as a handful to as many as several hundred, with about seventy-five protesters on most days.[53] The protests became the start of the environmental justice movement, despite the fact that they did not achieve the primary goal of stopping the landfill. Success was possible because organizers understood the important objective of organizing: build on an established repertoire of action but create significant uncertainty about how those actions might be used to produce disorder.

During the protests, civil rights leaders successfully walked a delicate line to politicize African Americans in the county, with the goal of increasing voter turnout in the upcoming election, while not alienating the white supporters from Warren County. White residents of the county were instigators and leaders of the opposition, and significant numbers of white residents participated in the protests. Specifically, nearly one-third of the adults arrested were white, and slightly more women were arrested than men (see table 4.2). While the majority of the white adults were not from Warren County, nearly one-third of the whites arrested were Warren County residents. This means that forty-two white adult residents of Warren County attended a black church, listened to black preachers and civil rights leaders, learned nonviolent civil disobedience techniques from black activists, and lay down on the road next to black residents from Warren County. Many more white residents participated in all aspects of the protests but were not arrested, so an accurate count cannot be made.

Whites and blacks were familiar with the pattern for activism, honed twenty years earlier. Meetings at the local black Baptist church, the high visibility of well-known African American activists, the incorporation of prayer into all the protests, and a long-distance march—from Warrenton to Raleigh, all were part of an established repertoire of civil rights activism. Several hundred people attended the "mass meetings" held daily at Coley Springs with "motivational" speeches and prayers, led by local pastors and national figures. Several anti-toxic activists spoke at the churches, including Lois Gibbs of Love Canal and William Sanjour, an EPA scientist and vocal opponent of the administration, who told the crowd about the EPA's conclusion that all landfills eventually leak. The meetings also provided a place to "pass the basket," and inform participants of the plan that had been decided by the organizers, Frinks, White, and Ferruccio. The style of the marches from the church to the landfill entrance mimicked the earlier civil rights marches. The group used similar chants and songs, as well as invented new words for old melodies. Prayer was an integral component of each

Table 4.2. Race of Adults Arrested during Warren County Protests by Place of Residence.

| | PLACE OF RESIDENCE | | | |
RACE	Warren County	North Carolina	Out of State	Total
Blacks	190	37	14	241
Whites	42	84	3	129
Native Americans	37	3	0	40
Total	269	124	17	410

Source: North Carolina Department of Crime Control and Public Safety, *Special Incident Report: PCB Incident in Warren County*, 17 November 1982.

march, as it had been at the mass meetings in the church. One event, based on the infamous Selma-to-Montgomery march, included a sixty-mile walk, over several days, from Warren County to Raleigh, where the protesters presented their cause at the state capital and the EPA office in Research Triangle Park, just outside Raleigh. The landfill presented an opportunity for innovative action, a slight twist to the sit-in of the 1960s. When the trucks rolled toward the landfill, many chose to lie down on the road to block the entrance to the landfill. Civil disobedience was new to the white protesters, but civil rights leaders skillfully guided them through it. The tactic of symbolically blocking the source of the contamination disrupted the orderly flow of the soil and delayed the project. The dramatic actions helped maintain a high uncertainty level and anxiety about complete disorder. The arrests served to increase visibility, build a constituency for the opposition, and cause even more uncertainty about the outcome of each day.

The trucks completed delivery of the soil, and the initial protests ceased on 6 November 1982. A few months later, when another opportunity for disruptive action occurred, the established repertoire of civil rights activism guided the protests, despite the fact that the participants were white. On 28 February 1983 Ken Ferruccio, Patricia Hubbard, and Rufus Harris of Hazardous Waste Organizing Alliance were arrested after pitching a tent in the access road to the landfill in protest of the state's mishandling of a water build-up in the landfill. Immediately before the trucks began bringing the soil, rain had saturated the landfill, causing a delay in final capping due to a water build-up. On March 3, thirty protesters held up pumping of the water and nine were arrested. On March 4, Ferruccio, Hubbard, and Harris removed a pipe from the leachate collection system because they claimed the state would not fix the broken system unless drastic action was taken. They faced the paradox of disruptive action. In order to raise visibility, they had to raise the stakes and chose to destroy property, not as vandals, but with the intention of being caught. When $5,000 in bail was posted, Ferruccio refused to leave jail and began a nineteen-day hunger strike to protest the inadequate procedures of removing and treating the water.[54]

The solidarity built during the protests reflects the skilled coalition building by the civil rights leaders. However, it also signaled that the initial events were more than protests against racism. While the Warren County case has been presented as blacks fighting against the landfill in order to stop the racist siting, the landfill controversy was much more complicated. During the protests, racism was part of the controversy, both as the reason for the landfill siting in the county and the reason blacks could not be elected. However, white residents of the county felt marginalized because of poverty while both blacks and whites were convinced that the county was politically weak because of its rural population and its distance from the triangle boom. In the rural South in 1982 these two divergent perspectives led to a loose and very fragile alliance, united on a very specific issue but not necessarily a foundation for broad-based coalition. One elderly white woman who lived her whole life in Warren County participated in the protests although she did not commit civil disobedience. She was not interested in increasing black political power; in fact, she was very agitated by the fact that after 1982 the majority black electorate in the county elected blacks to office. Although she had "many black friends" and admired the black man who worked in her yard, she resented the idea that "now Warren County is operated by the blacks." She did not hold Leon White or Ben Chavis in high regard, but she backed the protests fully "because they were putting it in the poorest county and people were suffering enough."[55] The organizing success in Warren County came, in part, from the strategic linking of multiple social positions into one seemingly unified front.

When the local opposition linked with the civil rights activists for strategic advantage, the NIMBY frame shifted from a local opposition to a more robust and wide-ranging collective action frame. The necessary social networks were available in an atmosphere of opened political opportunities. The collective disruptive action nurtured in Warren County, grounded in a sense of political powerlessness, resonated with communities throughout the country facing the realities of implementing the new cradle-to-grave waste policies. The civil rights involvement in Warren County started a systematic look at the potential for discrimination in waste management. The possibility of inequity in risk distribution became an important aspect of the burgeoning environmental justice movement. For local white participants, their political powerlessness was tied to ruralism and poverty. The environmental racism frame was a powerful organizing idea for the collective action in Warren County, but it also created the source of a major conflict in the environmental justice movement. Activists became entrenched in trying to determine which measure of marginalization was a better indicator of location of environmental hazards. This ongoing conflict within environmental justice began in Warren County as these two unlikely bedfellows forged their coalition.

5

The Environmental
Justice Movement
Maturation and
Limitations

By the 1990s, two major accomplishments indicated that environmental justice had an established presence on the political stage. In September 1993 the EPA established the National Environmental Justice Advisory Council (NEJAC) "to provide independent advice and recommendations to the Administrator on areas relating to environmental justice." In February 1994 President Clinton signed Executive Order (EO) 12898, "Federal Actions to Address Environmental Justice in Minority Populations and Low-Income Populations." The EO called for "each Federal agency [to] make achieving environmental justice part of its mission by identifying and addressing, as appropriate, disproportionately high and adverse human health or environmental effects of its programs, policies and activities on minority populations and low-income populations."[1] The EO established an Interagency Working Group (IWG), under EPA leadership, and required the development of specific strategies for incorporating environmental justice into each agency. It also mandated future data collection and analysis to include environmental justice considerations as well as an increase in appropriate public participation and access to information. An editorial in the *New York Times* praised Clinton for taking much-needed action: "[W]hen Ronald Reagan and George Bush occupied the White House, neither the environment nor racial justice ranked high on the official agenda. . . . President Clinton is thus to be commended for offering a measure of atonement in

the form of an executive order . . . asking all Federal agencies to insure that their programs do not inflict disproportionate environmental
harm on the poor or on minorities."[2] Environmental justice had come
a long way in the twelve years since Warren County. Although the
long-term impact of IWG and NEJAC was uncertain because both were
only advisory and could easily be revoked, the official recognition and
institutional attempts to address environmental justice marked a new
era for the movement. Attempts to pass legislation had failed, but the
formal structures of IWG and NEJAC indicated a maturation of the environmental justice movement.[3]

The collective identity that emerged from Warren County influenced the structure of the demands made by movement organizers by
contributing to the crystallization of new meanings about environmental risks. Environmental justice activists worked on a vast array of issues, in rural, urban, and suburban settings across the country, at local, regional, and national levels, and with a wide range of tactics. The
movement met the challenge of all social movements by creating "the
illusion of determined, unified, self-motivated political actors, [and act-
ing] publicly as if they believed that illusion."[4] Despite the diversity
of backgrounds and approaches, the environmental justice movement
united around three ideas: environmental problems are intimately entwined with social problems; the current environmental framework ex-
acerbates both environmental problems and social problems; and the
environmental establishment has neglected these relationships, in part,
because of their elitism and exclusive practices. The central tension in
the environmental justice movement focused on defining the intersection between environmental problems and social issues and the mechanisms that intensified those problems. The environmental identity from
Warren County, with its innovative framing of environmental problems as manifestations of civil rights injustices, profoundly impacted
the movement's engagement with these tensions. The impact of these
conflicts on environmental justice has not gone unnoticed by movement observers.[5] The emphasis on distributive and procedural justice
that emerged from Warren County contributed to a transformation of
environmentalism while simultaneously limiting the movement in the
design of solutions. The limitations moved environmental justice activists toward a reconceptualization of environmental policy with the goal
of eliminating risk rather than eliminating inequity in the distribution
of risk. The reconceptualization required a de-emphasis on equity and
had the potential to undermine the foundation of the movement. As a

result, environmental justice precariously straddled the two positions, empowered by an inequity frame that also hindered its effectiveness.

Inequitable Distribution
of Environmental Risks

In Warren County, civil rights activists constructed an environmental identity in opposition to environmental agencies, shaped by both the shifting cultural conceptualization of risk and by their experience in the civil rights movement. The new framing opened the eyes of civil rights activists. For example, before his involvement in Warren County, Golden Frinks hadn't thought much about waste facilities. He had heard about Love Canal in the news, but he thought the new landfills were supposed to prevent Love Canals from happening in the future. As a resident of Edenton, North Carolina, he knew about the illegal dumping of the PCB-contaminated liquid, but had not been directly impacted and did not follow the details of the plan for remediation. It just had not occurred to him that the demographics of the community might influence the government's choice of a landfill site. As soon as Frinks made his foray into Warren County through Floyd McKissick, he began to imagine that other Warren Counties existed and to realize he needed to learn more about hazardous waste, a subject that had not been part of his many decades of civil rights activism. "I did not know anything about it, so I did a little research. I called Atlanta and told Albert [Love] what I was involved in and wanted him to put it in the ear of [Joseph] Lowery. That I thought it was a good movement and thought he should become involved. I also wanted him to find out if there were other toxic waste dumps in black communities. They found it in South Carolina."[6]

Golden Frinks was not the only civil rights leader involved in the Warren County protests to ask if other landfills were located in predominately black communities. Civil rights leaders emerged from participation in Warren County and realized that it could not have been a unique situation. The landfill controversy in Warren County showed the possibility that environmental risks could be inequitably distributed and that regulations designed to protect all citizens protected some more than others. A central strategy of the burgeoning environmental justice movement was to document the primary claim in order to build the necessary empirical credibility for the new framing of environmental problems. The two canonical studies in support of these claims came directly from the experience in Warren County. The 1983 General

Accounting Office (GAO) report and the 1987 United Church of Christ (UCC) report concluded that waste sites were more likely to be found in communities with large proportions of racial and ethnic minorities.[7] These two studies cemented the environmental racism frame and became the foundation of the movement's credibility. The Warren County protests directly shaped the scope and design of the studies and subsequently shaped the movement strategy. The civil rights framing inherited from the Warren County events underpinned some of the success from the strategies based in these studies while it also restricted the movement's achievements.

In 1983 civil rights leaders did not have funding for research, but they did have political clout through leadership in the Congressional Black Caucus (CBC). Congressman Fauntroy (D-DC), then chair of the CBC and participant in the protests, used his position in the House and the tumult over waste implementation to leverage an investigation by the General Accounting Office (GAO).[8] The Warren County collective action frame impugned the government, especially environmental agencies, for siting decisions. As a government watchdog organization, the GAO was the perfect vehicle to provide needed oversight. The GAO limited the investigation to the demographic characteristics of communities surrounding commercial hazardous waste sites in the Southern states that make up Region 4 of the EPA. The landfill in Warren County, owned and operated by the State of North Carolina for the sole purpose of containing the PCB-contaminated soil from the road shoulders, was technically not a commercial facility or a hazardous waste site from a strict regulatory viewpoint. These distinctions were unimportant to the challenges levied against the entire waste management system implemented by EPA.[9] Landfills, as the backbone of waste management, were supposed to protect people and the environment from toxic contamination using a permit review process designed by regulatory agencies. Civil rights activists, performing in a familiar role of watchdogs over government enforcement, wanted the GAO investigation to provide oversight of the agencies responsible for these decisions. In requesting the GAO report, civil rights leaders did not challenge the principles of the waste system and expansion of waste it enabled but added another dimension to the growing criticism of the administration's implementation of waste policies. In their first foray into the policy arena, environmental justice activists conceptualized the problem with a narrow understanding of racism. The focus was on identifying the propensity for waste sites to be located near communities with a high number of minority residents as an indication that siting decisions were directly driven by racist views.

The focus in the GAO study on the southern states in EPA Region 4 (Alabama, Florida, Georgia, Kentucky, Mississippi, North Carolina, South Carolina, and Tennessee) enabled congressional review of the specific agency responsible for the Warren County landfill permit decision. Oversight of the implementation of government regulations in the South had additional meaning to the civil rights leaders who had participated in the Warren County protests as part of their voting rights campaign waged throughout the South in 1981 and 1982. For them, discriminatory siting was linked to lack of political power among blacks due, in part, to ongoing violations of voting rights. The regional focus on the South cemented the issue of inequitable environmental risks with the civil rights agenda of empowerment for blacks. In 1990, several years after the GAO report, the landmark book *Dumping in Dixie: Race, Class, and Environmental Quality* reified the importance of the South in understanding inequitable distribution of risks. In his study, sociologist Robert Bullard used a broader definition of the region employed by the Census Bureau, which included the states in EPA Region 4 plus eight additional states and the District of Columbia. He argued that the relationships between discrimination and environmental quality in the 1980s were best studied in the South. Bullard observed, "The southern United States appears to be the center of the black environmental equity movement."[10] The South remained a recurring theme for the environmental justice movement and was tied directly to political empowerment. In 1991 Jesse Jackson pledged the National Rainbow Coalition to work on behalf of environmental justice and to "organize a Southern Crusade." For Jackson, the focus on the South highlighted that the "South ha[d] half the nation's toxic waste dumps. The most working poor. Half the nation's poor children."[11] The South continued to be vital to nationwide elections.

In the 1983 report, the GAO identified four waste facilities in the South that required permits from the EPA. Chemical Waste Management, established in Sumter County, Alabama, in 1977 and operating with interim status as of the GAO report, was the site where most residents of Warren County initially wanted the PCB waste sent as an alternative to constructing the landfill in Warren County. There were two facilities in South Carolina. One, SCA Services, also had interim status. The other facility in South Carolina had been established in 1972 as an off-site landfill for disposal of waste from Industrial Chemical Company and operated with interim status until the state prohibited additional disposal in 1982. The landfill in Warren County was the fourth facility in the GAO report. Using data from the 1980 census, the study found that "at three of the four sites . . . the majority of the population in the census areas . . . where the landfills are located is Black. Also, at all four sites the Black population in the surrounding census areas has a lower mean income than the mean income for all races combined and represents the majority of those below poverty level."[12] It appeared from this initial look that regulators were not only undermining the entire permit process but were also allowing a disproportionate amount of risk to fall on blacks and the poor.

After the release of the report, Leon White and Ken Ferruccio presented the findings to communities dealing with toxic waste issues. They used the GAO report to spread the message that the social and political position of communities would influence regulatory agencies responsible for permitting waste facilities or overseeing remediation. As activists requested information about Warren County and the GAO report, the problem identified in the GAO report appeared broader than commercial hazardous waste sites in the South. Also, since the study had not produced statistical correlations between sites and communities with a majority of people of color, organizers were constantly under fire from regulators, who could easily challenge the conclusions of the report. Ferruccio and White worked with Ben Chavis, after he became executive director of the United Church of Christ's (UCC) Commission on Racial Justice, to obtain UCC funding for a larger and more sophisticated study.[13] The UCC was thinking strategically when they initiated the investigation since the circumscribed scope and methodology used in the GAO study made its claims vulnerable.

The UCC report, *Toxic Wastes and Race in the United States*, became the authoritative voice for researchers and activists in the movement. This study was a landmark; all subsequent research about equity in the distribution of environmental risk either refined, substantiated, or rejected the UCC's methodology or conclusion.[14] The UCC's report reinforced the movement's critique of environmental decisions creating "sacrifice zones," areas burdened with all the social costs of waste management, due to their demographic characteristics, despite the broad distribution of benefits. The first national-scale study of the demographic characteristics of communities near waste sites also reinforced the strategy of empirical investigations. The researchers investigated the 415 commercial hazardous waste facilities in operation in 1986; these were the transfer, storage, and disposal facilities (TSDFs) permitted under RCRA. The study also looked at "uncontrolled toxic waste sites," closed or abandoned sites identified by the EPA to pose a threat to human health or the environment. By 1986 the EPA had a list of nearly twenty-thousand sites to be evaluated for inclusion on the National Priority List of sites eligible for Superfund remediation. The findings related to commercial hazardous waste sites were significant: "The results of the study suggest that the disproportionate numbers of racial and ethnic persons residing in communities with commercial hazardous waste facilities is not a random occurrence, but rather a consistent pattern. Statistical associations between race and the location of these facilities were stronger than any other association tested. . . . This was clearly the case with respect to socio-economic status."[15] The study offered more equivocal conclusions about uncontrolled waste sites, but nevertheless concluded, "The Black population is not only concentrated in urban areas but disproportionately so in urban areas with large numbers of uncontrolled toxic waste sites."[16]

No one was much surprised by the general thrust of these findings that people of color tend to be poor and live in neighborhoods with poor environmental quality.[17] However, the arguments of environmental justice activists gained force when the UCC released the study with a press conference at the National Press Club. Ben Chavis reported that their study had identified "environmental racism."[18] During the preliminary work to get the funding from the UCC, Ferruccio, White, and Chavis used the term "environmental racism" quite liberally to describe the phenomenon they wanted to document. However, when this emotionally charged terminology hit the press, and had evidence to substantiate its validity, a new era in environmentalism was born. By recasting environmental problems in terms of race, it forced environmental agencies and organizations to question the underlying assumption that environmental protection would always benefit everyone. The evidence seemed to indicate that the system of waste management implemented by regulators would benefit some at the expense of others. Environmental racism, as it was proclaimed after the UCC study, implicated the government in exacerbating the already difficult conditions under which many people of color were forced to live. Environmental organizations also were complicit through their belief in the management system established under TSCA and RCRA and their neglecting to even consider that there could be socially stratified benefits and burdens from that system.

Environmental racism as the identified problem was present in a nascent form in the Warren County protests but was solidified and crystallized with the UCC report. The power came from "the degree to which 'race' looms large in public consciousness."[19] Its implication that racism resulted from "malicious individual acts"[20] led to swift, adamant denials by environmental agencies of intentionally targeting areas with large minority populations for waste facilities. In 1987, when the UCC published its report, movement participants argued that environmental racism was a direct result of decisions by environmental agencies, not a system of institutions and cultural meanings that produced discriminatory structures and practices. The idea that decision makers targeted a community with a waste site because of its racial composition became a rallying call for the movement, the quintessential example of environmental racism.[21] Waste sites played a central role in the public's perception of environmental risk, and regulators were deeply vulnerable to attacks on the waste management system.

The development of the environmental racism idea was directly connected to the role of civil rights leaders in the initial Warren County actions as they tried to obtain a level playing field for blacks in electoral politics. The theoretical idea of race as a set of social relations, a constructed identity with very fuzzy boundaries, would only take their cause so far. The UCC report purported to use the definition of racism advanced by the National Council of Churches: "Racism is more than just a personal attitude; it is the institutionalized form of that attitude."[22] Regardless, the investigators argued that there was a direct link from decision makers to location of waste sites and reduced complex social relations to seemingly objective measures.[23] The more constricted idea of racism galvanized the movement, gave moral underpinning to its claims, led to deep soul searching within the environmental movement, and sparked significant changes in environmental organizing. The restricted understanding of racism also created obstacles and conflicts for the movement, opening the movement to significant challenges. As quantifiable evidence of environmental racism became more important to the movement strategy, the skepticism of science fueled critiques of methodologies used in the UCC study and other research. New evidence was used to argue that inequitable risk did not exist or that racism was not necessarily the explanation for the inequities uncovered.[24] The Warren County legacy that emphasized inequitable distribution of environmental risk and differential implementation of environmental protection made the movement vulnerable to these challenges.

The methodological critiques included challenges in four areas: the definition of an affected community, measurements of race and class, criteria for comparison, and measurements of risk. First, defining the boundaries of communities affected by environmental burdens was not a straightforward task. It was probable that all citizens in a specified political jurisdiction (e.g., county) would not carry the same burden from a particular environmental risk. The type of risk, the potential routes of exposure to the risk, and the potential movement of risks though various environmental media all determine the area that would be impacted. Also, siting often occurred near the borders of political jurisdictions. These locations diffused objections to unwanted land uses and also complicated the use of political boundaries to determine an affected area.[25] The emerging geographic information systems technology enabled researchers to define affected areas without depending on predetermined spatial categories (e.g., political jurisdictions or census geography). Even with this new, sophisticated methodology, determining where to draw the line for "near a facility" was fraught with difficulties.[26]

Second, studies used several methods to measure the two most important independent variables, race and class. Studies that examined historical changes in community demographics encountered difficulties because in 1980 the Census added the use of multiracial identification and, for the first time, allowed self-identification of race. In some situations, the number of categories used to describe racial minorities influenced the outcome.[27] Measuring white and nonwhite might have one result, but using white, black, Hispanic, Hispanic nonwhite, Asian/Pacific Islander, and Native American could produce a different result for the same question. The common approach of using income and housing values as proxies for class could be problematic. Both variables correlated strongly with location of industrial land uses, which was a predictor of waste facilities, and could yield spurious results. All of these issues were further complicated by the correlations between race and income, making it difficult to tease out the role each variable had on the location of risks. The inherent reductionism of the approach did not lend itself to the fussiness of the social manifestations of these categories. Environmental justice research focused on determining how much each variable contributed to the environmental burden of an area. For researchers, the core issue was whether racism was really the root of the problem or if the inequity could be explained by poverty. Environmental justice researchers continued to find evidence that "race has an additional effect on the distribution of environmental hazards that is independent of class."[28] However, other research suggested that income had more of an effect than race.[29]

The third set of methodological problems emerged when researchers tried to determine the criteria for defining communities as "minority" or "low income." Would a 50 percent population in either category be necessary or would the population simply have to be higher than a comparison community, or higher than an average for a particular geographic locale? For example, how would a researcher categorize a county that had a higher minority population than the state average, but less than many counties in other states? The geographic scale of the analysis also influenced the findings: when measured at one scale, race or income may not correlate with location of waste facilities, but might show strong correlations at a larger scale.[30]

Lastly, researchers also found different relationships depending on the type of environmental hazard examined. An analysis of NPL sites could yield very different conclusions about environmental racism than an analysis of commercial hazardous waste facilities.[31]

As a result, by the mid-1990s, many studies undermined the central strategy of the movement. The challenge was formidable, and reliance on evidence of direct discrimination in environmental decisions became more difficult for movement activists. In one such study, researcher Vicki Been found correlations between race and the location of waste facilities.[32] However, she demonstrated that the demographic correlations were a result of dynamics of the housing market, and she argued that this was not environmental racism. Environmental justice activists attacked the narrow conception of racism and insisted that the findings did demonstrate discrimination based on race because the housing market she described was governed by discriminatory practices. Been's study was vilified, but she was, in part, responding to the terms of the debate established by environmental justice activists through the GAO report and the UCC study. Been's challenge forced environmental justice to step out of the constricted view inherited from Warren County. As a result, many researchers tried to move the environmental justice debate away from "fetishizing siting" in order to examine the multiple, interacting factors that led to disparate outcomes in environmental decisions.[33] Environmental justice activists, however, held close to the idea that regulators operated on the principle of "PIBBY—Put It in Blacks' Backyard" and resisted the attempt to show that environmental injustices came from "ambiguous and complicated entanglements" of variables.[34]

The strategy of using scientific measures of environmental racism was not easily abandoned because it also led to some successes in the policy arena. The language of objectified scientific knowledge drove policy discussions that were located in the social institutions built to support the modernization process. In 1990 Paul Mohai and Bunyan Bryant, two scholars from the University of Michigan, organized a conference, Race and the Incidence of Environmental Hazards, as a "vehicle where scholar-activists could come together and share their latest findings . . . and take steps to disseminate information about this important issue."[35] The credentials of the conference organizers and attendees afforded them significant legitimacy, and they harnessed this position to bolster the environmental racism frame in both academic circles and the policy arena. Mohai and Bryant acknowledged the direct impact of the GAO and UCC reports and by implication the impact of Warren County on the conference proceedings: "The evidence in these reports appeared stunning and compelling and suggested that people of color have a greater stake in the environment than their white counterparts. This evidence raised serious doubts about the conventional wisdom regarding the lack of concern of minorities about environmental quality issues . . . and eventually led us to convene a retrieval/dissemination Conference."[36] The Michigan conference organizers argued that the form of environmental protection implemented by federal agencies provided better protection for some than others. As an outcome of the conference, attendees decided to write to the EPA, Department of Health and Human Services, and the Council on Environmental Quality to demand that these government agencies acknowledge the disproportionate impact of environmental contamination on people of color and provide additional research, enhanced communication with minority and low-income communities, inclusion of environmental equity in impact assessments, involvement of minority institutions in the development of environmental equity programs and policies, and the development of a policy statement on environmental equity.[37]

In response, EPA administrator William Reilly established a workgroup to "review and evaluate the evidence that racial minority and low-income people bear a disproportionate risk burden" and to examine EPA programs that "might give rise to differential risk" with the focus of developing "approaches to correct such problems." While the report urged the agency to conduct further studies concerning disproportionate impacts and hire more people of color, activists were angry with the lack of substantive recommendations, especially since the workgroup failed to consider lead poisoning, where the evidence of disproportionate impacts was particularly strong. Congressman Waxman, then chair of the House Health and Environment Subcommittee, uncovered an internal agency memorandum delineating methods for EPA staff to diffuse the power of the activists by building alliances with mainstream civil rights organizations before the "minority fairness issue reaches a flashpoint. . . . when activist groups finally succeed in persuading the more influential groups . . . to take ill-advised actions."[38] The memo outlined a communications plan that activists interpreted as a public relations campaign to obfuscate and defuse the legitimate grievances they had against the EPA.

The activists' emphasis on direct and discrete incidences of environmental racism was successful in forcing a quick response by the EPA, but ultimately the agency resisted the idea that their programs ignored and even exacerbated disproportionate risks. The final report from the workgroup agreed that "[r]acial minority and low-income populations experience disproportionate exposures to selected air pollutants, hazardous waste facilities, contaminated fish and agricultural pesticides in the workplace" but quickly qualified the finding.[39] Disproportionate exposure was attributed to "historical patterns affecting where [minorities] live and work and what they eat." In this way, the report gave some credence to the idea that environmental racism was the result of racist practices infused throughout multiple social institutions that led to white privilege.[40] As one commentator on the draft report argued, "There is overwhelming evidence documenting that the roots of institutional racism are deep and have been difficult to eliminate in the American society . . . racism influences where an individual lives, works and plays. Racism also influences the likelihood of exposure to environmental toxins and the accessibility to health care."[41] The EPA implied, however, that disproportionate exposure to environmental hazards because of "historical patterns" for residences, workplaces, and recreation was not environmental racism. Its emphasis on larger cultural processes was not an attempt to embrace the complexity of processes that enable racism but rather to deflect attention away from its policies and programs. The agency identified the source of the problem as external to the EPA, thereby relieving it of the power and responsibility to make any changes.

Environmental justice advocates insisted that the EPA was obfuscating the real problem of direct and linear discrimination. According to Robert Bullard, "Environmental racism does not exist if we are to believe the EPA *Equity* report. The report attributes class factors as the reason for the elevated risks borne by people of color."[42] The final report actually reinforced the agency's refusal to accept the underlying premise of inequitable distribution of environmental protection. For example, after comments on the draft report were made, the workgroup added more caveats to the risk assessment section: "These revisions [to the risk assessment process] could be useful in determining whether there are any population groups at disproportionately high risk."[43] Even had administrators at the EPA been inclined to satisfy their critics, it would have been impossible for them to embrace the idea of direct environmental racism. To do so would have been an admission that racism infused government institutions, in general, and that environmental protection policies, in particular, contributed to the problem.

The EPA denied the accusations of environmental justice activists by focusing on whether there was intent to discriminate. Without proof of intent, the agency could defuse the environmental racism rhetoric and shift the burden of proof back to activists. Activists responded to the denial of intentional racism by arguing that environmental racism was the unintentional result of standard practices but were limited in their effectiveness, in part, because of the movement's legacy of emphasizing direct linkages between race and environmental burdens. The EPA report stated that "the differences in exposure rates are complex and deeply rooted in many aspects of society," but environmental justice activists argued that the "aspects of society" identified by EPA "are known to people of color as 'racism' and the issue is whether EPA policies are reinforcing environmental racism."[44] Activists continued to insist that the results were the most appropriate litmus test for environmental racism and argued that the agency's focus on intent allowed for an easy denial of a complicated process of racism. However, activists were caught in a bind by using a constricted definition of race for their own empirical underpinning while at the same time challenging the use of that idea in the agency's work.

Participation and
Environmental Decision Making

The reports about inequitable siting led civil rights activists to ask why the environmental regulatory framework resulted in concentrated hazardous waste in communities of color. To them, it seemed that the solution to hazardous waste problems was built on the backs of people of color and needed to change. The problem expanded to include discriminatory enforcement of regulations when a *National Law Journal* article in 1992 concluded, "White communities see faster action, better results and stiffer penalties than communities where blacks, Hispanics and other minorities live. This unequal protection often occurs whether the community is wealthy or poor."[45] EPA administrator Reilly refuted the claims of the article and argued that the methods were flawed, but environmental justice activists embraced the findings that regulatory agencies did not include community concerns in permitting and enforcement decisions. One environmental justice activist told the EPA that minorities "suffer from the end results of [your] actions, but are never full participants in the decision-making which leads to them."[46] In addition to amassing evidence of the disproportionate burden of environmental risks, environmental justice quickly moved into strategies that emphasized increased participation in environmental decision making. Environmental justice activists focused their strategy for procedural changes in two areas: the full infusion of people of color into positions of leadership and the development of processes designed to allow meaningful citizen input. Since environmental agencies and environmental organizations were both responsible for the regulatory structure that gave minorities additional environmental burdens, environmental justice activists demanded that both arenas transform their decision-making processes.

Environmental Organizations

Environmental organizations had many different missions, strategies, tactics, and organizational structures and were at times in conflict with one another.[47] However, environmental justice advocates collapsed these differences and created the unitary entity "mainstream environmentalism." Environmental justice characterized the monolithic environmental organization as a large, Washington-based, bureaucratic organization with professional staff and predominately white, middle-class membership, and a history of racist exclusionary practices. Environmental justice advocates understood mainstreamers as advocating for reform-based solutions to environmental problems without taking into consideration the impacts those solutions might have on the poor and communities of color.[48] Perhaps most troubling to critics of mainstream environmentalism was the use of professional tactics such as lobbying and negotiating. These tactics made them part of the same system that produced environmental injustices and prevented mainstreamers from fully understanding and embracing diverse communities.[49] For critics from environmental justice circles, the mainstreamers had abandoned their roots as a social movement and embraced interest group politics. However, the origins of these groups were more complex than this neat picture describes. Reform had always been part of the mission of some of the most prominent groups. For example, the Sierra Club—the quintessential mainstream organization—lobbied the Washington power brokers since the Hetch Hetchy controversy in 1908. Another example, the Wilderness Society, was founded in 1935 with the purpose of passing a bill in Congress to set aside public lands as wilderness and persevered for nearly thirty years until their politicking had paid off.

Mainstreamers did use interest group politics from the beginning, but the "professionalization and institutionalization"[50] tactics of the largest environmental organizations intensified after 1980 and buttressed their access to congressional representatives, committee staffers, and agency personnel. Burgeoning memberships and budgets cemented the authority enjoyed by mainstream organizations. During the 1980s, in response to the Reagan assault on environmental regulations, coupled with direct mail campaigns, memberships in the large environmental organizations that made up the Washington lobby grew exponentially so that, by 1990, over 7.1 million people belonged to a national environmental organization that used either lobbying, advocacy, direct action, or a combination of all three. Along with increased memberships, budgets also grew, totaling $478 million for the national-level groups. The Nature Conservancy ($152 million) and National Wildlife Federation ($87.2 million) had the largest budgets in 1990.[51] As a result, the environmental organizations with the largest memberships and budgets became synonymous with a unitary environmental identity. Ideologies and strategies remained diverse despite the seeming unity. For example, Greenpeace and the National Wildlife Federation had the largest memberships but operated with highly divergent goals and tactics. Environmental justice activists reacted against the singular and privileged voice that the legitimacy of environmental groups enabled.

In 1981 a group of ten of the largest environmental organizations began meeting to discuss common goals and possible synergistic activities in hopes of strengthening their effectiveness in the face of the staunch anti-environmental philosophy of the Reagan administration.[52] In 1985 the "Group of Ten" published the *Environmental Agenda for the Future* to articulate "where the environmental movement should be going and what goals it should be pursuing." They argued that "a successful strategy . . . must appeal to the broadest spectrum of the American people"⁵³ yet made no mention of the poor or minorities. The *Agenda* approached each of the issues with two assumptions: environmental problems impacted everyone equally and solutions advocated in the *Agenda* would protect everyone to the same degree. The chapter entitled "Toxics and Pollution Control" contained recommendations to increase information and to improve citizen involvement in decisions about facilities but omitted a discussion about disproportionate siting. The authors wanted, instead, to strengthen the RCRA regulations that environmental justice advocates argued led to disproportionate siting in minority communities. Most surprisingly, the "Urban Issues" chapter neglected to include a discussion of the impact that environmental problems had on the poor and minorities despite the fact that cities had increasingly higher concentrations of poor and people of color. In response to the neglect by mainstreamers of urban issues impacting the majority of city dwellers, environmental justice activists argued that mainstreamers overlooked their communities because they cared more about animals and trees than people. The *Agenda* did extensively address human impacts of environmental risks, not just impacts on the nonhuman environment, and reflected the ambivalence that environmentalists had toward the city environment. The separate chapter on urban issues showed that cities were central to their understanding of environmental issues, but the omission of the impact that environmental issues had on the largest segment of the urban population illustrated that mainstreamers did not understand the complexity of the relationships between social structures in cities and environmental problems.

Environmental justice advocates responded to the hegemony of environmental organizations with an adamant demand for inclusion: "We will not take any more of being left out of environmental decision making."⁵⁴ The long history of deliberate racist acts that excluded people of color from environmental organizations along with the blatant racism of revered leaders of environmentalism reinforced the idea that mainstreamers had intentionally shut out people of color and their concerns. The Sierra Club became the archetypal environmental organization challenged by environmental justice advocates, who thought the club focused on nature, not people. The club's long tradition of advocating for strong environmental regulations to protect human health paled because of its roots in Romanticism and the preservation movement. The club also had white-only membership until the mid-twentieth century.[55] John Muir, the founder of the Sierra Club, who was deeply revered by many mainstreamers, had written that Negroes were lazy and that Indians were savages. Historian Carolyn Merchant summarized Muir's approach: "[His] environmental ethic . . . embraced nonhuman nature from bears to orchids to rattlesnakes as 'fellow mortals,' but his theocentric ethic, which was grounded in a God manifested within nature, did not explicitly include the entire human community."[56] Muir's ethical arguments for preserving wild areas continued to inform contemporary environmental sensibilities that favored communities over individuals so that maintaining the health of an ecosystem took precedence over other goals.[57] The holistic ethic often pitted environmentalists against minority communities and underscored the idea that nature, not people, mattered to mainstreamers.[58]

In 1990 a group of environmental justice activists wrote a scathing letter to the Group of Ten, telling them that "[r]acism is the root cause of your inaction around addressing environmental problems in our communities."[59] For the authors of the letter, the veiled racism of omission was an integral part of the environmentalist identity of the mainstreamers. The systems constructed in the name of environmentalism reinforced the existing racist structures and practices as well as created new ones. Environmental justice activists wanted to dismantle the environmentalism of the mainstreamers and build one that had a community-based multiracial constituency, addressed issues of concern to people's daily lives in those communities, and used direct action strategies led by community members, not paternalistic Washington-based groups. Environmental justice activists saw their environmental focus only as a new articulation of the community-based work they had been doing all along. "Unlike the EPA, communities of color did not discover environmental inequity in 1990. They have been living (and many dying) with inequitable environmental quality for decades."[60]

A strong articulation of an environmental justice identity required cultivation of leaders from impacted communities. The most critical element of this strategy was the First National People of Color Environmental Leadership Summit (known thereafter as the Summit), organized under the leadership of the UCC in October 1991. As a defining moment for environmental justice, the Summit championed the new environmental identity and built solidarity among the disparate groups that made up the movement. The organizers of the Summit claimed the events in Warren County crystallized the formation of their ideas and sculpted the goals and structure of the Summit. While the UCC credited "the protests and actions in all people of color communities throughout the United States [for] inspire[ing] the Summit,"[61] Ben Chavis opened the Summit drawing a direct line from the Warren County landfill protests to the Summit. He tied the lineage to Dollie Burwell, who had been instrumental in organizing participants for the marches and protests in Warren County. Chavis reinforced the idea that Burwell and "other African American sisters like her, along with Reverend Leon White . . . caused us to take seriously the life and death consequences of this struggle."[62] For Chavis, Burwell's leadership in Warren County was an illustration of the Summit's goal of cultivating the leadership of people of color in environmental organizing. The situation in Warren County, however, was much more complicated than Chavis led attendees to believe. Warren County organizers walked the unstable and challenging line of nurturing blacks in leadership positions while also attempting to hold together a multiracial coalition with both black and white leadership. The drive to dismantle the hegemony of environmentalism fueled the movement's need to present a more simplified version of the complex and precarious relationships that enabled the Warren County events. Burwell, however, understood the fullness of her experience in 1982. On one hand, though a latecomer to the Warren County organizing, Burwell was a key player in bringing African Americans to the protests because of the connections she made between the demonstrations and the voter registration drives she spearheaded. She emphasized that leaders like Reverend White did not create the powerful movement without the "strong black women [who] cooked, fed their families, washed the clothes, went to their jobs and still had the time and commitment to go to jail, fighting for environmental justice." She also understood that the Warren County protests against the landfill were tied to the struggle for political voice for blacks in the county. Despite the fact that the landfill was built and the contaminated soil was entombed in it, Burwell told the crowd that the actions in Warren County were not in vain. "We elected for the first time an African American to the state house of representatives, state senate and an African American county sheriff. We gained African American control on our school board. The county commissioners appointed an African American county manger. And . . . I now am the Registrar of Deeds of Warren County." However, Burwell also knew that the Warren County protests resulted from blacks and whites working together for a common cause, a fact that could hopefully change the racial dynamics in the county. She acknowledged the deep debt that they owed to "one of my white brothers in Warren County," Ken Ferruccio. Burwell told the Summit delegates that Ferruccio's commitment to the struggle was inspiring. He had held a hunger strike while in jail in 1983 after others had given up, and he had lost his job at a local community college because of his tenacious challenges against the state government, holding them accountable to protect residents of Warren County. [63]

The need to present a unified environmental leadership for people of color usurped Burwell's words about the collaboration between blacks and whites. The legacy of exclusion from environmentalism propelled the Summit toward demanding a central role in environmental decision making for people of color. As Eleanor Holmes Norton, member of Congress from the District of Columbia, articulated at the Summit, "We will not be defined out of any issues."[64] Richard Moore, a vocal critic of the mainstreamers, reflected on the Summit for an interview in *Sierra,* the club's monthly magazine, "It's about us speaking for ourselves. It's not about what's taking place under the table, it's about what's taking place on top."[65] In order to achieve this goal, the organizing committee for the Summit invited activists of color as full delegates and white activists as observers.

Organizers did invite mainstreamers to speak, and the leaders of the Sierra Club and the Natural Resources Defense Council (NRDC) addressed the potential for building bridges between mainstreamers and environmental justice activists. Michael Fischer of the Sierra Club suggested that making national environmental organizations the enemy played into the Reagan/Bush administration's divide-and-conquer strategy. Fischer argued that, far from being an adversary, the Sierra Club was a comrade that used a similar structure advocated by the Summit delegates. "The executive director is not the policy-making head of the Sierra Club at all. Ours is a volunteer led, volunteer driven grassroots activists network."[66] He pleaded with the attendees for help "to open up the eyes and to open up the hearts of our members" and insisted that the Sierra Club would be much more receptive than previously experienced. John Adams of NRDC told the crowd that the mission of the NRDC encompassed a public health agenda, distancing his organization from the common understanding that mainstreamers only cared about trees and animals. At the same time, Adams quickly gave credit to the Summit for revolutionizing environmentalism and offered the NRDC's support.

These pledges of support did not forestall a "very tense session with leaders from mainstream environmental organizations" at the Summit, reflecting the deeply felt distrust of mainstreamers by environmental justice advocates. [67] A key message of the Summit was that leadership by environmental justice activists, informed by life experiences that resulted from a particular social location, was essential to overcome the imbalance of the white-only leadership that had dominated environmentalism. They claimed that their perspective could not be fully understood or articulated by others who did not live with the experience of bigotry and prejudice. Translation inevitably introduced the subtlety of white privilege. Only those whose daily lives were directly impacted by these experiences had the authority to articulate an appropriate path for change. Bullard developed this theme in his influential *Dumping in Dixie*, insisting that mainstreamers did not have the mechanisms to work with people of color and the issues germane to their lives. The environmental justice movement emphasized the cultivation of people of color in leadership positions as a remedy to the problem of incommensurability.

Environmental Agencies

In 1990 the Paños Institute published *We Speak for Ourselves: Social Justice, Race and Environment* to document the "marriage of the movement for social justice with environmentalism." In the report, a cartoon depicted the EPA and environmentalists using the same rhetoric, "You have to be patient, these things take time." (See fig. 5.1.) For environmental justice advocates, the views and actions of environmental organizations and government agencies were equivalent because government and nongovernment environmentalism joined together to forge policies that had social and racial implications. In developing environmental protection policies, neither the organizations nor the agencies considered the possible impacts on the poor or minorities. Environmentalists, inside and outside government, engaged in decision-making processes that either denied access to citizens, especially those with fewer resources and power, or simply ignored the voices of the marginalized.

The formal structures for public participation did not lead to the inclusion of the poor and people of color in environmental discussions. For example, the National Environmental Protection Act of 1969 (NEPA) mandated formal public participation procedures that required citizen review of environmental impact assessments. The

Figure 5.1. Paños Institute depiction of EPA and environmental organizations. *Cartoon by Mark Gutierrez in* We Speak for Ourselves *(Washington, DC: Paños Institute, 1991), 22.*

goal of NEPA was to empower average citizens, but instead NEPA encouraged a legalistic approach that demanded significant expertise and expense. The highly technical knowledge and skills required to negotiate the NEPA process overshadowed the intent to increase public participation and perpetuated exclusion from decision making by those without resources. Mainstream environmentalism accepted these procedures and the equivalent state laws as meaningful participation. They hailed the environmental impact review process as a turning point in environmental decision making because it mandated that all stakeholders be involved in a thorough and comprehensive review of decisions that impacted environmental quality. The reality, however, was very different. In many situations, citizens most deeply affected had no meaningful input into the decisions. A landmark 1991 court ruling in California showed the extent of the exclusion that still existed. ChemWaste had conducted an environmental impact review for a proposed hazardous waste incinerator in Kettleman City but refused the request of citizens to translate the 1,000-page report into Spanish; ChemWaste gave the citizens a five-page summary in Spanish. The area impacted by the incinerator already hosted a hazardous waste landfill, had a population of 40 percent monolingual Spanish-speakers, and 70 percent who spoke Spanish at home. The court ruled against the company, arguing that NEPA processes had not been followed.[68] The resistance of the county and the waste company to translation of the documents seemed egregious, particularly because it was a relatively simple action to take.

The Kettleman City outcome provided a potentially easy solution for government agencies to assuage environmental justice activists. The EPA's environmental equity report in 1992 had few substantive recommendations; communications was the one area where the agency made specific suggestions. "Great opportunities exist for EPA and other government agencies to improve communication about environmental problems with members of low-income and racial minority groups. The language, format, and distribution of written materials, media relations and efforts in two-way communication all can be improved. In addition, EPA can broaden the spectrum of groups with which it interacts."[69] The EPA could take a fairly strong stand, calling for more inclusive communication techniques, because taking action in this area did not require an admission of intentional discrimination. The idea of providing information in an appropriate format and language fit well with the theory of the regulatory structure that had already been established. There was no need to radically reinvent environmental protection if translation of documents and less technical language would satisfy dissenters.

Environmental justice advocates equivocated on procedural remedies. They criticized the EPA for overemphasizing process-oriented solutions at the expense of substantive changes to policies yet, at the same time, focused a significant part of their strategy on procedural equity. Robert Bullard explained procedural equity as "the 'fairness' question: the extent to which governing rules and regulations, evaluation criteria, and enforcement are applied in a nondiscriminatory manner."[70] For Bullard and others, environmental injustices emerged directly from decision processes that did not embody democratic practices. Processes for meaningful and inclusionary participation were needed to change the outcomes. Holding public hearings at accessible places and times and providing information in appropriate languages were just the beginning. Environmental justice advocates argued that the official methods of involving citizens were perfunctory efforts to get support for decisions that had already been made. Warren County had demonstrated the phenomenon at its worst. The EPA considered the public hearing process as a movement beyond the letter of the law because TSCA, unlike RCRA, did not require it. However, David Kelly's remark that the landfill would be sited "regardless of public sentiment" had belied their intentions. As the environmental justice movement matured, a public official would never actually say that public opinion did not matter, but the heart of environmental justice conflicts often rested in divergent ideas about the purpose and structure of public participation.

Just as Warren County residents found very little access to environmental decision makers, the lack of mechanisms in place to address environmental justice frustrated many other activists in communities throughout the country. The EPA report, published in response to the letter from the Michigan group, made clear that a new mechanism for input was needed. The workgroup that issued the report was comprised only of EPA employees and had no input from citizens. In fact, plans included the release of the final report without a public comment period for the draft report. Although there was no statutory requirement, it had become standard practice to invite public comments on draft reports. The topic of the report itself would seem to cry out for public comment, and the irony of the omission was not lost on environmental justice activists. The agency was not following its own recommendation that the "EPA should expand and improve the level and forms with which it communicates with racial minority and low-income communities and should increase efforts to involve them in environmental policy-making."[71] As a result, activists began to think that access to policy makers through a more formal structure was necessary.

The Clinton/Gore transition team first formalized the idea of an advisory board to provide advice to the EPA about environmental justice issues.[72] They recommended a membership to only "include indigenous peoples and representatives of community-based groups experiencing disproportionate impact," but when the administrator formed the National Environmental Justice Advisory Council (NEJAC), membership was extended to all stakeholders' groups, including regulated industries, for example, Waste Management, Inc., Motorola, and Monsanto. It was common practice for regulated industries to provide input to the agency. EPA administrator Carol Browner anticipated that the group of activists, academics, state and local government employees, and the industry interests might find working together difficult and addressed the first meeting of NEJAC beseeching members to "develop an atmosphere where different perspectives are shared and differences are honored. . . . [and] to resolve differences and find areas of common agreement in a way that is responsive to the people of this country."[73] Concerns about working together to create meaningful recommendations continued through the first several meetings of NEJAC, as the structure of the council and its subcommittees was organized. For environmental justice advocates on NEJAC, the details regarding selecting members, structuring the subcommittees, and choosing a chair were central to their vision. Changing disparate environmental risks meant eliminating exclusionary practices from environmental institutions and infusing them with democratic practices.

The differences in approaches culminated when EPA administrator Browner appointed John Hall, then the head of the Texas environmental regulatory agency, as chair of NEJAC. The action demonstrated to activists that the EPA still determined the shape of the input, but activists wanted NEJAC to be the voice of "environmental democracy . . . from the bottom up, not from the top down."[74] The problem was exacerbated because Hall led a government agency charged with making decisions that affected communities impacted by environmental injustice. Hall stepped down as soon as the environmental justice activists on NEJAC stated their objections. Despite his resignation as chair, the group decided to move ahead with a formal motion expressing their "concern regarding the improper message being sent in the formation of the first NEJAC meeting."[75] The vote on the motion—nine yeas, two nays, and three abstentions—showed the depth of the conflicts. Richard Moore of the Southwest Network of Environmental and Economic Justice became the new chair. His environmental justice resume made him a perfect choice from the perspective of the activists. He had co-authored the Michigan letter that resulted in the EPA's first report, co-authored the letter to mainstream environmental organizations demanding inclusion of people of color into the environmental agenda, and was a prolific writer on behalf of the cause. In his new role as chair, Moore emphasized his vision that "NEJAC is tackling questions of democracy" and urged council members to listen to the many different points of view that would be expressed as part of the NEJAC proceedings.[76]

NEJAC became a cornerstone of the activists' strategy for inclusion. Administrator Browner told NEJAC members that the agency needed "to involve stakeholders in resolving environmental justice issues. Effective participation must become a reality." The EPA, Browner stated, cannot "be responsive to the needs of all people without NEJAC's help."[77] NEJAC focused on providing recommendations to the agency for effective public participation processes for all of the agency's programs through the Subcommittee on Public Participation and Accountability. The subcommittee emphasized that participation issues cut across all other environmental justice topics addressed by NEJAC subcommittees (Enforcement, Health, International, Indigenous People, and Waste and Facility Siting). The subcommittee initially focused on the development of a model public participation process to be distributed throughout the agency and incorporated into the Interagency Working Group for use in other federal agencies. The complexity of the issue, however, soon created participation issues for NEJAC itself, and the subcommittee moved its focus to developing "a process to incorporate public participation in all activities of the NEJAC through key activities."[78] NEJAC needed better communication among the members and a better model for public participation. While there was ample time at each meeting for public comments, there was no systematic way to incorporate these comments into the NEJAC agenda. Members worried that perfunctory use of public comments made them as elitist as those they had criticized. The radical integration of citizen input into the agenda-setting and decision-making process envisioned by environmental justice activists was missing from the movement's primary vehicle for influencing policy. Environmental justice, through the NEJAC format, faced the challenge of building legitimacy without falling into the rigidity of institutionalization.[79]

Radical Critique or Policy Reform

The environmental justice movement argued that environmental risks were inequitably distributed, adversely affecting people of color and the poor more than other populations. The difficult question of how to measure the actual distribution of environmental burdens paled in comparison to developing a system to ensure that no community bore more of a burden than another community. Detractors of environmental justice contended that any new system would simply redistribute the risks that were already disproportionately impacting people of color and the poor. Environmental justice activists insisted that redistribution of risk was not the logical solution to the problem of inequity. Ben Chavis adamantly denied that moving waste facilities into predominately white and wealthy communities was the inevitable end point of the environmental justice movement. He emphasized this position to attendees of the Summit. "We are not

organizing an anti-white movement. We are organizing an anti-injus-
tice movement."[80] He told delegates and observers that "[w]e are not
saying 'take the poisons out of our community and put them in a white
community.' We are saying that no community should have these poisons."[81] Moreover, according to Chavis, the problem of inequitable
distribution of risks was related to another issue, the role of corporations in creating environmental policies: "[T]he larger [environmental]
movement out there . . . ha[s] refused to challenge the petrochemical
industry; they have refused to challenge the multinational corporations. Many multinational corporations and petrochemical companies
sit on their board of directors."[82]

Activists challenged environmental policies "predicated on continued waste expansion" with the assistance of the scholarly writings
of academics. Bullard maintained that race was the primary factor underlying the distribution problem but also contended that "no community, rich or poor, black or white, should be allowed to become a
'sacrifice zone.'"[83] The "dominant environmental protection paradigm"
must be dismantled, he argued, not only because it leads to unequal enforcement and disproportionate distribution of risks, but also because it
"fails to develop pollution prevention as the overarching and dominant
strategy."[84] Others argued that achieving genuine environmental justice
required a democratic practice that reached into production processes.
Geographer Laura Pulido, for example, insisted that "greater democracy in private production decisions" would only be a first step toward
attaining environmental justice. In addition, "a redistribution of wealth
and power" along with a restructuring of "uneven development" both
in the United States and internationally was necessary in order to secure environmental quality for the oppressed and exploited.[85] The radical critique insisted that environmental justice required not only a new
environmental protection paradigm but also the complete restructuring
of the current economic system.

Although environmental justice kept one foot squarely planted in
the distribution analysis, economic restructuring and democratization
of production became part of the movement. The foundation of the
movement, rooted in the specific collective action in Warren County,
forced it to straddle the two contradictory goals of reforming environmental protection decision processes and redesigning the system that
created the need for environmental regulations. On the one hand, the
emphasis on distributive justice resulted in mobilization efforts based
on the evidence of environmental inequities. Also, procedural justice

led to a focus on amplifying previously neglected voices. On the other hand, as the Warren County case and subsequent research highlighted, the implementation of the new waste policies created the need for more waste facilities and exacerbated the problem of inequitable risk distribution. The equity issues limited the radical critique as the procedural changes became absorbed by the regulatory structure, and the radical critique undermined the civil rights approach by de-emphasizing the inequities of distribution and stressing reduction of risks for all citizens.

The Summit demonstrated the inherent conflict in the environmental justice movement. Jesse Jackson, a keynote speaker at the event, put environmental justice squarely in the center of progressive politics and brought significant political power to the movement. Jackson became an important political figure in 1988 when he won 29 percent of the Democratic party primary vote, showing that a black candidate could run a serious national campaign. His appeal in the primary "was due, in part, to his own ability to understand and tap those substantive issues that have cut across a broad cross-section of America's dispossessed and disadvantaged."[86] After the election of George H.W. Bush in 1988, Jackson embraced environmental issues as part of his platform of ensuring "equal protection under the law, equal opportunity, equal access and a fair share." At the Summit, Jackson emphasized the same themes that defined his nationwide "Toxic Tour" of poor minority communities in the spring of 1990, commemorating the twentieth anniversary of Earth Day. He told Summit attendees, "Tonight we gather to fight for the most basic right. . . . Tonight we gather fighting for the right to breathe free. . . . But without the right to breathe, nothing else really mattered. . . . We cannot let workers get trapped in this debate about jobs or lungs. We should have jobs and a healthy environment. We need an economy that can grow and flourish without destroying the land and the people on it." Jackson stressed the universality of environmental issues and underscored the impacts of the current environmental protection paradigm on everyone. "You can't say it's just a black thing, or a brown thing, or a red thing. You can't say it's just a reservation thing. For they may dump toxic waste on the poor side of town today, but as surely as the wind blows, as surely as it's one planet Earth, what affects any of us in the morning affects the rest of us by sundown. We either live together as brothers and sisters, or perish apart as fools. That is why there can be no elite environmental movement—it must be universal. . . . Poison should not belong to any of us."[87]

Robert Bullard, the sociologist who spearheaded much of the scholarly interest in environmental justice, also spoke at the Summit. He demonstrated the desire of environmental justice to emphasize racial equity rather than broad progressive politics. He pointedly addressed the "race v. class" argument in his remarks, warning the Summit delegates not to be swayed by economic explanations for environmental burdens in their communities. "We can clearly document that the environmental problems that confront our communities cannot be reduced solely to class; it is not just a poverty thing. Middle class African American communities are just as affected by environmental racism as poor, poverty-stricken urban ghettos and rural poverty pockets in the Deep South. It is not a class thing. Racism cuts across class. And we have to understand that and drive that point home every time some white media person tries to spin it into 'it's a class thing.'"[88]

The tension in the environmental movement was embodied in the "Principles of Environmental Justice," the primary document issued by the Summit delegates. The organizers of the Summit wanted to foster solidarity by creating a document about the meaning of environmental justice on which all the diverse attendees could agree. Despite the fact that the attendees shared the identity of "leaders in the environmental justice movement," they had a vast range of experiences of environmental injustice and a diverse set of cultural understandings about the environment. Organizers drafted six versions of the principles prior to the meeting, but still the plenary session about the principles was tense and difficult. The resulting document not only reinforced solidarity, a necessary ingredient for successful movements, but also explained to a wider audience a unified set of beliefs and desires of the movement. The seventeen principles have been reprinted in nearly every book about environmental justice published since the meeting, even books that critique the movement, as an expression of the underlying ideas of the movement.

The statements emphasized two dimensions of environmental injustice. On one hand, they tied environmental justice to the civil rights approach that emphasized distribution and equal access. The principles declared that environmental injustices violate the UN Declaration on Human Rights and proclaimed the right to a pollution-free life. The right to sovereignty was emphasized because the indigenous people in the movement tied their right to self-determination to their particular understanding of the land and natural world. Rights, according to the principles, should be afforded to workers and victims of environmental injustices, not just to "trees" or other objects of nature that were declared to have legal standing by mainstream environmentalism. However, the principles also encapsulated a radical critique of the environmental protection paradigm. Vernice Miller, one of the architects of the principles, said, "[T]he fact that the Principles present a fundamental moral challenge to our existing capitalist economy cannot be overemphasized."[89] Several of the principles explicitly challenged environmental policy to change the basic economic and social structures that supported the environmental policy framework. For example, the sixth principle fully embraced the idea of stopping all risks, rather than redistributing them. "Environmental justice demands the cessation of the production of all toxins, hazardous wastes, and radioactive materials, and that all past and current producers be held strictly accountable to the people for detoxification and containment at the point of production." The fourteenth principle "oppos[ed] the destructive operations of multi-national corporations" and underscored the idea that restructuring production systems was central to achieving environmental justice, not using environmental policies to contain risks after production.

The principles defined a movement that focused on transforming the standard assumptions about environmental protection that informed regulations. However, during the 1990s the movement worked to reform the regulatory structure so that the concerns of the poor and minorities would be integrated into deliberations. Despite the stated goals of environmental justice as articulated through the principles, activists put little effort into restructuring production systems because the focus on procedural reform limited the ability of the movement to address the issues of distribution of risk. In part, the activists were responding to the resistance of regulatory agencies to any effort to define disproportionate impact. Once environmental justice advocates gained legitimacy in the eyes of the regulatory agencies, they needed to find areas of agreement and cooperation. The best place to start was to focus on participation in environmental decision making. For activists, creating radically new ways of participating in environmental decisions was the first step toward democratization of the production processes that generated risks.

The changes that were achieved did little to further the larger objectives of eliminating risk in the production processes. In the few instances where environmental justice ideas were infused into the regulatory framework, the modifications improved the participation procedures but did not reconceptualize environmental protection as a problem of production. For example, the 1995 Environmental Justice Strategic Plan of the EPA, produced in compliance with Executive Order 12898, articulated methods to integrate environmental justice into programs and procedures at the agency. The goal of the strategic plan was that "no segment of the population, regardless of race, color, national origin, or income, as a result of EPA's policies, programs, and activities, suffers disproportionately from adverse human health or environmental effects, and all people live in clean, healthy, and sustainable communities." The primary mechanism for achieving the goal was to assure active and full participation in environmental decisions by community members. The plan outlined specific improvements to increase participation by residents who were impacted by decisions resulting from the myriad of environmental laws enforced by the agency. The plan did not question the current structure of regulation, nor did it suggest that the primary purpose of the agency should shift away from managing existing risks to trying to eliminate them. In another example, the EPA's Office of Solid Waste and Emergency Response (OSWER), charged with implementation of RCRA, issued environmental justice accomplishment reports that emphasized participation "early in the process" as a major achievement of the agency. OSWER did not suggest that RCRA needed to be reconceptualized to include participation in decisions prior to the generation of waste.[90]

The Pollution Prevention Act of 1990 is another example of the emphasis on process obscuring the possibility of outcomes that restructure industrial processes. The goal of the act was to develop practices that "reduce the amount of any hazardous substance, pollutant, or contaminant entering any waste stream or otherwise released into the environment (including fugitive emissions) prior to recycling, treatment, or disposal; and reduce the hazards to public health and the environment associated with the release of such substances, pollutants, or contaminants." The goals seemed to dovetail with the more radical arm of environmental justice. However, many environmental justice advocates did not support the EPA's pollution prevention efforts. First, activists working on specific threats to local communities worried that pollution prevention would substitute for compliance and enforcement, possibly leaving their communities at higher risk, depending on the pollution prevention practice put into place. Also, they remained skeptical that pollution prevention would lead to the elimination of pollution because they did not trust the collaboration between government and industry. Business stakeholders on NEJAC even said that they did "not hold successful pollution prevention efforts to the criteria that they eliminate pollution, only that they reduce environmental and health impacts below the baseline of applicable regulatory standards."[91] Many in government and industry argued that reaching for the unachievable goal of eliminating pollution would take time and resources away from sound risk management, leading to even higher burdens in communities that suffer disproportionately. The act underscored that pollution prevention should be voluntary, with support and incentives from government. Environmental justice advocates did not put much faith in the voluntary approach, nor did they believe that the act spurred the agency and its regulated industries to embrace a zero emission goal.

EPA's stress on participation was a direct response to the demands of environmental justice advocates, but it also helped the agency manage the environmental justice problem in two other ways. In focusing on participation, the agency diverted attention away from challenges to the dominant environmental protection paradigm that called for a complete transformation from control after contamination occurred to elimination of the risks from production processes. Also, rigorous democratic practice might not actually lead to the elimination of disproportionate adverse human health and environmental effects. Without guidance on how to determine whether a community was disproportionately impacted, the agency would not have to offer proof that its primary method had generated a change in the distribution of the risks. They could continue to point toward their efforts at incorporating environmental justice into their programs and procedures while avoiding any radical shift in the environmental protection paradigm.

6 | Warren County Revisited

The landfill controversy in Warren County did not end after the protests in the early 1980s. The landfill remained, and citizens continued to live with the anxiety that its contents would move into the environment, either through leakage into the groundwater or seepage from the cap into the air. For residents of Warren County, the landfill remained a menace lurking behind the entrance barrier to the facility. The public health threat was always present despite the many successes they could enumerate from their protests against the landfill. In 1993, when the state announced that the landfill contained one million gallons of water, threatening the ability of the liner to contain the contaminated soil, most people in Warren County were not surprised—they were outraged. Residents had long believed that in the haste to complete the removal of soil from the road, the state had not built the landfill securely, nor had the EPA provided appropriate oversight. Residents also were convinced that the state did not follow the proper protocols for maintenance and monitoring of the site. The discovery of the threat to the landfill's integrity confirmed their suspicions and sparked a renewed campaign against the state. This time citizens could build on their success from earlier years. The national environmental justice movement that had emerged in the intervening ten years shaped both the response of citizens to the landfill crisis and the outcome of the confrontation. The multiracial coalition that was responsible for the initial organizing played a central role on the national environmental justice stage, and this enabled them ten years later, to successfully demand major substantive and procedural concessions from the state regarding remediation at the landfill. The efforts of Warren County residents to remediate the landfill illustrate how the environmental justice movement empowered residents and challenged the environmental establishment to include disproportionate environmental effects and exclusive practices into environmental discourse.

Two ideas from environmental justice, multiracial coalitions and social production of scientific knowledge, informed the renewed activism in the 1990s. First, as environmental justice matured, they used science to mount campaigns and underscored the uncertainty that scientific rationale encompasses as well as to demonstrate how the social position of the scientist influenced the type of questions, assumptions, and methods employed. For environmental justice, this meant that science attached to official institutions was always suspect and that citizen control over production of scientific knowledge was necessary. Second, environmental justice had to maintain a difficult balance between the development of a broad-based constituency and the nurturance of the long overdue leadership from people of color in environmentalism. In the second phase of activism, citizen-based science and identity politics collided and unveiled the internal tensions in environmental justice. Where environmental justice reinforced a constricted understanding of social location, based on a reductionist approach, dissent was silenced. As a result, the activists almost missed the opportunity to resolve the crisis at the landfill and, in part, contributed to a reinforcement of the idea that environmental risks and social problems should be addressed separately. The final phase of the Warren County story demonstrates that the framing of distributive justice and procedural justice in the environmental justice movement have contradictory implications for the potential of radically re-envisioning environmental policy.

Linkages between Distributive Justice and Procedural Justice

When water was first discovered at the Warren County landfill in 1993, the state proposed a two-hundred-thousand-dollar plan to address the problem by installing a new pump, filtering the sediments contaminated by PCBs, spraying the filtered water over the top of the landfill, and shipping the residues to a facility permitted to manage PCB waste, either a landfill in Alabama or an incinerator in Arkansas. Residents objected vehemently to this plan and to the process used to decide on a course of action. The state's approach violated both of the major concepts of environmental justice. First, residents did not want to burden another community with additional toxics, particularly because they knew the high likelihood that the community near the waste facility would be predominately poor and minority. Not only did the empirical research since the first GAO report show that waste facilities were distributed disproportionately, but the specific sites the state suggested had active environmental justice organizations fighting against the waste facilities. Specifically, the landfill in Alabama that the state had in mind was the same one that residents had initially wanted to use for the contaminated soil instead of building a landfill in Warren County. They had long ago come to understand that sending toxics to another community would only move the problem of inequity to another location. The residents of Warren County refused to be part of perpetuating the approach to waste management that moved toxic threats from one poor minority community to another and pitted communities against each other. The environmental justice movement had built the solidarity that halted these types of cleavages.

Second, environmental justice activists demanded full participation in any decisions that would impact their communities. The demand for participation stemmed from several underlying principles in the environmental justice construct. Environmental justice activists claimed that only people who lived the experience of contamination and discrimination could construct appropriate solutions. Also, environmental decisions were made in the language of scientific knowledge, and activists had come to see that science was deeply influenced by the belief systems of the scientists. Therefore, activists knew that citizens had to be part of producing any new scientific knowledge about the landfill. The movement had highlighted for ten years the role that exclusion played in distributive inequity. In 1993, when the landfill crisis was exposed, the movement had succeeded in moving the procedural justice component of their demands onto the national stage. The EPA formed the National Environmental Justice Advisory Council (NEJAC) and several legislative proposals were being floated, each calling for a more primary role for citizens in decision making. The laws did not pass, but several of the ideas were translated into the Executive Order, signed in 1994, that established additional avenues for citizen input. For environmental justice activists, including the citizens of Warren County, full participation in decision making demanded access well beyond improved communications, translations, public hearings, and document review. Residents wanted a fundamental shift in the decision-making processes to include citizens as equal partners. It was no longer acceptable for government to make a decision and, after the fact, solicit feedback that might or might not be used to fine-tune the decision that had already been made. Citizens envisioned a process in which the state and the citizens would together develop a plan of action that everyone could live with. They did not want to be in an advisory role but wanted to be decision makers to the same extent that the state experts were. For residents, the procedural justice demands were the key to creating a solution with distributive justice as its cornerstone. In the second phase of activism in Warren County the residents succeeded in creating a citizen participation structure that surpassed a traditional advisory role and gave the residents significant input and near veto power over all decisions regarding the landfill. The citizens had access to outside, independent expertise, and were eventually successful in pushing the state to pursue treatment of the landfill contents to detoxify them by a process that ensured that no contaminated materials would leave the site.

The first step toward achieving the fundamental shift in the citizen participation process occurred with a letter from Ken Ferruccio to Jonathan Howes, then secretary of the Department of Environment, Health, and Natural Resources (DEHNR), demanding a process to allow for citizen review and approval of any action taken by the state. He began by emphasizing the historical significance of Warren County and identifying the problem as tied to environmental racism. "We of Warren County . . . ignited the spark, that lit the fuse, that blew the powder keg in 1982. . . . The light and heat from those explosions fueled forever concepts that for too long had been kept apart: environmental justice, environmental civil rights."[1] The state was not required by law to create a citizen participation process but agreed to do so, in part, because of the potential for recreating the events of 1982, when the ongoing battle over the siting of the landfill had produced demonstrations by civil rights leaders. Environmental racism claims gave residents of the county power to make demands for meaningful input into any decisions that affected the landfill. Further, the iconic position that Warren County held in the environmental justice movement gave residents considerable power and legitimacy. The secretary responded by promising to "create a first-of-its-kind joint advisory committee comprised of local citizens and State officials to develop a process by which the water can be removed."[2] The idea, as understood by residents, was that decisions would be made together, with state officials and local citizens as equal members of the decision-making body.

The structure of participation that citizens envisioned, too, was shaped by how they understood the success of the 1982 events. Activists emphasized the centrality of the multiracial coalition to the success in organizing the first phase of activism. As the environmental justice movement developed, multiracial coalitions continued to be emphasized as a significant part of the solution to build a bridge between environmental issues and social issues. According to Dorceta Taylor, a vocal critic of elitism in the environmental movement, environmental justice should "mobilize community-wide coalitions built across race, ethnic and class lines and between interest groups and factions . . . [because] fairness and justice are issues all can agree on as ones which are important in building a desirable society."[3] At the same time, racial identity quickly became the primary organizing framework for the political activism of the environmental justice movement, enabling people of color to validate their experiences of environmental racism and to become vocal members of an expanded environmental movement. Environmental justice activists did not want to reinforce the static ideas of race that had enabled the construction of racism and its many manifestations. In addition, the environmental racism framework empowered blacks to be vocal advocates for environmental protection and encouraged transparency in environmental decision making. However, the identification of environmental racism coupled with the solution of multiracial coalitions created significant tension within the environmental justice movement. As the second phase of activism develop in Warren County, these two competing views on identity led to an expanded political participation in environmental decision making and a simultaneous contraction of democratic practice.

The initial group had a broad membership but was dominated by local residents. The most active and vocal community members were Ken and Deborah Ferruccio and Dollie Burwell, who had worked closely together in 1982 when the large protests were held and had continued active involvement in the environmental justice movement. Since that time, Ken and Deborah Ferruccio became very involved in the antitoxic movement, especially the influential North Carolina Waste Awareness and Reduction Network (NC WARN), and a variety of waste-siting conflicts throughout the state. Dollie Burwell had been elected as Registrar of Deeds for the county in 1982, in part because of her activism with the landfill. She sustained a connection with the UCC's Commission on Racial Justice during the time of its influential environmental justice study and also played an integral part in organizing the first National People of Color Environmental Leadership Summit in 1991 and formulating of the "Principles of Environmental Justice" document. Her prominence as a black woman leader in the all-important Warren County project gave her access to the environmental justice structures newly emerging in the national policy arena, and she served on the National Environmental Justice Advisory Council (NEJAC) from 1996 to 1998.

The joint advisory committee in Warren County was immediately renamed the Citizens/State Joint Warren County PCB Landfill Working Group, referred to as the Working Group. This change, while seemingly a semantic detail, reflected the citizens' demands to be equal partners in the decision-making process. Securing scientific expertise away from state control was imperative to the process since citizens understood scientific knowledge as socially embedded, not as an objective, disinterested enterprise. With the aid of outside expertise, citizens infused the discussion about the landfill with an alternative set of values from those of the state. As a result, the goal of the Working Group shifted from overseeing the dewatering of the landfill to finding and implementing a detoxification process for the materials in the landfill. Moreover, the Working Group was able to ensure that no contaminated materials were removed from the landfill for shipment to another community.

Concessions by the state to seek detoxification did not come easily. The initial purpose of the committee, as envisioned by Secretary Howes, was not to find a detoxification process, but for "citizens and the state together to develop, monitor and review the process by which the water will be removed from the landfill." Howes concurred that any movement of materials off-site would be unfortunate, but claimed that "no technically feasible means to handle onsite the sediment . . . has been identified."[4] In agreeing to the creation of the Working Group, the DEHNR acknowledged that "environmental justice/environmental equity is a major issue" but was also adamant that detoxification should proceed as "appropriate and feasible," not "at any cost."[5]

Jim Hunt was the governor of North Carolina during the original protests in 1982. He left office in 1984 after eight years (because North Carolina law prohibits more than two consecutive terms), then returned for two more terms in 1992 and again in 1996. In 1983, immediately after the landfill was capped, the governor appointed a group to examine the possibility of treating the soil in the landfill, but the composition, format, and structure of that group did not foster meaningful citizen participation. The report of the governor's group was issued in early 1984 and recommended proper upkeep, appropriation of enough funds for safe maintenance in the future, and the dissolution of the ad hoc group with "continue[d] surveillance of developments in PCB detoxification, with representation from the appropriate state agencies as well as liaison with EPA, Warren County and the research community." No follow-up action was taken, but ten years later, in 1993, with the opportunity from the water emergency at the landfill, residents focused on the promise Governor Hunt had made in a 1982 letter to the citizens of Warren County: "The state will push as hard as it can for detoxification of the landfill when and if the appropriate and feasible technology is developed."[6] Citizen members of the Working Group never relented in their demand for detoxification, and the procedural concessions made by the state eventually led to this outcome.

The first substantive victory for citizens related to the water debacle in the landfill was the approval of an independent science advisor paid for by the state but answerable to the residents. For citizens, this was absolutely necessary since meaningful participation could not proceed without the production of science informed with citizens' values. While Secretary Howes had, in principle, agreed to "outside review," finding the funding for a qualified consultant was another matter. Eventually, in March 1994, after tenacious insistence by citizen members of the group, DEHNR funded one year of work for the landfill project with $100,000. This allocation was to cover capital improvements to initiate removal of water (still the official position of the state) and payment to the science advisor. The initial funding started a process that enabled residents to shift away from the dewatering plan and to force their vision for a just outcome of detoxification.

In March 1994 Ken and Deborah Ferruccio contacted their antitoxics comrade Billie Elmore, director of NC WARN, who suggested Pauline Ewald for the position of science advisor. Residents were very confident in Ewald; she had strong science and community advocacy qualifications and a reputation for standing up to regulatory agencies. Her experience with dioxin issues was particularly important to members of the Working Group because during the ten years after the landfill was capped, the science regarding dioxin and dioxin-like chemicals developed, indicating a strong possibility that dioxin was in the landfilled soil. Dioxin-like compounds are a class of halogenated aromatic organic compounds that have a similar chemical structure, similar physical-chemical properties, and evoke a similar range of toxic responses. Thirteen of the 209 PCBs are considered dioxin-like chemicals. In addition, other dioxin-like compounds can be produced during the production of PCBs. In 1979, when the PCBs from the transformers were illegally dumped on the side of the roads, very little was understood about dioxin and its relationship to PCBs, so regulators did not test for other dioxin-like chemicals in the soil. Residents wanted the state's assessment to include a full review of the chemical characteristics of the soil in the landfill, in part, because they believed the soil contained significant levels of various dioxin-like compounds. The potential for the presence of dioxin in the landfill deepened the anxiety about potential threats to public health from the landfill after dioxin was dubbed "the most toxic chemical known."[7]

The state members agreed to Ewald as a way of moving the project along, not because they agreed that dioxin was an important issue in the situation at the landfill. Immediately, the group hit a wall in working together, with the science advisor supporting the residents. They attempted to draft a mutually satisfactory sampling plan but could not agree on the inclusion of split samples to be evaluated at an independent lab and reviewed by Ewald. The state's resistance only fueled the perception that it had something to hide and did not, in reality, accept the idea of an equal partnership with residents. At the June 1994 meeting, residents confirmed their intention to conduct an action of civil disobedience if split samples were not taken, and only then did the state acquiesce.

After the initial sampling, the state found no PCBs, dioxins, or furans in the leachate, but did report eleven to thirteen parts per quadrillion (ppq) of dioxin in the monitoring wells. They concluded that the positive results in the monitoring wells were due to either contamination from outside the landfill or lab error from contaminated equipment; they wanted to test again.[8] Ewald issued a damning report of dioxin and a range of dioxin-like compounds in surface soils outside the landfill and in sediments of the nearby stream. The Division of Solid Waste Management was furious, particularly because the conclusions in Ewald's report seemed biased and unrelated to the data. Her report focused on a general description of the toxicity of dioxins without specific reference to the risks at the site and recommended a specific technology, Base-Catalyzed Decomposition (BCD), to remove the chlorine from the dioxin-like compounds in the soil at the landfill. The state contended that Ewald's conclusions could not be drawn from the data reported but were, in fact, predetermined.[9]

Citizen members of the Working Group agreed that choosing a particular technology might be premature but continued to insist that detoxification was the primary goal. The findings of the science advisor, in whom they had placed enormous trust, were enough for citizens to conclude that a serious risk from contamination did exist. The state never accepted the Ewald report, refused to accept that dioxin was an issue to consider, and rejected the idea that detoxification of the landfill was necessary for public health reasons. They did, however, partially agree to the principle of detoxification when they argued against selection of a particular technology in favor of full review of available technologies as a continuation of the initial effort of the governor's appointed group in 1984. Although the technical report began the state's shift away from the dewatering plan, the Working Group also called on the support of powerful politicians. Eva Clayton, the congressional representative for Warren County, was a black woman who had won her first election after the 1982 protests, partially because of increased black voter registration and turnout. She wrote a scathing letter to the secretary of the DEHNR, reinforcing that the landfill situation could become a national-level civil rights cause once again.[10]

Ewald's contract was not renewed in 1995 because the state refused to work with her. Citizens were convinced that Ewald had reported the truth and that the state did not want the truth to be known. Employing the argument that it would maintain credibility with the community, the citizens were able to keep the independent science advisor's position. Inclusion of an expert advisor continued to help drive the citizens' agenda, and the Working Group hired two science advisors, each with a different expertise, to address the multiple issues from the landfill. Joel Hirschhorn had a doctorate in materials engineering in addition to extensive experience with remediation, technology assessment, and risk assessment. He had worked at the Office of Technology Assessment and was lead author on many of their reports on hazardous waste and toxic chemicals. Patrick Barnes was a geologist whose experience would be helpful in understanding the site characteristics and the current situation at the landfill. State officials were still strongly supporting dewatering and installation of an upgraded pump in the current leachate collection system, so, for the state, the geologist was potentially more appropriate. However, many citizens were impressed with Hirschhorn's expertise in and support of detoxification as well as his extensive qualifications in the area of "environmental technologies."

The state's resistance to detoxification continued; they argued that this expensive approach was not necessary because the landfill presented no real risks to the community. The regulators were schooled in the logic of risk analysis, and they wondered if detoxification might cause significant risks that would outweigh the very negligible risks posed by the landfill. Residents were particularly frustrated with this line of reasoning since they interpreted Governor Hunt's promise to detoxify as independent of the conditions at the landfill. Residents always felt the landfill posed serious health risks to their community, despite the formal risk analysis employed by the state. Of equal importance to the assessment of the landfill problem was the further decline in their already troubled economy, which the standard risk-assessment techniques did not take into account. There are one hundred counties in North Carolina, and in 1980 Warren was ranked ninety-seventh in wealth—only three counties had a lower economic standard. By 1990 it had reached the bottom—it was the poorest county in the state. The inequities were highlighted by the economic boom in the triangle area (Raleigh, Durham, Chapel Hill), just sixty miles away, which continued throughout the 1980s and 1990s. Massenberg Kearney, who lived adjacent to the landfill and was a member of the Working Group, expressed his concern in this way: "Our neighbors died of cancer. We all use filtered water, but it didn't help them . . . I used to raise cows here, but I can't anymore because the contamination from the landfill . . . I just want my family to be able to stay on this land. The landfill is here because the community is poor. If we had more money, we could have fought the dump. Things just got worse after the dump was put in."[11]

Any action that the state took, or did not take, that slowed detoxification was seen as obstructionist, and when Hirschhorn recommended further study of the landfill to determine its condition, citizens in the Working Group were completely frustrated. They had put their faith in one advisor, but now another one was telling them that the first one had not done an adequate job. Who were they to believe? Could it be that Hirschhorn did not bring a citizen-based perspective to his analysis? Hirschhorn's challenge to the Ewald report, however, was tempered by his critique of the state's response to the report. On one hand, the state was not forceful enough in criticizing the report's deficiencies; on the other hand, the state ignored the possibility that dioxins were found off-site and did not attempt to find a reason for their presence.

Residents were eager to move forward with detoxification and wanted the BCD process, but Hirschhorn successfully convinced them that a full examination of the landfill's status was needed to determine the current risks posed by the landfill and to compare these risks to those involved with the different remediation processes. The formal risk-assessment techniques of environmental decision making also shaped his approach: "Every remedial action poses some risks. But if the landfill itself poses a high[er] risk, there will be a sound reason to detoxify."[12] Coming from the science advisors, this approach was now easier to accept.

Hirschhorn's assessment of the leachate collection system concluded that the water in the landfill was most likely from the heavy rain that occurred during the construction of the landfill. The state, he argued, was negligent in the construction of the landfill because they allowed the water to build up, and the EPA was also negligent for not monitoring the construction more closely. His most damning conclusion was that the design and operation of the leachate collection system was seriously flawed. The original plan for the landfill called for a perforated pipe system, but the "as-built" drawing showed that no such system was installed. Although the state claimed that they had received permission from the EPA for the change in design, neither the state nor the EPA ever located the documentation. The system that was installed, according to the Hirschhorn report, had never operated properly. The fluctuating water in the monitoring wells, he also argued, indicated that the landfill was leaking through the bottom liner. Since the original plan called for a more extensive leachate collection system and there was indication of contamination moving out of the landfill, Hirschhorn argued that the landfill never was a "state-of-the-art" facility as was promised by the state and EPA. Government agencies were culpable, therefore, in misrepresenting their actions, of making promises that they did not keep, and of putting the community at risk.

The highly critical report enabled citizens to move one step closer to their stated goal of detoxification. In April 1996 the Working Group approved a proposal for the two science advisors to conduct a full site investigation as a first step toward detoxification. Given Barnes's background in geology and experience in site assessment, his firm took the lead in conducting the investigation. The scientific investigation was grounded in the understanding that the selection of the Warren County site was not based on good scientific data. First, the report stated that "the State selected the site, either in part or in large measure, because of an African-American community that could not effectively fight the site selection process." Secondly, "the location was complicated by a difficult to assess hydro-geological setting that was, in fact, never fully or accurately characterized prior to the decision to locate the landfill there."[13]

The investigation found data to indicate several problems with the landfill. The report affirmed Hirschhorn's earlier investigation, damning the leachate collection system, and stated that "the State had not complied with certain important legal requirements." Evidence from groundwater testing supported the claim that leachate from the landfill had moved into the subsurface immediately adjacent to the landfill. Evidence from the air-monitoring system suggested that PCBs were probably moving through breaches in the top liner. Analysis of the chemical composition of the landfill contents reported that "a significant amount of 2,3,7,8-TCDD was found, namely 24 ppq, which is unusual for dioxin/furan impurities for PCBs." This analysis resonated strongly with citizens who had long felt unsure of exactly what was put into the landfill. Most of the soil had been taken off the roadsides contaminated with PCB liquid from the illegal dumping in 1979, but some of it was obtained from Fort Bragg, near Fayetteville, North Carolina. Activists had argued that the material from Fort Bragg was different from the original PCB-contaminated soil. The report stated, "No specific data has been found in the files on exact chemical compositions of the Fort Bragg material," and concluded with "the possibility that there might be a source of the dioxins other than PCBs."[14]

The most problematic finding with respect to the water in the landfill, however, related to Barnes's analysis of water levels in the landfill and the monitoring wells in relation to seasonal rainfall variations. The evidence suggested a "very strong correlation between the natural hydrologic cycle and the water in the landfill," indicating that the materials in the landfill were not isolated from the environment as the engineering design had intended, but that rainwater was entering and moving through the landfill.[15] State officials were "taken aback" by this finding and for the first time thought perhaps there was evidence to suggest a breach in landfill integrity.

In the end, the information and assessments from both Hirschhorn and Barnes enabled the citizens to continue to push for their ultimate goal of detoxification. In particular, they provided extensive data leading to the "overall conclusion . . . that the landfill has lost integrity and containment efficiency" and that "detoxification of the landfill . . . [is] the only reliable long-term solution to address the threats posed by a low quality landfill containing large amounts of PCBs and dioxins."[16]

The pressure on the state to begin a detoxification project intensified as a result of these investigations. The citizens used the power they had gained through the environmental justice framework to infuse the production of scientific knowledge with a new set of values. The role of the citizens' science advisors demonstrated that the investigation by state experts was driven by their view of risk. When a different understanding of risk was brought to bear, the investigation completely changed: new questions were asked, new measurements were made, data was interpreted with alternative criteria, and the investigators' results led to very different conclusions. The approach worked, and in 1997 the state acquiesced to using the BCD technology for detoxification. Governor Hunt was then at the end of his political career, and his 1982 promise to Warren County citizens for detoxification was looming as a possible blemish on his historical record. The political costs were too high; he directed DEHNR to move ahead and make the problem go away. DEHNR's agreement was not so much an acknowledgment of a risk but what was characterized by Mike Kelly as "the right thing to do." The Working Group had chosen BCD as the appropriate technology, and Hirschhorn estimated a $24-million price tag for design, demonstration tests, treatment, and restoration.[17] Funding was the major sticking point, but it was a time of state budget surpluses, and the Working Group had a very strong ally, Frank Ballance, in the General Assembly. Hunt included $15 million in his 1999 budget, pledging to fulfill the promise he had made. The state hoped to find the additional $9 million elsewhere.[18] The Assembly approved $7 million, but $1.4 million of it was diverted to help with the cleanup from Hurricane Floyd in September 1999. An additional $1 million was taken from the state's white goods program, designed to divert appliances from landfills, and the General Assembly approved $4.5 million more in 2001. It looked like a $24-million project would have to be whittled down to a $12-million project. Treatment of the soil began in August 2002 and was scheduled to be completed by spring 2003. The BCD process was designed to treat the soil to 200 parts per million (ppm) for PCBs and dioxins/furans, a level ten times below regulatory requirements.[19] The residents also achieved their goal of eliminating the need to send contamination to another community; all the treatment was done on-site.

Unintentional Ramifications and the
Dissolution of Radical Critique

The environmental justice movement succeeded in challenging environmentalism to include the concerns of the poor and people of color. Redefining participation and inclusion was at the heart of the movement's goals. On one level, the Warren County residents used this strategy successfully and were victorious in obtaining their stated goal of landfill detoxification. The Warren County case illustrates, however, that the dominant approach used by environmental justice had the effect of reinforcing the myth that environmental degradation and social marginalization were not intimately entwined. The potential solution of multiracial coalitions was limited by a rigid understanding of the identity of legitimate victims of environmental injustices rather than fluid identities that many environmental justice advocates understood to "unite a diversity of people and allows for individual racial group identification."[20] The Warren County citizens faced a daunting and complex problem: how to have a multiracial coalition while nurturing people of color in leadership positions in environmental decision making?

The idea of black leadership was vital to the environmental justice movement for three reasons. First, people of color had been systematically excluded from environmentalism. Second, since the experience of racism could not be translated, no one else could validly speak for people of color. Lastly, if whites were leaders in the movement, people of color feared their own leadership would be usurped, as had happened in so many other situations in the past. The conflict between multiracial coalition building and the racial identity of leaders emerged in two contexts in the Working Group. The governance structure of the Working Group and the role of the science advisor both contributed to the dissolution of solidarity among the black and white citizen activists.

In March 1994 the initial structure of the Working Group allowed for very broad participation by community members, with a total of sixteen, including eight residents of Warren County and the chair of the County Commissioners. It was co-chaired by Dollie Burwell and Ken Ferruccio. They were reasonable choices since both had worked together during the 1982 protests and had been involved with the UCC's Commission on Racial Justice report. Both were articulate, tenacious, and dedicated to the project of detoxification. When Henry Lancaster, a high-ranking black official in the Hunt administration, was added as a third co-chair, he was supposed to help solve some of the problems in communication between the state and the citizens. Yet several members were wary of adding a state employee to an official position. Conflicts among the three co-chairs intensified, and Ferruccio accused Burwell and Lancaster of pushing him out. The animosity heightened to a point where Ferruccio decided to leave the position of co-chair at the end of 1996 but remained an active member.

The Working Group was initially scheduled to complete its work in December 1996, but as the end came near and they had not finished the project, the group needed to reconstitute itself and gain the approval of the governor. The remaining co-chairs, Burwell and Lancaster, proposed that the original eight citizen members be reduced to four. However, at the December meeting, the Working Group not only defeated the decrease in citizen members but also prevailed in increasing the number to nine. They decided to place an advertisement in the local paper to find new people to work on the project and instructed Lancaster to submit the proposal to the secretary for approval. The group waited for the secretary's decision for six months, during which time they did not meet, despite several requests by members. When the co-chairs informed the group that they had met with Secretary Howes on May 29, and the secretary was awaiting a proposal for a new structure of the Working Group, citizen members were perplexed and outraged. Why hadn't the co-chairs represented the wishes of the group to the secretary? Could it be that the "first-of-its-kind" advisory committee, created to foster a new form of citizen participation in government decision making, was silencing potential members? When a meeting still had not been called by July, Ferruccio wrote a scathing memo to the co-chairs, claiming that they had been co-opted by the state because they wanted to maintain their positions of power. Ferruccio, a white man from Ohio, claimed to be speaking on behalf of the marginalized residents of Warren County, victimized by "policies [that] are discriminatory and are based on a willingness to enslave and sacrifice people, especially people of color, by keeping them in ignorance of the facts, often through the help of people of color."[21]

The Working Group was eventually reconstituted with eight members so that the broader membership could continue reviewing technology for detoxification of the landfill. Dollie Burwell continued as co-chair and Mike Kelly, special assistant to Secretary Howes, took Lancaster's position as the other chair. Funding was secured from the General Assembly. As the detoxification process moved forward, the state argued that the Working Group was no longer necessary and a more traditional Citizen Advisory Board (CAB) would suffice. Not everyone embraced the name change, and the Ferruccios, who had been central to the entire effort, "work[ing] long and hard to get to this point,"[22] completely rejected it. For Ferruccio, "the state and federal government would continue to control the decision-making process through their state co-chair and through their NEJAC affiliated local co-chair. . . . The Citizen Advisory Board in Warren County is simply a function of the federally institutionalized environmental justice community, centralized . . . through NEJAC."[23]

These direct attacks on Burwell and Lancaster claimed "reverse environmental racism," and the challenge to leadership by a black woman and black man was deeply troubling to members of the group. Despite the real and difficult personality conflicts in the group, the new format did demonstrate that the CAB was now part of the establishment. This position in the established order was possible, in part, because environmental justice had gained enormous power on the state and national level, and this power was directly related to partisan politics. Ferruccio took an extreme position on this development. He said, "It is therefore to the economic advantage of the NEJAC nexus to link environmental problems to environmental racism as a rationale for justifying minority control of alleged liberation mechanisms . . . [and] polluters are protected and environmental problems perpetuated in exchange for trickle-down economic and political benefits to minority leaders."[24]

He was adamant that Burwell's political connections limited her ability to represent citizens because she was using her position to further her political career or the political career of others. After she lost her Registrar of Deeds position to Elsie Weldon in the election of 1996, she went to work for Congresswoman Eva Clayton. The Ferruccios were not the only citizen members of the group who felt uncomfortable with the close ties Burwell had to the political establishment. In November 1996 Burwell and Barnes met with Eva Clayton and state senator Frank Ballance without the knowledge of the Working Group or the participation of the other science advisor. Jim Warren, representing the state anti-toxic coalition, NC WARN, alleged that any contact with the government should be sanctioned by the other citizen members, lest there be secretive deals made and "hidden agendas" pursued that diverted the Working Group away from its main goal of detoxifying the landfill. Although Jim Warren was convinced that Burwell never "lost her commitment to detoxification," the meetings did not fit with the operating procedure used by the group.[25] The political connections of members of the Working Group created competing and contradictory reactions, reflecting the tension in environmental justice about the appropriate relationship of a social movement to the established political order. The close relationship Burwell had with both Ballance and Clayton did enable the group to move appropriation bills through the General Assembly; however, just a month after these questionable meetings with elected officials, the co-chairs proposed a diminished role for citizen members in the Working Group. This timing was not lost on other members.

As the conflicts over governance deepened, tension about the science advisors also contributed to the dissolution of a fluid identity that enabled a multiracial coalition. Since science as a socially embedded endeavor played a prominent role in developing a solution, the racial identity of scientists, as a marker of their ability to fully represent citizens, became important. A new science advisor was needed after the Ewald debacle, and the review of candidates left two choices. Patrick Barnes was a geologist with Barnes, Ferland and Associates, Inc. (BFA), an African American–owned environmental consulting business, and Joel Hirschhorn was an engineer who had worked on technology review and risk assessment. Barnes presented himself to the Working Group as a strong candidate because of his extensive work in site assessment, but he also had credentials from his lived experience. As he told the Working Group, Barnes had "an understanding of the distribution of environmental contamination, especially as it relates to minority communities. As a black environmental consulting firm, BFA is dedicated to assisting Grassroots organization[s] as they seek answers to the environmental problems facing minority communities."[26] Here was a perfect opportunity for the Working Group to contribute to the goal of increasing the number of people of color in technical and decision-making positions in environmental agencies and organizations. While tokenism was not desired, a highly qualified black geologist was too good to pass up. However, not everyone was pleased with this approach to choosing a science advisor, particularly Ken Ferruccio, who held that "environmental justice in Warren County requires that we hire the most qualified person for science advisor, that we exclude racial and political considerations, and that we judge applicants only on documented merits."[27]

Of course, in the world of the black members of the Working Group, the idea of "excluding race" was impossible; race existed as a consideration because racial discrimination persisted. Yet, how could they address the seemingly contradictory impulses in the environmental justice movement: nurture black environmental leadership while also developing a multiracial coalition?

The Working Group avoided a direct discussion of this tension. After they voted, nine to six, in favor of Hirschhorn, Henry Lancaster, a black deputy secretary for DEHNR, met alone with Bill Meyer, director of solid waste management and the lead state member on the Working Group, to craft a structure for a joint science advisor position.[28] The state was inclined to work with Barnes because he was more approachable, but they did not want to alienate the Working Group, who had voted for Hirschhorn. Since Lancaster worked for the state, despite his legitimate voice in the environmental justice movement by virtue of his black identity, most citizens did not trust him. If Lancaster wanted to eliminate Hirschhorn, many citizens thought he must be the biggest threat to the state's perception of the problem. They thought that Hirschhorn must embody the citizen view more purely and his unadulterated approach must be kept at all costs.[29] The state was able to garner support with the help of Burwell, who had favored Barnes, in part, because she was dedicated to encouraging African American leadership in environmental decision making. The proposal was not well received by Hirschhorn or Ferruccio, but in the interest of moving forward, the Working Group decided to hire both of the consulting firms, hoping to benefit from their complementary qualifications while also ensuring the involvement of an African American scientist.

The tensions over the science advisors were also related to different work styles. Hirschhorn had been unrelenting in his attacks on the state and was unwilling to work collaboratively. For example, he oversaw the state's air-monitoring tests. While at the site, he observed but said nothing. The following day, he denounced the state's tests as incomplete and inaccurate. State officials were upset that he had spent the entire day at the site and did nothing proactively to improve the monitoring process, made no suggestions, gave no comments. Instead of taking the opportunity to make a change, the state saw Hirschhorn's actions as only trying to find additional reasons to bolster the argument that the state did not know what it was doing.[30] Barnes was less confrontational, even though the site assessment report that he oversaw offered severe criticism of the state and the EPA. Now that the group was moving toward detoxification, Barnes was more willing to work with the state. He did not always agree, often offering significant challenges to the state's position, but could more easily work out compromises.[31]

Black residents in the Working Group allied with Barnes, and the white residents with Hirschhorn, resulting in an additional racial division within the group. Hirschhorn felt that he was discriminated against because he was white and often claimed his qualifications were superior to Barnes's. Deborah Ferruccio concurred: "He is the national expert in detoxification technologies. He has a doctorate and many publications in peer-reviewed journals about these topics."[32] The sense of superiority was particularly troubling to black members of the group, especially Burwell and Lancaster, who wrote to Hirschhorn, castigating him for his "unfair and baseless" allegations against Barnes. They continued to stress that each had different skills and experience to bring to the project—Hirschhorn's technical expertise in detoxification processes, and Barnes's geological expertise for site assessment. Dollie Burwell and Henry Lancaster wrote to Hirschhorn: "It is our opinion that neither of you are superior to the other and such comments have strong racist undertones. This is particularly distressing given the PCB landfill detoxification is such an important environmental justice project."[33]

Adding to this animosity, Hirschhorn rejected the economic development dimension of the project, which was central to the Working Group's environmental justice mission. The plan for implementation included an Environmental Job Training program to "strengthen the ability of Warren County workers to compete for jobs associated with the PCB Landfill Detoxification and Redevelopment Project"[34] with funding from the EPA and HUD. Also, Barnes spent much of his time in Warren County meeting with local businesses to help them compete for construction bids at the site. Hirschhorn rejected these activities by saying, "In my view the [Working Group] should and must remain limited to dealing with the safety and detoxification of the landfill. If people want to pursue civil rights, environmental justice and economic development, then they should use means other than the [Working Group]."[35] These comments perplexed members of the Working Group because they understood environmental justice to emphasize the relationship between economic justice and environmental quality. For these activists, any community work related to the landfill had to be tied to economic development efforts. If these activists knew anything, it was that environmental problems and issues of civil rights and economic opportunities could not be separated.

Conclusion

The environmental justice framework, both through its problem definition and proposal for solutions, broadened participation in the decision making about the landfill and led to major substantive successes on behalf of environmental quality for residents of Warren County. The soil was detoxified without shipment of contamination off-site, and investment in job training for residents of Warren County was obtained. The dedicated efforts of many activists over ten years made these outcomes possible.

Despite the many successes that can be enumerated, there was still some skepticism. Massenberg Kearney, while delighted that work was progressing, was holding off judgment on the success of the project until everything is finished: "I'll believe it when I see it." The Ferruccios still argued that the detoxification process will not yield the desired results because the science advisor, Patrick Barnes, was in the state's pocket. Without the independent oversight that Hirschhorn would have offered, they believed there was no way to know if the activities at the site are safe and if the procedure will render the site clean.

Many involved in the process expressed some surprise that the detoxification had actually started because there were so many opportunities during the decade for the entire process to unravel. The animosity about leadership and science advisors was virulent, but an intra-citizen rift also grew as black members of the group grappled with the development of a unitary racial identity. When members wanted to send out a press release, pointing out the landfill problems and the need for funding for detoxification, Burwell claimed that newspapers were not the best form of communicating with residents of Warren County because "my people don't read," suggesting that the majority of African Americans in Warren County were illiterate. Another black member of the group, a reticent but thoughtful man who lives adjacent to the landfill, stormed out of the meeting, telling Burwell, "I don't know about your people, but my people know how to read."

While distrust of the state contributed significantly to the tension and difficulty in resolving the issues, conflicts among citizens over the role of identity in environmental justice proved equally as troubling. These tensions were personality-driven, in part, but were also tied to the politics of environmental justice. As Jim Warren reflected on the process, "They [blacks on the Working Group] were under enormous pressure from the environmental justice community. All eyes were on them. There had to be black leadership on this project because of that pressure."[36]

Perhaps a direct and up-front discussion about the role of affirmative action in the project would have helped ease the tension, but in the end the racial animosity, driven by both racism and pressure from the outside, enabled the state to avoid the sticky problem of the risks from the landfill. While science was used to force an alternative perspective on risk, decision makers maintained that the landfill problem was not related to environmental risks but was solely driven by issues outside the purview of an environmental regulatory agency. The state never acknowledged that there was a significant risk from the landfill, and the decision to detoxify was driven by a desire to keep a lid on racial politics. The logic of siting, the inherent problems with attempting to entomb waste in perpetuity, and the perpetuation of waste policies predicated on expected waste expansion, therefore, never had to be brought into question. Not only did identity-based politics limit the ability for radical challenge to waste policy, the state's insistence that "of course it became a racial thing" belittled the legacy of racism. As the second phase of activism in Warren County illustrates, environmental justice, while an enormously powerful organizing principle, can have the unintended consequence of reinforcing the very problem it is attempting to dismantle.

7 | Epilogue

Twenty-four years after the initial Warren County events, environmental justice has had a major impact on contemporary environmentalism. Decision makers have been forced to include in their deliberations the potential negative impacts on minority and poor communities. However, the challenge to fundamentally shift the environmental policy paradigm toward preventing environmental burdens through a transformation of production rather than managing environmental risks has been less successful. Despite the limited success, the change in the environmental arena as a result of the environmental justice movement provides reason to hope. Environmental justice embraces the premises of the "risk society" postulated by traditional environmentalism while it also challenges the idea that the universality of risks should be emphasized over the local manifestations, which are always reflective of social stratification. Only by fusing risk consciousness with the multiple manifestations of inequities in power, knowledge, and resources can production processes be transformed.[1]

When Jesse Jackson told the Summit attendees that everyone is impacted by pollution, he was articulating one side of the environmental justice equation. However, environmental justice has also demonstrated that risk is defined and managed by social and political institutions that are infused with layers of values, beliefs, and judgments. The systems of domination that result in stratified distribution of costs and benefits, therefore, cannot be ignored when risk issues are considered. Since risks depend on the distribution of knowledge and the construction of knowledge, access and identities from different social locations are central to risk societies. In Warren County, both aspects of dealing with risk—universal/equal and local/unequal—were present and nurtured. The movement that emerged expanded not only the number of people who directly embrace the environmental identity but diversified the constituents for a transformed approach to protection. While these two manifestations of risk can often pull the movement in divergent directions, the potential of the movement lies in its ability to simultaneously hold both seemingly contradictory views.

A recent development in the environmental justice chronicle illustrates the potential that can come from the expanded support for environmental protection. In 1997 the EPA issued a draft guidance for complaints filed under Title VI of the Civil Rights Act of 1964 alleging discriminatory effects resulting from the issuance of pollution control permits by state and local governmental agencies that receive EPA funding. After issuance of a permit, a Title VI complaint could be filed, alleging that the permit caused "disparate adverse impacts." The guidance statement met with intense resistance from environmental justice activists and was considered a major step backward. In many ways, their assessment was accurate. The EPA policy on Title VI complaints undermined the ability of complainants to prevail and supported violators. For example, the policy stated that a complaint could only be filed by someone living in the affected area, but the agency did not define affected area, preferring to determine it on a case-by-case basis because each facility had impacts that disperse differently. Also, the EPA would only consider health impacts and not economic, social, and cultural impacts. Most troubling to environmental justice advocates, the EPA would not refuse a permit based solely on a Title VI violation but would only require mitigation as a remedy if a violation was found. For environmental justice activists, the result of "less discrimination is still discrimination." As one activist put it, the mitigation approach to Title VI violations actually "institutionalize[s] discrimination, allowing recipients' actions to be approved of by EPA even when they have demonstrable discriminatory impact."[2]

The EPA's policy on Title VI was not well received by local governments, either. For them, it created too much uncertainty for companies that needed permits to open new or expanded facilities. The U.S. Conference of Mayors passed a resolution demanding that the guidance document be withdrawn because it would discourage industry from redeveloping cities. The rallying call against the Title VI policy was led by Dennis Archer, mayor of Detroit at the time. He was convinced that companies would see the Title VI hurdle as too burdensome and opt out of new development in urban areas, negating efforts by cities across the country to attract developers back into urban centers.[3] Archer organized an Environmental Justice Roundtable with mayors from around the country to develop an alternative approach to the one suggested by EPA. At the event, EPA administrator Carol Browner tried to assuage the mayors by emphasizing the work the agency was doing with the redevelopment of the abandoned and contaminated sites in cities, also known as "brownfields." However, Archer was not convinced. "The ever-present risk to developers under this rule could have a chilling effect on much-needed urban redevelopment. . . . With the challenges already faced in developing brownfield sites, this further delay could tip the balance in favor of a business choosing a greenfield site."[4]

Mayor Archer's concerns sound remarkably similar to the sentiments of Carl Stokes, mayor of Cleveland in 1970, who thought that the nation's concern with environmental quality had usurped the needs of the urban poor for housing, food, and jobs. Archer in 2000 and Stokes in 1970 both wanted to encourage economic development in cities as the means to bring employment and economic opportunity to the poor, predominately black residents living in cities with a collapsed industrial sector. For Stokes and Archer, environmental policies that constrained economic development became an enemy of the poor and people of color, who were increasingly poor, urban dwellers with fewer and fewer options. In the 1970s the burgeoning air and water regulations threatened to shut down industry because of the high costs of pollution control equipment. For example, in 1970 U.S. Steel Corporation wanted to close its plant in Duluth rather than spend $8 million on pollution controls.[5] In the early twenty-first century, efforts to insure nondiscrimination through enforcement of Title VI could derail urban redevelopment through costly delays and by pushing development to sites outside industrial areas, where it was less likely for a Title VI complaint to be filed or upheld. For example, in 1997 a Title VI complaint was filed with the EPA claiming that the permits issued by the State of Louisiana to Shintech Corporation for the construction and operation of a new chemical-processing facility discriminated against the largely black population in Convent, Louisiana, where the plant was sited.

EPA never ruled on the complaint, but Shintech decided to withdraw its plans for the facility in that location. Supporters of Mayor Archer claimed that Louisiana lost desperately needed jobs and tax revenue, and the effect was to decrease the quality of life for the poor blacks in Convent, not improve it, as environmental justice advocates asserted.

While the two mayors articulated similar concerns about the effects of environmental policies on the poor, a major shift had occurred in the intervening three decades, making the environmental landscape significantly different. In 1970 very few people of color living in low-income communities rallied behind an environmental cause. By 2000 the environmental justice movement had created a vast constituency of individuals from poor communities across the country who enthusiastically embraced the idea that they could live in an economically vibrant and environmentally sound community. For environmental justice activists, actions on behalf of environmental quality were not necessarily "distractions from the problems of black and brown Americans," but were instead, an integral part of making daily life healthy, safe, and economically secure. The environmental justice movement nurtured the idea that the problems of poverty and environmental quality are inextricably intertwined so that many poor and people of color no longer accept the idea that the promise of jobs and economic development compensate for increased risks they bear from polluting industries. Environmental regulatory agencies continue to issue permits designed to keep the risk from contamination within manageable limits. This approach does not question the expansion of pollution generation or the distribution of the risks associated with potential contamination. As more constituents are unwilling to embrace this approach, the possibility of creating a new paradigm predicated on prevention rather than management can be imagined. Environmental justice does not always correspond to the unified movement purported by its advocates. However, Warren County—the unlikely coalition that formed there—brought new voices into environmentalism, opening the possibility that environmental protection may, in the future, be available to everyone.

Notes

CHAPTER 1: THE SIGNIFICANCE OF WARREN COUNTY

1. Legal actions were taken against the three Burnses and Robert Ward. The elder Burns spent five years in jail; the sentence for his two sons was suspended. Robert Ward was held liable for the cost of the cleanup. *United States District Court, E.D. North Carolina, Raleigh Division. United States of America, Plaintiff, State of North Carolina, Plaintiff-Intervenor, v. Robert Earl Ward, Jr.* and *Ward Transformer Co., Inc., Defendants and Third Party Plaintiffs, v. Norry Electric Corporation and Liberty Motor and Machinery Co., Third Party Defendants,* No. 83–63-CIV-5, 9 September 1985.

2. Dollie Burwell, interview by author, Macon, NC, 24 May 1994.

3. Environmental Justice Resource Center, *People of Color Environmental Groups Directory 2000* (Atlanta, GA: Environmental Justice Resource Center, 2000).

4. Dollie Burwell, "Reminiscences from Warren County, North Carolina," in *Proceedings of the First National People of Color Environmental Leadership Summit,* ed. Charles Lee (New York: Commission for Racial Justice, 1991), 126.

5. Robert Gottlieb, *Forcing the Spring: The Transformation of the American Environmental Movement* (Washington, DC: Island Press, 1993), 246.

6. U.S. Environmental Protection Agency, *Environmental Equity: Reducing Risks for All Communities,* vol. 1, *Workgroup Report to the Administrator,* EPA 230-R-92–008 (Washington, DC: General Printing Office, 1992), 6.

7. Aldon Morris, *The Origins of the Civil Rights Movement: Black Communities Organizing for Change* (New York: Free Press, 1984), ix.

8. Ibid., xi.

9. Sydney Tarrow, *Power in Movement: Social movements, collective action and politics* (Cambridge: Cambridge University Press, 1994), 3–4.

10. Ken Geiser and Gerry Waneck, "PCBs and Warren County," *Science for the People* 15 (1983): 13–17. As reprinted in Robert Bullard, ed., *Unequal Protection: Environmental Justice and Communities of Color* (San Francisco: Sierra Club Books, 1994), 43–52.

11. Ibid., 52.

12. Robert Bullard, *Dumping in Dixie: Race, Class, and Environmental Quality* (Boulder, CO: Westview Press, 2000), 5.

13. Ibid., 29–30, 40.

14. For an example of a website, see the Sierra Club at http://www.sierraclub.org/environmental_justice/stories/northcarolina.asp. There are alternative stories of origin but these are less salient. For some, Martin Luther King's support of garbage workers in Memphis prefigures environmental justice. Luke and Foster point to several factors or "tributaries" that were precursors to environmental justice. Luke Cole and Sheila Foster, *From the Ground Up: Environmental Racism and the Rise of the Environmental Justice Movement* (New York: New York University Press, 2000).

15. Taylor claims that these concerns functioned as "submerged frames" of the civil rights master frame. Dorceta Taylor, "The Rise of the Environmental Justice Paradigm: Injustice Framing and the Social Construction of Environmental Discourses," *American Behavioral Scientist* 43, no. 4 (January 2000): 508–80.

16. For discussion of the cultural impact of the environmental movement see Sylvia Noble Tesh, *Uncertain Hazards: Environmental Activists and Scientific Proof* (Ithaca, NY: Cornell University Press, 2000), 100–119.

17. For examples, see Donald Worster, *Dust Bowl: The Southern Plains in the 1930s* (New York: Oxford University Press, 1979); Andrew Hurley, *Environmental Inequalities: Race, Class and Industrial Pollution in Gary, Indiana, 1945–1980* (Chapel Hill: University of North Carolina Press, 1995); and Richard White, *The Organic Machine: The Remaking of the Columbia River* (New York: Hill and Wang, 1995).

18. James Noel Smith, ed., *Environmental Quality and Social Justice in Urban America* (Washington, DC: Conservation Foundation, 1974).

19. Clem L. Zinger, *Environmental Volunteers in America* (Washington, DC: National Center for Voluntary Action, 1973), 17.

20. While environmental activists had long embraced this idea, Ulrich Beck first articulated its importance in the development of industrial capitalism and its potential for transformative politics. In *Risk Society: Towards a New Modernity* (Thousand Oaks, CA: Sage, 1992), he argues that an era marked by environmental contamination dissolves class distinctions because, eventually, no one can escape the effects of pollution. The so-called "Boomerang Effect" means that even producers and those who profit from production will feel the "latent side effects" of modernization.

21. Thomas Bradley, "Minorities and Conservation," *Sierra Club Bulletin*, April 1972, 21.

22. Don Combs, "The Club Looks at Itself," *Sierra Club Bulletin*, July/August 1972, 35–39.

23. "The Environmental Cause Is No Cop-out for the Affluent," *Audubon*, November 1971, 35–39.

24. *Time*, 3 August 1970, 42.

25. Daniel Zwerdling, "Poverty and Pollution," *The Progressive*, April 1971, 25–29; "Where Pollution Control Is Slowing Industrial Growth," *U.S. News*

and World Report, 23 April 1971, 47–50; Henry Wallack, "Paying for the Clean-up," *Newsweek*, 26 January 1970, 72.

26. Public opinion polls bear this out. Overwhelmingly, people support stronger environmental protection, and the strength of that support has grown significantly since the 1960s. Riley E. Dunlap, "Trends in Public Opinion toward Environmental Issues: 1965–1990," *Society and Natural Resources* 4 (1991): 285–312.

27. For the resource mobilization school of social movements, see John McCarthy and Mayer N. Zald, eds., *Social Movements in an Organizational Society* (Oxford: Transaction Press, 1987).

28. For an overview of new social movements, see Alberto Melucci, "New Social Movements: A Theoretical Approach," *Social Science Information* 19 (1980): 199–226; Claus Offe, "New Social Movements: Challenging the Boundaries of Institutional Politics," *Social Research* 52 (1985): 817–65. For a comparison of the two approaches see Bert Klandermans and Sidney Tarrow, "Mobilization into Social Movements: Synthesizing European and American Approaches," in Bert Klandermans, Hanspeter Kriesi, and Sidney Tarrow, eds., *From Structure to Action: Comparing Social Movement Research across Cultures, International Social Movement Research* 1 (1988), 1–38.

29. Craig Calhoun, "New Social Movements in the Early Nineteenth Century," *Social Science History* 17 (1993): 385–427. For a critique of the new social movement approach see Sidney Tarrow, *Struggle, Politics and Reform: Collective Action, Social Movements and Cycles of Protest* (Ithaca: Cornell University, Western Society Papers, 1989); Doug McAdam, Sidney Tarrow, and Charles Tilly, *Dynamics of Contention* (Cambridge: Cambridge University Press, 2001).

30. Tarrow, *Power in Movement.*

31. Alberto Melucci, *Nomads of the Present: Social Movements and Individual Needs in Contemporary Society* (Philadelphia: Temple University Press, 1990); Alain Touraine, *The Return of the Actor: Social Theory in Postindustrial Society* (Minneapolis: University of Minnesota Press, 1984).

32. Tarrow, *Power in Movement.*

33. John W. Kingdon, *Agendas, Alternatives and Public Policies*, 2nd ed. (New York: Longham Press, 2003), 3.

34. Alan Scott, *Ideology and Social Movements* (London: Unwin Hyman, 1990).

35. David Nabuib Pellow, *Garbage Wars: The Struggle for Environmental Justice in Chicago* (Cambridge, MA: MIT Press, 2002), 164.

36. Laura Pulido, *Environmental and Economic Justice: Two Chicano Struggles in the Southwest* (Tucson: University of Arizona Press, 1996), 24–30.

37. Gottlieb, *Forcing the Spring*, 264.

38. Tarrow, *Power in Movement*, 16.

39. Ibid., 108

40. Erving Goffman, *Frame Analysis: An Essay on the Organization of Experience* (New York: Harper, 1974), 21.

41. Taylor, "Environmental Justice Paradigm," 516.

42. Ibid., 562.

43. David Schlosberg, *Environmental Justice and the New Pluralism: The Challenge of Difference for Environmentalism* (Oxford: Oxford University Press, 1999), 111.

CHAPTER 2: REGULATING TOXIC CHEMICALS, PCBS, AND HAZARDOUS WASTE

1. In the years after World War II, the use of synthetic chemicals in both production processes and consumer goods proliferated. In 1940 one billion pounds of synthetic organic compounds were produced. In 1950 production had increased to 30 billion pounds. In 1968 a total of 120 billion pounds was produced, a 15 percent increase over 1967 and a 161 percent increase in one decade. In the same year, about nine thousand synthetic organic compounds were in commercial use. Approximately three to five hundred new compounds entered commercial use each year. The "petroleum invasion" consumed clothing, building supplies, furniture, appliances, cleansers, and almost every category of consumer goods. The total plastic production in the United States rose 103 percent between 1962 and 1968 and was expected to rise 10 percent each year during the 1970s. All the data is taken from the Council on Environmental Quality, *Toxic Substances* (Washington, DC: U.S. Government Printing Office, April 1971). The iconic film *The Graduate* (1967) demonstrated the degree to which synthetics had captured the American economy when the young protagonist was told to build his future on plastics.

2. Linda Lear, *Rachel Carson: Witness for Nature* (New York: Henry Holt, 1997).

3. The "risk society" thesis is attributed to both Ulrich Beck and Anthony Giddens. Beck argues that the increase in risk awareness comes from the actual outcomes and unfulfilled promises of modernization. Giddens, however, argues that modernization, especially through scientization, has produced the ability to perceive the world differently and that scientific skepticism, increased fragmentation, and the compression of time and space have changed the social perception of threats. Although the specific path of its manifestation may differ for the two scholars, both Giddens and Beck see the pervasiveness of risk in organizing society as a product of the modernization process. Anthony Giddens, *Runaway World: How Globalization Is Reshaping Our Lives* (London: Routledge, 2000); Ulrich Beck, *Risk Society: Toward a New Modernity* (Thousand Oaks, CA: Sage, 1992). For an overview of the literature on the sociology of risk see Deborah Lupton, *Risk* (New York: Routledge, 1999).

4. Lupton, *Risk*, 31.

5. Sylvia Noble Tesh, *Uncertain Hazards: Environmental Activists and Scientific Proof* (Ithaca, NY: Cornell University Press 2000), 132–37.

6. Iain Wilkinson, *Anxiety in a Risk Society* (London: Routledge, 2001).

7. *Federal Register* 43 (17 February 1978), 7150–64.

8. United States Environmental Protection Agency, Office of Pollution Prevention and Toxics, *Management of PCBs in the United States* (Washington, DC: EPA, 30 January 1997).

9. CEQ, *Toxic Substances*, v.

10. John E. Blodgett, ed., *Legislative History of the Toxic Substances Control Act: Together with a Section-by-Section Index* (Washington, DC: Environment and Natural Resources Policy Division of Library of Congress, December 1976), 4.

11. Ibid., 210.

12. Joel Reynolds, *The Toxic Substances Control Act of 1976: An Introduction, Background and Analysis* (New York: Columbia Law School, 1977), 23.

13. Jane E. Brody, "Vinyl Chloride Exposure Limit Is Opposed by Industry," *New York Times*, 26 June 1974, 30.
14. Reynolds, *The Toxic Substances Control Act*, 32.
15. John O'Connor, "TV: 'The Way of Cancer,'" *New York Times*, 15 October 1975, 87.
16. Reynolds, *The Toxic Substances Control Act*, 41.
17. For a critique of risk assessment, see Tesh, *Uncertain Hazards*, 66–80.
18. A similar incident occurred in 1979 in Taiwan, where about 2,000 people consumed rice oil contaminated with PCBs. Morton Mintz, "Industrial Chemical PCB Is Linked to Liver Cancer," *Washington Post*, 13 September 1976, A1, A6.
19. Richard Severno, "E.P.A. Aide Warns of Toxic Leakage," *New York Times*, 20 November 1975, 20.
20. U.S. Environmental Protection Agency, *Hudson River PCBs Site, New York, Record of Decision* (Washington, DC: EPA, February 2002).
21. Blodgett, *Legislative History*, 133.
22. James R. Allen and D. A. Barsotti, "The Effects of Transplacental and Mammary Movement of PCBs on Infant Rhesus Monkeys, *Toxicology* 6 (Nov.-Dec. 1976): 331–40.
23. General Accounting Office, *Toxic Substances: EPA's Chemical Testing Program Has Made Little Progress* (Washington, DC: GAO, 25 April 1990).
24. General Accounting Office, *Toxic Substances: Effectiveness of Unreasonable Risk Standard Unclear* (Washington, DC: GAO, 20 July 1990).
25. Andrew Hanan, "Pushing the Environmental Regulatory Focus a Step Back: Controlling the Introduction of New Chemicals under the Toxic Substances Control," *American Journal of Law and Medicine* 18 (1992).
26. The regulations issued in February 1978 for disposal of PCBs allowed only rags, soil, and other debris to be disposed of in landfills. See *Federal Register*, 1978.
27. General Accounting Office, *EPA Slow in Controlling PCBs* (Washington, DC: GAO, December 1981).
28. U.S. EPA, Office of Pollution Presentation and Toxics, *PCB Question and Answer Manual: An EPA TSCA Assistance Document* (Washington, DC: EPA, 1994).
29. U.S. Senate, *TSCA Oversight Hearings before the Subcommittee on Environmental Pollution of the Committee on Environment and Public Works*, 95th Congress, 2nd session (20–21 July 1978), 111.
30. Ibid., 21. The final inventory rule involved two phases. During the first phase, completed 1 June 1979, manufacturers and importers reported 43,000 chemicals. The second phase added chemical substances that were processed, used, or imported as part of a mixture or an article for commercial purposes and raised the total number of chemicals on the inventory to 55,103, published on 28 July 1980. As of October 1, 1985, the inventory contained 62,980 chemicals. The majority of the increase came from corrections to the original inventory, but 2,460 were new chemicals. Without a mechanism to track changes in production data, the agency could not determine the full level of risk or the costs associated with regulation. By 1985, with little action taken on any of the chemicals, the inventory was nearly obsolete. EPA wanted a smaller inventory with tracking mechanisms. The proposed update exempted four categories of chemicals (polymers, inorganic chemicals, microorganisms, and naturally occurring substances) and any chemical manufactured in quantities of

less than 10,000 pounds annually at an individual production site. The rules also required that manufacturers report production information every four years. EPA promulgated a rule (40 CFR part 710, subpart B), referred to as the Inventory Update Rule (IUR), on 12 June 1986 in the *Federal Register* 51:21438.

31. TSCA Section 4 (e). The law required the following agencies represented on ITC: Council on Environmental Quality (CEQ), Department of Commerce, U.S. Environmental Protection Agency, National Cancer Institute, National Institute of Environmental Health Sciences, National Institute for Occupational Safety and Health, National Science Foundation, and Occupational Safety and Health Administration. The following agencies were made liaison members: Agency for Toxic Substances and Disease Registry, Consumer Product Safety Commission, Department of Defense, Department of the Interior, Food and Drug Administration, National Library of Medicine, National Toxicology Program, and U.S. Department of Agriculture.

32. U.S. Senate, *Oversight Hearings*, 18.

33. National Research Council, *Toxicity Testing: Strategies to Determine Needs and Priorities* (Washington, DC: National Academy Press, 1984), 1.

34. General Accounting Office, *Toxic Substances: Status of EPA's Review of Chemicals under the Chemical Testing Program* (Washington, DC: GAO, October 1991).

35. Hanan, "Pushing the Environmental Regulatory Focus."

36. General Accounting Office, *Toxic Substances Control Act: Preliminary Observations on Legislative Changes to Make TSCA More Effective* (Washington, DC: GAO, July 1994).

37. Edward J. Woodhouse, "External Influences on Productivity: EPA's Implementation of TSCA," *Policy Studies Review* 4 (February 1985): 497–503.

38. Office of Technology Assessment, *The Information Content of Premanufacture Notices* (Washington, DC: OTA, April 1983). In the oversight committee hearings, Robert Hayden from the United Steel Workers claimed that 80 percent of the PMNs contained claims of confidentiality, but he did not provide information on how he arrived at that number. U.S. Senate, *Oversight Hearings*, 21.

39. Martin V. Melosi, *Sanitary City: Urban Infrastructure in America from Colonial Times to the Present* (Baltimore, MD: Johns Hopkins University Press, 2000), 351–55.

40. Eileen M. McGurty, "City Renaissance on a Garbage Heap: Newark, NJ, and Solid Waste Planning," *Journal of Planning History* 2, no. 4 (November 2003).

41. Melosi, *Sanitary City*.

42. Cost estimates included capital investments of $940 million, operating expenditures of $620 million, and regulatory costs of $20 million. U.S. EPA, *Report to Congress: Disposal of Hazardous Wastes* (Washington, DC: EPA, 1973), 26–30.

43. Ibid., 3, 7.

44. General Accounting Office, *How to Dispose of Hazardous Waste: A Serious Question that Needs to be Resolved* (Washington, DC: GAO, December 1978), 1.

45. General Accounting Office, *Statement of Eleanor Chemlimsy, Director, Program Evaluation and Methodology Division, before the Environment, Energy, and Natural Resources Subcommittee, Committee on Government*

Operations, House of Representatives, on the Condition of Information on Hazardous Waste, 25 September 1986, 4–11.

46. The budget problems began with the Carter EPA and worsened under Reagan. In 1979 the Office of Management and Budget was focused on halting inflationary repercussions of regulations and cut the small request for the hazardous waste program by 65 percent, which made RCRA a mere 3 percent of the total EPA budget. General Accounting Office, *Hazardous Waste Management Programs Will Not Be Effective: Greater Efforts Are Needed* (Washington, DC: GAO, 23 January 1979), 14–15. On anti-inflation, see Samuel Epstein, Lester Brown, and Carl Pope, *Hazardous Wastes in America* (San Francisco: Sierra Club, 1982), 228. After Reagan's election, total EPA spending decreased drastically, from $130 million in 1980 to $94 million in 1984, and RCRA's budget suffered accordingly. Daniel A. Mazmanian and David Morell, *Beyond Superfailure: America's Toxics Policy for the 1990s* (Boulder, CO: Westview Press, 1992), 91. The program remained under-funded until Congress authorized direct funding through the RCRA amendments in 1984. Within a year after passage, RCRA had the third largest operating budget at EPA. General Accounting Office, *Hazardous Wastes: New Approach Needed to Manage the Resource Conservation and Recovery Act* (Washington, DC: GAO, July 1988), 14.

47. GAO, *Hazardous Waste Management Programs,* 5.

48. Ibid., 14.

49. Andrew Szasz, *Ecopopulism: Toxic Waste and the Movement for Environmental Justice* (Minneapolis: University of Minnesota Press, 1994), 35.

50. General Accounting Office, *Hazardous Waste: Groundwater Conditions at Many Land Disposal Facilities Remain Uncertain* (Washington, DC: GAO, February 1988).

51. U.S. Environmental Protection Agency, *The Prevalence of Subsurface Migration of Hazardous Chemical Substances at Selected Industrial Waste Land Disposal Sites* (Washington, DC: EPA, October, 1977).

52. David Anderson, K. W. Brown, and Jan Green, "Effect of Organic Fluids on the Permeability of Clay Soil Liners," in U.S. EPA, *Land Disposal of Hazardous Waste* (Cincinnati: EPA, March 1982).

53. Peter Montague, "Four Secure Landfills in New Jersey—A Study of the State of the Art in Shallow Burial Waste Disposal Technology," (Princeton, NJ: Department of Civil Engineering and Center for Energy and Environmental Studies, School of Engineering/Applied Science, Princeton University, 1 February 1981).

54. William Sanjour, "Statement of William Sanjour, Chief, Hazardous Waste Implementation Branch, U.S. EPA, before the Subcommittee on Natural Resources, Agriculture Research and Environment Committee on Science and Technology, House of Representatives," 30 November 1982, http://pwp.lincs.net/sanjour/default.htm (accessed 3 October 2005).

55. General Accounting Office, *Assessment of EPA's Hazardous Waste Enforcement Strategy* (Washington, DC: GAO, September 1985).

56. General Accounting Office, *Hazardous Wastes: Many Enforcement Actions Do Not Meet EPA Standards* (Washington, DC: GAO, June 1988).

57. Mazmanian and Morell, *Beyond Superfailure,* 106

58. As of 1997, only 8 percent had completed cleanups. General Accounting Office, *Hazardous Waste: Progress under the Corrective Action Program Is Limited* (Washington, DC: GAO, October 1997), 7.

59. Szasz, *Ecopopulism.*

60. Over the next two years television news coverage totaled over 190 minutes. See Szasz, *Ecopopulism*.

61. The Love Canal story is recounted in many sources; for example, Szasz, *Ecopopulism*; Lois Marie Gibbs and Murray Levine, *Love Canal: My Story* (Albany: State University of New York Press, 1982); and Allan Mazur, *A Hazardous Inquiry: The Rashomon Effect at Love Canal* (Cambridge, MA: Harvard University Press, 1998). Many scientists doubt that there ever was a real health crisis at Love Canal. For a summary of these arguments, see Tesh, *Uncertain Hazards*, 21–23.

62. The CBS segment was six and a half minutes, and the NBC one was three minutes and ten seconds. *Vanderbilt Television News Archive* (Nashville, TN).

63. Sheila Rule, "Fire Breaks Out amid Chemicals at Site in Jersey," *New York Times*, 22 April 1980, B3.

64. Harold C. Barnett, *Toxic Debts and the Superfund Dilemma* (Chapel Hill: University of North Carolina Press, 1994), 69.

65. Strict liability held responsible parties liable even if a company had adhered to all applicable laws at the time of the contamination. Without strict liability, almost any potential responsible party could avoid penalty by claiming non-negligence. Under joint and several liability, a responsible party could be required to pay the entire cleanup costs even if that party had only contributed a small fraction of the wastes at the site. This standard gave the government an incentive to identify and pursue companies with large assets even if they were small contributors to the contamination. In *Chem-Dyne*, the court ruled that the burden of proof was on the potentially responsible party (PRP) to show its contribution of harm. Without this evidence, the court could impose joint and several liability. In *A&F Materials*, the court could hold each PRP responsible even if that meant joint and several liability, based on the facts of the case. John M. Hyson, "'Fairness' and Joint and Several Liability in Government Cost Recovery Actions under CERCLA," *Harvard Environmental Law Review* 21 (1997): 152–53.

66. George J. Mitchell, "Not a Super Fund," *New York Times*, 8 December 1980, A27.

67. Mazmanian and Morell, *Beyond Superfailure*, 27.

68. R. McGreggor Cawley, *Federal Land, Western Anger: The Sagebrush Rebellion and Environmental Politics* (Lawrence: University Press of Kansas, 1993).

69. Quoted in Richard N. L. Andrews, "Deregulation: The Failure at EPA," in *Environmental Policy in the 1980s: Reagan's New Agenda*, ed. Norman J. Vig and Michael E. Kraft (Washington, DC: CQ Press, 1984), 163.

70. Quoted in Barnett, *Toxic Debts*, 71.

71. Office on Technology Assessment, *Technologies and Management Strategies for Hazardous Waste Control* (Washington, DC: OTA, 1983), 63.

72. General Accounting Office, *Superfund: Missed Statutory Deadlines Slow Progress in Environmental Programs* (Washington, DC: GAO, November 1988), 8.

73. Barnett, *Toxic Debts*, 81.

74. Phillip Shabecoff, "New Environmental Chief Vows to Lift Regulatory 'Overburden,'" *New York Times,* 21 June 1981, 36.

75. Szasz, *Ecopopulism*, 123–30.

76. Barnett, *Toxic Debts*, 86.

77. James J. Florio, "Congress as Reluctant Regulator: Hazardous Waste Policy in the 1980s," *Yale Journal of Regulation* 3 (1986): 351–82.
78. Congressional Budget Office, *Analyzing the Duration of Cleanup at Sites on Superfund's National Priorities List* (Washington, DC: CBO, March 1994), 8.
79. The removal of the soil was completed on 6 November 1982. Roadside PCB Spill (NCD 980602163) was officially delisted on 7 March 1986, one of the first seven sites delisted from the Final NPL. *Federal Register* 51 (45): 7934–35. The delay was related to testing issues as well as managerial problems. Five sites were delisted prior to the NC site: County Golf Course, St. Louis (MID980794531), on 8 September 1982 and four on 30 December 1982: Luminous Process Inc. (GAD 990855818), Chemical Metals Industries (MDD98055478), Walcott Chemical Company (MSD980601736), and Chemical and Minerals Reclamation (OHD980614549). These five sites were on the initial NPL and were delisted before issuance of the Final NPL on 8 September 1983. The NC site had not been delisted prior to the Final NPL, so the NC site was included on it and was, therefore, in the first group of delisted sites from the Final NPL. See http://cfpub.epa.gov/supercpad/cursites/csitinfo.cfm?id=0403068.

CHAPTER 3: THE COLLECTIVE ACTION FRAME OF "NOT IN MY BACKYARD"

1. Environmental Protection Agency, *Public Hearing before the Environmental Protection Agency on the Matter of the Application to Dispose of Soil Contaminated with PCBs at a Selected Site in Warren County, North Carolina,* 4 January 1979, RC-CCPS File 697, State of North Carolina Archives, Raleigh, North Carolina, 100.
2. Charles White in EPA, *Public Hearing,* 149.
3. Herbert Hyde, Memorandum to Governor James B. Hunt, 23 January 1979, RC-CCPS File 697, State of North Carolina Archives, Raleigh, North Carolina.
4. North Carolina, Department of Crime Control and Public Safety, *Final Environmental Impact Statement for the Removal and Disposal of Soils Contaminated with PCBs along Highway Shoulders in North Carolina* (Raleigh, NC, 13 November 1980), 9.
5. Nearly 40 percent of the toxic waste disposed of nationwide between 1984 and 1987 under the federal Superfund removal program ended up at the landfill. The 2,700-acre landfill also sits directly over the Eutaw Aquifer, which supplies water to a large part of Alabama.
6. Kelly Alley, Charles Faupel, and Connor Bailey, "The Historical Transformation of a Grassroots Environmental Group," *Human Organization* 54, no. 4 (1995); Connor Bailey, Charles Faupel, and James H. Gundlach, "Environmental Politics in Alabama's Blackbelt," in *Confronting Environmental Racism: Voices from the Grassroots,* ed. Robert D. Bullard (Boston: South End Press, 1993).
7. Susan Hunter and Kevin M. Leyden, "Beyond NIMBY: Explaining Opposition to Hazardous Waste Facilities," *Policy Studies Journal* 23, no. 4 (1995): 601ff.
8. Paul Slovic, "Perceptions of Risk," *Science* 236 (1987): 280–85.
9. Kent E. Portney, *Siting Hazardous Waste Treatment Facilities: The NIMBY Syndrome* (New York: Auburn House, 1991).

10. David Snow and R. Benford, "Ideology, Frame Resonance and Participant Mobilization," *International Social Movement Research* 1 (1988): 197–217; David Snow and R. Benford, "Master Frames and Cycles of Protest," in *Frontiers in Social Movement Theory*, ed. Aldon Morris and Carol McClurg Mueller (New Haven: Yale University Press, 1992), 135–55.

11. Sydney Tarrow, *Power in Movement: Social Movements, Collective Action and Politics* (Cambridge: Cambridge University Press, 1994), 16.

12. Snow and Benford, "Master Frames."

13. For the role of experiential knowledge in environmental activism, see Giovanna DiChiro, "Nature as Community: The Convergence of Environmental and Social Justice," in *Uncommon Ground: Toward Reinventing Nature*, ed. William Cronon (New York: W. W. Norton, 1995).

14. Ed and Florence Somerville, interview by author, tape recording, Afton, NC, 30 August 1994.

15. Massenberg Kearney, interview by author, Afton, NC, 2 February 2003.

16. Luther Brown, interview by author, tape recording, Soul City, NC, 8 June 1994.

17. Robert Austin in EPA, *Public Hearing*, 113.

18. William Brauer in EPA, *Public Hearing*, 132.

19. Stanton Miller, "The PCB Imbroglio," *Environmental Science Technology* 17, no. 1 (1983): 11–14; Julian Josephson, "Phasing Out PCBs: Whatever the Outcome of the Debate over Their Health Effects, They Must Go," *Environmental Science Technology* 18, no. 2 (1984): 43–44; "Polychlorinated Biphenyls: How Do They Affect Human Health?" *Health and Environment Digest*, August 1988; Kristine Napier, "PCBs: The Mythical Monsters," *ACSH News and Views*, March/April 1988, 3–4; "PCB Cancer Reassessment Completed," *IEHR Bulletin*, October 1991.

20. C. Greg Smith, interview by author, Raleigh, NC, 24 May 1994.

21. Ibid.

22. Martin Halper, interview by author, Washington, DC, 14 December 1994.

23. Environmental Protection Agency, "PCB Marking and Disposal Regulations Final Action Support Document," *Federal Register* 43:7150, 17 February 1978.

24. Andres Szasz, *Ecopopulism: Toxic Waste and the Movement for Environmental Justice* (Minneapolis: University of Minnesota Press, 1994). In 1984 the California Waste Management Board produced a study through a public relations and political consulting company. The so-called Cerrell Report outlines the demographic and social qualities of communities that were more likely to accept waste facilities. By that time, the resistance to sitings had created a logjam in implementing the waste management system, but in 1979 there was little reason to expect this type of response. The report found that the communities least likely to resist were older, conservative, and lower socioeconomic neighborhoods. The report concluded, "Middle and higher socioeconomic strata neighborhoods should not fall at least within (five miles) of the proposed site." If implemented, the board would be targeting the poor, not choosing sites for their technical merits. The impact of the report on citizens groups cannot be overstated. California Waste Management Board, "Political Difficulties Facing Waste-to-Energy Conversion Plant Siting," 1984.

25. Martin V. Melosi, *The Sanitary City: Urban Infrastructure in America from Colonial Times to the Present* (Baltimore, MD: Johns Hopkins University Press, 2000), 271–73.

26. Ken Ferruccio, interview by author, tape recording, Warrenton, NC, 24 May 1994.

27. Environmental Protection Agency, Memorandum to State of North Carolina, 27 December 1979, North Carolina Division of Solid Waste, File Room, Raleigh, North Carolina.

28. State of North Carolina, Department of Crime Control and Public Safety, *Addendum to Final Environmental Impact Statement for the Removal and Disposal of Soils Contaminated with PCBs along Highway Shoulders in North Carolina* (Raleigh, NC, February 1981).

29. EPA, *Public Hearing*, 66.

30. Deborah Ferruccio, interview by author, tape recording, Warrenton, NC, 24 May 1994.

31. *Warren County v. State of North Carolina*, 79 560 Civ 5, 28 (Easter District, 25 November 1981).

32. Deborah Ferruccio, interview; Ken Ferruccio, interview; Luther Brown, interview.

33. Ken Ferruccio, interview.

34. "Dump Decision Delayed," *Warren Record*, 25 January 1979; Deborah Ferruccio, Letter to Editor, *Warren Record*, 25 January 1979.

35. Sylvia D. Bumgardner in EPA, *Public Hearing*, 123–24.

36. James B. Hunt, "Open Letter to the Citizens of Warren County," *Warren Record*, 20 October 1982.

37. Robert Buchner, interview by author, Chatham County, NC, May 1994; Don Griffin, interview by author, tape recoding, Charlotte, NC, 19 January 1994; Charles Jeffries, interview by author, tape recording, Durham, NC, 18 January 1994.

38. Jule Boulding, interview by author, 27 August 1994.

39. Warren County Economic Development Commission, "Warren County Fact Sheets," (Warrenton, NC, 1991).

40. Paul Luebke, *Tar Heal Politics: Myths and Realities* (Chapel Hill: University of North Carolina Press, 1990), 58–70.

41. Ibid.

42. EPA, *Public Hearing*, 104–5.

43. Gregory Newsome, Letter to John White, 5 January 1979, North Carolina Division of Waste Management, Solid Waste File Room, Raleigh, NC.

44. Linda Carter in EPA, *Public Hearing*, 142.

45. CCPS, *Final EIS*; Tom Oliver, "Warren Wants Soul City Land to Bring Jobs," *Durham Herald*, 29 December 1982.

46. Ken Ferruccio, interview.

47. Herman R. Clark, Letter to Residents of Warren County, 15 September 1982, RC- CCPS File 697, State of North Carolina Archives, Raleigh, North Carolina.

48. Deborah Ferruccio, interview.

49. Helen Howard, "Opponents Focus on Discrepancies," *Warren Record*, 4 January 1979; Jack Harris, interview by author, 16 June 1994.

50. Harris, interview.

51. Deborah Ferruccio, interview.

52. White in EPA, *Public Hearing*, 10–11.

53. Mary Guy Harris, interview by author, tape recording, Red Hill, NC, 2 September 1994.

54. Brown, interview.

55. Bauer in EPA, *Public Hearing*, 80.

56. EPA, *Public Hearing*, 181.
57. Smith, interview; Deborah Ferruccio, interview.
58. EPA, *Public Hearing*, 140.
59. Sylvia Day Bumgardner, Letter to Editor, *Warren Record*, 4 January 1979, 2.
60. Smith, interview.
61. *Durham Herald*, 22 December 1978, as quoted in EPA, *Public Hearing*, 215.
62. *Warren County v. State.*
63. Robert W. Lake, "Rethinking NIMBY," *Journal of the American Planning Association* 59, no. 1 (Winter 1993): 87–93.

CHAPTER 4: CONSTRUCTING ENVIRONMENTAL RACISM

1. For the anti-toxics movement, see Andrew Szasz, *Ecopopulism: Toxic Waste and the Movement for Environmental Justice* (Minneapolis: University of Minnesota Press, 1994).
2. For brokering linkages between movements, see Doug McAdam, Sidney Tarrow, and Charles Tilly, *Dynamics of Contention* (Cambridge: Cambridge University Press, 2001), 157–59.
3. Social movements, both the so-called old and new, include formal and informal mobilizing structures. While formal organizations often become important at later stages in a social movement, perhaps even leading to an interest group structure, informal social networks are central to the formation of movements. These informal networks played a role in the formation of the earlier class-based movements, civil rights movements, and the more recent life-style-focused movements. See Sidney Tarrow, *Power in Movement: Social Movements, Collective Action and Politics* (Cambridge: Cambridge University Press, 1994), 135–50.
4. McAdam, Tarrow, and Tilly, *Dynamics of Contention*, 89–98.
5. Steven R. Weisman, "Reagan Says Blacks Were Hurt by Works of the Great Society," *New York Times*, 16 September 1982, A1.
6. As quoted in Manning Marable, *Race, Reform, and Rebellion: The Second Reconstruction in Black America, 1945–1982* (Jackson: University Press of Mississippi, 1984), 195.
7. Ibid.
8. John Robinson, "Blacks in N.C. Muster Forces to Shield Civil Rights," *Raleigh News and Observer*, 31 January 1982, 25-I.
9. Robert C. Mitchell, Angela G. Mertig, and Riley E. Dunlap, "Twenty Years of Environmental Mobilization: Trends among National Environmental Organizations," *Society and Natural Resources* 4 (1991): 219–34.
10. Riley E. Dunlap, "Trends in Public Opinion toward Environmental Issues: 1965–1990," *Society and Natural Resources* 4 (1991): 285–312.
11. The preclearance provisions applied to nearly nine hundred jurisdictions, including the entire states of Alabama, Alaska, Georgia, Louisiana, Mississippi, South Carolina, Virginia; forty counties in North Carolina; four counties in Arizona; one county in Hawaii; and one in Idaho. The 1970 and 1975 amendments added coverage to the entire states of Arizona and Texas and sections of New York, Wyoming, California, New Hampshire, Maine, Massachusetts, Florida, Michigan, and South Dakota. United States Commission on Civil Rights, *The Voting Rights Act: Unfulfilled Goals* (Washington, DC: Commission, 1981), 14.
12. Ibid., 73.

13. In March 1965, just months before the act was passed, 29 percent of voting-age blacks were registered to vote in the South, compared to 73 percent of the white voting-age population. By 1967 a 78 percent increase in black registered voters had been achieved, with over half of the voting-age black population registered. Richard L. Engstrom, "Black Politics and the Voting Rights Act, 1965–1982," in *Contemporary Southern Politics*, ed. James F. Lea (Baton Rouge: Louisiana State University Press, 1988).

14. Commission, *Voting Rights Act*, 19–21.

15. Ibid., 11–15.

16. United States House of Representatives, Hearings before the Subcommittee on Civil and Constitutional Rights of the Committee on the Judiciary, Ninety-seventh Congress, First Session on Extension of the Voting Rights Act, 1981, 2070–2071.

17. The extension of the VRA involved three issues: How long should the preclearance provisions be extended (if at all)? Should the criteria for release of a covered jurisdiction from the preclearance requirement be loosened to allow for easier "bail out"? Should Section 2 explicitly say that an election practice existing at the time of the initial VRA need only have the effect of discrimination to be rendered illegal? This last issue became a concern after the 1980 Supreme Court case, *Mobile v. Bolden*, challenging the at-large city elections in Mobile, Alabama, which concluded that proof of intent to discriminate was required under the original act. The result of *Mobile* was that an election practice that was in place prior to 1965 could remain unless intent could be shown, but if a jurisdiction wanted to institute the same practice after 1965, the DOJ could review the change under the preclearance provision and use a results test to determine if it was discriminatory.

18. Steven V. Roberts, "Voting Law Compromise Clears Senate Panel," *New York Times*, 5 May 1982, A23.

19. Sheila Rule, "Blacks and Reagan's Goal on State's Rights, *New York Times*, 11 March 1981, B20.

20. Police estimated 1,000 participants; organizers claimed 3,500. Reginald Stuart, "March Is Begun in Alabama to Back Voting Rights Law," *New York Times*, 7 February 1982, 24.

21. There were a total of 156 witnesses at the House hearings for the 1982 extension, as compared to 74 in 1965, 24 in 1970, and 57 in 1975. Nearly 48 percent of those 156 witnesses were members of civil rights organizations. Dianne M. Pinderhughes, "Black Interest Groups and the 1982 Extension of the Voting Rights Act," in Huey L. Perry and Wayne Parent, eds. *Blacks and the American Political System* (Gainesville: University Press of Florida, 1995), 218.

22. For the legal history of redistricting see Andrea L. Wollock, *Reapportionment: Law and Technology* (Denver, CO: National Conference of State Legislatures, 1980). For preclearance in North Carolina, see United States Department of Justice, Division of Civil Rights, Voting Rights Section, File No. 82–2368.

23. The district did not elect a black representative in 1982. Tim Valentine, from Rocky Mount, won. After the 1990 census, new districts were drawn that put Warren County into District 1. District 1 then became a majority black district and elected Eva Clayton, a black woman from Warren County, who had served as chair of the county board of commissioners, 1982–92.

24. Jack Harris, interview by author, tape recording, Warrenton, NC, 16 June 1994.

25. Luther Brown, interview by author, tape recording, Soul City, NC, 8 June 1994.
26. Ken Ferruccio, interview by author, tape recording, Warrenton, NC, 24 May 1994.
27. Golden Frinks, interview by author, tape recording, Edenton, NC, 19 January 1995.
28. For a discussion of how risk dissolves social divisions see Ulrich Beck, *Ecological Politics in the Age of Risk* (Cambridge: Polity Press, 1995). For a critique of the environmentalist view of risk see Mary Douglas and Aaron Wildavsky, *Risk and Culture: An Essay in the Selection and Interpretation of Technological and Environmental Dangers* (Berkeley: University of California Press, 1982).
29. For example, Laura Westra and Bill E. Lawson, eds., *Faces of Environmental Racism: Confronting Issues of Global Justice*, 2nd ed. (Lanham, MD: Rowman and Littlefield, 2001), xviii. United Church of Christ Commission on Racial Justice, *Toxic Wastes and Race in the United States* (New York: Commission, 1987).
30. Leon White, interview by author, Oak Level UCC Church, Manson, NC, 22 May 1994.
31. "Minister to Leave Jail, Preach against Dump," *Raleigh News and Observer*, 19 September 1982, 24A.
32. Richard Hart, "PCBs Change 'Leap of Faith' to Full Battle," *Raleigh News and Observer*, 3 October 1982, 28A.
33. Richard Hart, "39 Arrested in Third Day of PCB Landfill Protests," *Raleigh News and Observer*, 18 September 1982, 1A, 8A.
34. Lennox S. Hinds, *Illusions of Justice: Human Rights Violations in the United States* (Iowa City: University of Iowa, School of Social Work, 1978); "Chavis Battling Reagan Policies," *Raleigh News and Observer*, 4 April 1982.
35. Richard Hart, "39 Arrested."
36. Tarrow, *Power in Movement*, 109.
37. Col. D. L. Matthews, interview by author, tape recording, Hope Mills, NC, 15 June 1994.
38. There is no evidence of public actions: no letters, no quotes in the paper, no participation in public hearings. She may have been involved in a more private way, but certainly not as a public leader.
39. Mary Guy Harris, interview by author, tape recording, Red Hill, NC, 2 September 1994; Frinks, interview.
40. Marable, *Race, Reform, and Rebellion*.
41. Don Griffin, interview by author, tape recording, 19 January 1995; Matthews, interview; Jane Sharp, interview by author, tape recording, Chapel Hill, NC, 20 January 1995.
42. North Carolina Department of Crime Control and Public Safety, *Special Incident Report: PCB Incident in Warren County*, 17 November 1982.
43. Aldon Morris, *The Origins of the Civil Rights Movement* (New York: Free Press, 1984).
44. Walter E. Fauntroy, interview by author, tape recording, Washington, DC, 14 December 1994.
45. Fauntroy, interview; Marable, *Race, Reform, and Rebellion*.
46. Marguerite Ross Barnett, "The Congressional Black Caucus: Illusions and Realities of Power," in *The New Black Politics: The Search for Political Power*, ed. Michael B. Preston, Lenneal J. Henderson, and Paul Puryear (New York: Longman Press, 1982).

47. General Accounting Office, *Siting of Hazardous Waste Landfills and Their Correlation with Racial and Economic Status of Surrounding Communities* (Washington, DC: GAO, 1 June 1983); United Church of Christ, Commission on Racial Justic, *Toxic Wastes and Race in the United States* (New York: UCC, 1987).

48. For a discussion of how the environmental movement brought these ideas into the general public's perspective see Sylvia Noble Tesh, *Uncertain Hazards: Environmental Activists and Scientific Proof* (Ithaca, NY: Cornell University Press, 2000), 135–37.

49. Dollie Burwell, interview by author, Oak Level UCC Church, Manson, NC, 22 May 1994.

50. David Levy, interview by author, tape recording, Washington, DC, 15 December 1994.

51. Jane Sharp, interview by author, tape recording, Chapel Hill, NC, 30 August 1994.

52. Tarrow, *Power in Movement*, 108.

53. NC Department of Crime Control, *Special Incident Report*.

54. The site was vandalized twice. A monitoring well was destroyed, requiring an entirely new well and causing considerable delay in construction. Also, the week before the trucks were scheduled to bring in the contaminated soil, the plastic liner was slashed twenty-three times. The repair cost $8,000 and delayed the project another five days while the damaged areas were sealed and then inspected by the EPA The state then hired an armed security company to patrol the landfill construction area at night. William W. Phillips, Letter to Al Hanke, North Carolina Department of Environment and Natural Resources, Solid Waste Division, Warren County PCB Landfill File, Raleigh, NC, 31 August 1982; James Scarborough, Record of Communication with O. W. Strickland, Warren County PCB Landfill File, 23 August 1982.

55. Belle Bright, interview by author, tape recording, Warrenton, NC, 31 August 1994.

CHAPTER 5: THE ENVIRONMENTAL JUSTICE MOVEMENT:

MATURATION AND LIMITATIONS

1. Executive Order 12898, "Federal Actions to Address Environmental Justice in Minority Populations and Low-Income Populations" (11 February 1994).

2. "Environmental Justice," *New York Times*, 11 February 1994, A34.

3. James P. Lester, David W. Allen, and Kelly M. Hill, *Environmental Injustices in the United States: Myths and Realities* (Boulder, CO: Westview Press, 2001).

4. Doug McAdam, Sidney Tarrow, and Charles Tilly, *Dynamics of Contention* (Cambridge: Cambridge University Press, 2001), 159.

5. Pulido showed that the dominant understanding of race in contemporary society limited the research about the distribution of environmental risks. Laura Pulido, "Rethinking Environmental Racism: White Privilege and Urban Development in Southern California," *Annals of Association of American Geographers* 9, no. 1 (2000): 12–40. Szasz and Meuser also argued that environmental justice discourse overlooks the implications for the globalized economy. Andrew Szasz and Michael Meuser, "Environmental Inequalities: Literature Review and Proposals for New Directions in Research and Theory," *Current Sociology* 45, no. 3 (July 1997): 99–120.

6. Golden Frinks, interview by author, tape recording, Edenton, NC, 19 January 1995. Reverend Albert Love was on the staff of the Southern Christian Leadership Conference.

7. General Accounting Office, *Siting of Hazardous Waste Landfills and Their Correlation with Racial and Economic Status of Surrounding Communities* (Washington, DC: GAO, 1 June 1983); United Church of Christ, Commission on Racial Justice, *Toxic Wastes and Race in the United States* (New York: UCC, 1987).

8. As the investigative arm of Congress, GAO evaluates federal programs, audits federal expenditures, and issues legal opinions. In July 2004 the name was changed to General Accountability Office.

9. The protesters were convinced that the landfill would eventually accept commercial waste despite the promises of regulators. The belief that commercial waste operation at the landfill was inevitable became part of the official narrative about Warren County. References to the history of the environmental justice movement invariably explained—without evidence to cite—that the Warren County landfill was about to become a commercial facility; for example, "The landfill would receive 6,000 truckloads of PCB-laced roadside dirt from the midnight dumping episode. But that would not come close to exhausting the proposed landfill's capacity; it would stay open and continue to accept massive amounts of industrial wastes on a commercial basis." Szasz and Meuser, "Environmental Inequalities," 100.

10. In his study, Bullard uses the U.S. Census definition of the South, which includes the EPA Region 4 states plus eight additional states and the District of Columbia. By this definition, "[t]he South has the largest population of any region in the country. More than 75.4 million inhabitants, nearly one-third of the nation's population, lived in the South in 1980. . . . The South also has the largest concentration of blacks in the country. In 1980, more than 14 million blacks lived in the region. Blacks were nearly one-fifth of the region's population. In the 1970s the region's black population increased by nearly 18 percent. In 1980, six of the southern states had black populations that exceeded 20 percent (35.2 percent of the population in Mississippi, 30.4 percent in South Carolina, 29.4 percent in Louisiana, 26.8 percent in Georgia, 25.6 percent in Alabama, and 22.4 percent in North Carolina)." Robert Bullard, *Dumping in Dixie: Race, Class, and Environmental Quality*, 3rd ed. (Boulder, CO: Westview Press, 2000), 22.

11. Charles Lee, ed., *Proceedings: The First National People of Color Environmental Leadership Summit* (New York: United Church of Christ, 1991), 75.

12. GAO, *Siting of Hazardous Waste Landfills*, 3.

13. Ken Ferruccio, interview by author, tape recording, Warrenton, NC, 24 May 1994.

14. For a comprehensive review of environmental equity research see Feng Liu, *Environmental Justice Analysis: Theories, Methods, and Practice* (Boca Raton, FL: Lewis Publishers, 2001).

15. UCC, *Toxic Wastes and Race*, 15.

16. Ibid., 18.

17. After the proliferation of zoning following the *Euclid* decision, the environmental quality of minority neighborhoods diminished from an intensification of industrial land uses. "Zoning . . . has been used to permit—even promote—the intrusion into black neighborhoods [of] disruptive incompatible uses that have diminished the quality and undermine the stability of those neighborhoods. . . . [A] number of cities . . . zoned low-income

residential areas occupied mainly, but not exclusively, by blacks for industrial or commercial use." Yale Rabin, "Expulsive Zoning: The Inequitable Legacy of *Euclid*," in *Zoning and the American Dream 101*, ed. Charles M. Haar and Jerold S. Kayend, reprinted in Clifford Rechtschaffen and Eileen Gauna, *Environmental Justice: Law, Policy, and Regulation* (Durham, NC: Carolina Academic Press, 2003), 27–28. Even Beck, who emphasized the universality of risks, acknowledged that they could have class-based distributions initially. However, he argued that, eventually, "poverty is hierarchic and smog is democratic." Ulrich Beck, *Risk Society: Towards a New Modernity* (Thousand Oaks, CA: Sage, 1992), 36.

18. Richard J. Lazarus, "Environmental Racism! That's What It Is," *University of Illinois Law Review* (2000): 255–74.
19. Laura Pulido, "A Critical Review of the Methodology of Environmental Racism Research," *Antipode* 28, no. 2 (1996): 145.
20. Pulido, "Rethinking Environmental Racism," 1.
21. Ibid., 17–20. Environmental justice scholar/activists did attempt to develop more complex explanations for disparate siting, but the movement focused on the direct explanations. See Paul Mohai, "Environmental Justice or Analytic Justice? Reexamining Historical Hazardous Waste Landfill Siting Patterns in Metropolitan Texas," *Social Science Quarterly* 77, no. 3 (September 1996): 500–507.
22. UCC, *Toxic Wastes and Race*, x.
23. For discussion of the legitimacy of using racial categories and the ethical considerations in their use see Stephen J. Gould, *Ever Since Darwin* (1977), 231–36; Newton G. Osborne and Marvin D. Feit, "The Use of Race in Medical Research," *Journal of the American Medical Association* 267 (8 January 1992): 275–79. For the implications for environmental justice research see Rae Zimmerman, "Issues of Classification in Environmental Equity: How We Manage Is How We Measure," *Fordham Urban Law Journal* 21, no. 3 (1994): 633–69.
24. For a summary of methodological issues in environmental justice research see Liu, *Environmental Justice Analysis*, 52–60.
25. Zimmerman, "Issues of Classification," 650.
26. D. J. Lober, "Resolving the Siting Impasse: Modeling Social and Environmental Locational Criteria with a Geographic Information System," *Journal of the American Planning Association* 61, no. 4 (1995): 482–95; J. Mennis, "Using Geographic Information Systems to Create and Analyze Statistical Surfaces of Population and Risk for Environmental Justice Analysis," *Social Science Quarterly* 83, no. 1 (March 2002): 281–97.
27. James T. Hamilton, "Testing for Environmental Racism: Prejudice, Profits or Political Power?" *Journal of Policy Analysis and Management* 14, no. 1 (1995): 107–32.
28. Bunyan Bryant and Paul Mohai, eds., *Race and the Incidence of Environmental Hazards: A Time for Discourse* (Boulder, CO: Westview Press, 1992), 169.
29. Hird's study of NPL sites contrasts with evidence showing that minorities bear the burden of environmental risks. He found that NPL sites tended to be in communities with "lower poverty rates, lower unemployment rates, lower percentages of nonwhites, and higher median housing values." John A. Hird, *Superfund: The Political Economy of Environmental Risk* (Baltimore, MD: Johns Hopkins University Press, 1994), 136. For an examination of the race/class debate see special issue of *Social Science Quarterly* 77, no. 3 (September 1996).

30. Susan L. Cutter, Danika Holm, and Lloyd Clark, "The Role of Geographic Scale in Monitoring Environmental Justice," *Risk Analysis* 16 (1996): 517–25. For an example of how scale can influence the equity analysis of waste facility siting see Eileen M. McGurty, "City Renaissance on a Garbage Heap: Newark, NJ and Solid Waste Planning," *Journal of Planning History* 2, no. 4 (November 2003). In Newark, New Jersey, an incinerator for county waste was sited in a predominately white and working-class neighborhood in a predominately black and poor city in a predominately white and middle-class county.

31. For examples of NPL studies see Rae Zimmerman, "Social Equity and Environmental Risk," *Risk Analysis* 13 (1993): 649–66; Hird, *Superfund*. For commercial hazardous waste facilities see UCC, *Toxic Wastes and Race*; and R. L. Anderton et al., "Environmental Equity: The Demographics of Dumping," *Demography* 31 (1994): 229–43.

32. Vicki Been, "Locally Undesirable Land Uses in Minority Neighborhoods: Disproportionate Siting or Market Dynamics," *Yale Law Journal* 10 (1994): 1383ff.

33. Pulido, "Rethinking Environmental Racism," 19; Robert D. Bullard, "Environmental Justice: It's More Than Just Facility Siting," *Social Science Quarterly* 77, no. 3 (September 1996): 493–99.

34. For more on PIBBY see Bullard, *Dumping in Dixie*, 5; for "ambiguous" see Vicki Been, "Analyzing Evidence of Environmental Justice," *Journal of Land Use and Environmental Law* 11, no. 1 (Fall 1995): 21.

35. Bryant and Mohai, *Race and the Incidence of Environmental Hazards*, 3–4.

36. Ibid., 3.

37. Ibid., 4–5.

38. As quoted in Robert D. Bullard, "Conclusion: Environmentalism with Justice," *Confronting Environmental Racism: Voices from the Grassroots* (Boston, MA: South End Press, 1993), 196.

39. U.S. Environmental Protection Agency, *Environmental Equity: Reducing Risks for All Communities*, vol. 1, *Workgroup Report to the Administrator*, EPA 230-R-92–008 (Washington, DC: General Printing Office, 1992), 12.

40. Pulido uses the idea of white privilege in environmental justice. She defines it as "hegemonic structures, practices and ideologies that reproduce whites' privilege status. In this scenario, whites do not *intend* to hurt people of color, but because they are unaware of their white skin privilege, and because they accrue economic and social benefits by maintaining the status quo, they inevitably do. . . . It is precisely because few whites are aware of the benefits they receive from being white and that their actions, without malicious intent may undermine the well-being of people of color, that white privilege is so powerful and pervasive." Pulido, "Rethinking Environmental Racism," 15.

41. U.S. Environmental Protection Agency, *Environmental Equity: Reducing Risks for All Communities*, vol. 2, *Supporting Documents* (Washington, DC: Government Printing Office, 1992), 107.

42. Ibid.

43. EPA, *Environmental Equity*, 1:4.

44. EPA, *Environmental Equity*, 2:98.

45. Marianne Lavelle and Marcia Coyle, "Unequal Protection: The Racial Divide in Environmental Law," *National Law Journal* 21 (September 1992): S2.

46. "Letter, Circa Earth Day 1990," in Rechtschaffen and Gauna, *Environmental Justice*, 21.

47. David Schlosberg, *Environmental Justice and the New Pluralism: The Challenge of Difference for Environmentalism* (Oxford: Oxford University Press, 1999), 3–4.

48. Laura Pulido, *Environmental and Economic Justice: Two Chicano Struggles in the Southwest* (Tucson: University of Arizona Press, 1996), 24–30.

49. Robert Gottlieb, *Forcing the Spring: The Transformation of the American Environmental Movement* (Washington, DC: Island Press, 1993); Margaret FitzSimmons and Robert Gottlieb, "A New Environmental Politics," in *Reshaping the U.S. Left: Popular Struggles in the 1980s*, ed. Mike Davis and Michael Sprinkler (London: Verso Press, 1988); Giovanna Di Chiro, "Defining Environmental Justice: Women's Voices and Grassroots Politics," *Socialist Review* 22, no. 4 (1992): 93–130.

50. Gottlieb, *Forcing the Spring*, 116.

51. Robert C. Mitchell, Angela G. Mertig, and Riley E. Dunlap, "Twenty Years of Environmental Mobilization: Trends among National Environmental Organizations," *Society and Natural Resources* 4, no. 3 (1991): 219–34.

52. Environmental Defense Fund, Environmental Policy Center, Friends of the Earth, Isaac Walton League, National Audubon League, National Parks and Conservation Association, Natural Resources Defense Council, National Wildlife Foundation, Sierra Club, and the Wilderness Society.

53. Robert Cahn, ed., *An Environmental Agenda for the Future* (Washington, DC: Island Press, 1985), 1.

54. Lee, *Proceedings*, 31.

55. Dorceta Taylor, "Blacks and the Environment," *Environment and Behavior* 21 (Winter 1989): 175–205.

56. Carolyn Merchant, "Shades of Darkness: Race and Environmental History," *Environmental History* 8, no. 3 (July 2003): 387.

57. Eugene Hargrove, "Forward," in *Faces of Environmental Justice: Confronting Issues of Global Justice*, ed. Laura Westra and Bill E. Lawson, 2nd ed. (Oxford: Rowman and Littlefield, 2001).

58. Pulido, *Environmental and Economic Justice*, 125–90.

59. "Letter, Circa Earth Day 1990," 22.

60. EPA, *Environmental Equity* 2:111.

61. Lee, *Proceedings*, vii.

62. Ibid., 125.

63. Ibid., 126.

64. Ibid., 13.

65. "A Place at the Table," *Sierra* 78, no. 3 (May/June 1993): 50–61.

66. Lee, *Proceedings,* 100.

67. Vernice Miller, "Building on Our Past, Planning for Our Future: Communities of Color and the Quest for Environmental Justice," in *Toxic Struggles: The Theory and Practice of Environmental Justice*, ed. Richard Hofrichter (Philadelphia, PA: New Society Publishers, 1993), 129.

68. Luke Cole and Sheila Foster, *From the Ground Up: Environmental Racism and the Rise of the Environmental Justice Movement* (New York: New York University Press, 2001), 1–9.

69. EPA, *Environmental Equity* 1:3.

70. Bullard, *Dumping in Dixie*, 116.

71. EPA, *Environmental Equity* 1:4.

72. Deeohn Ferris, "A Call for Justice and Equal Environmental Protection," in *Unequal Protection: Environmental Justice and Communities of Color*, ed. Robert D. Bullard (San Francisco: Sierra Books, 1994), 298–320.

73. EPA, "Proceedings of the National Environmental Justice Advisory Council Meeting," 20 May 1994, 4.

74. EPA, National Environmental Justice Advisory Council, Minutes, 3–5 August 1994, 4.

75. Ibid.

76. EPA, National Environmental Justice Advisory Council, Minutes, 23–25 October 1994, 1–2.

77. Ibid., 22.

78. EPA, National Environmental Justice Advisory Council, Minutes, 12–14 December 1995, ES-7.

79. The Weber-Michels model predicts a development of bureaucratization as social movements shift their goals toward maintaining their own organizations and away from the initial demands of the movement. However, Zald and his collaborators have shown that the degree of institutionalization is dependent on many conditions of the social movement organization. More recently Kriesi showed that, in addition to organizational structures, the life cycle of a social movement is dependent on political opportunity structure and the form of social networks. Mayer N. Zald, "Looking Backward to Look Forward: Reflections on the Past and Future of the Resource Mobilization Research Program," in *Frontiers in Social Movement Theory*, ed. Aldon D. Morris and Carol McClurg Mueller, (New Haven, CT: Yale University Press, 1992), 326–48; Hanspeter Kriesi, "The Organizational Structure of New Social Movements in a Political Context," in *Comparative Perspectives on Social Movements: Political Opportunities, Mobilizing Structures and Cultural Framings*, ed. Doug McAdam, John D. McCarthy, and Mayer N. Zald, (Cambridge: Cambridge University Press, 1996), 152–84.

80. Lee, *Proceedings*, 9.

81. Ibid., 8.

82. Ibid.

83. As quoted in Christopher H. Foreman, *The Promise and Peril of Environmental Justice* (Washington, DC: Brookings Institute, 1998), 117.

84. Bullard, *Unequal Protection*, xvi.

85. Laura Pulido, "Restructuring and the Contraction and Expansion of Environmental Rights in the United States," *Environment and Planning A* 26 (1994): 915–36.

86. Mfanya Donald Tryman, "Jesse Jackson's Campaigns for the Presidency," in *Blacks and the American Political System*, ed. Huey L. Perry and Wayne Parent (Gainesville: University of Florida Press, 1995), 67.

87. Lee, *Proceedings*, 73.

88. Ibid., 30.

89. Ibid., 54.

90. U.S. EPA, *OSWER Environmental Justice Success Stories Report (FY 2002–2003)* (Washington, DC: EPA, 2004).

91. EPA, National Environmental Justice Advisory Council, *Advancing Environmental Justice through Pollution Prevention* (Washington, DC: EPA, 2003).

CHAPTER 6: WARREN COUNTY REVISITED

Portions of the chapter are from "Identity Politics and Multiracial Coalitions in the Environmental Justice Movement" by Eileen McGurty from *"To Love the Wind and the Rain": African Americans and Environmental*

History, Dianne D. Glave and Mark Stoll, Eds., © 2005. Reprinted by permission of the University of Pittsburg Press.

1. Ken Ferruccio to Jonathan Howes, 17 May 1993, author's personal files.
2. Jonathan Howes to Ken Ferruccio, 21 May 1993, author's personal files.
3. Dorceta Taylor, "Can the Environmental Movement Attract and Maintain the Support of Minorities?" in *Race and the Incidence of Environmental Hazards: A Time for Discourse*, ed. Bunyan Bryant and Paul Mohai (Boulder, CO: Westview Press, 1992), 44.
4. Howes to Ferruccio, 21 May 1993.
5. John Humphrey, Statement on Status of PCB Landfill, March 1994, Warren County File, NC Solid Waste File Room, Raleigh, NC, 2.
6. "Hunt to Citizens of Warren County," *Warren Record*, 20 October 1982, 1, 14.
7. Dioxin-like compounds include polychlorinated dibenzo-*p*-dioxins (PCDDs or CDDs), polychlorinated dibenzofurans (PCDFs or CDFs), polybrominated dibenzo-*p*-dioxins (PBDDs or BDDs), polybrominated dibenzofurans (PBDFs or BDFs), and polychlorinated biphenyls (PCBs). These chemicals are all hydrophobic, resist metabolism, persist, and bioaccumulate in fatty tissues of animals and humans. Risk assessment of these chemicals is complicated by the fact that they are often found in mixtures. In order to address these complexities, the concept of toxic equivalency factor (TEF) was developed. TEFs compare the potential toxicity of each dioxin-like compound comprising the mixture to the well-studied and understood toxicity of the most toxic member of the group, 2,3,7,8-tetrachlorodibenzo-*p*-dioxin (TCDD). This one chemical, TCDD, is often simply referred to as dioxin. EPA, *Exposure and Human Health Reassessment of 2,3,7,8-Tetrachlorodibenzo-*p*-Dioxin (TCDD) and Related Compounds*, National Academy of Sciences (NAS) Review Draft, December 2003.
8. Jonathan Howes, Statement to Working Group, 20 January 1995, Warren County File, NC Solid Waste File Room, Raleigh, NC.
9. Sharon Rogers to Henry Lancaster, 27 January 1994, Warren County. Mike Kelly, interview by author, Raleigh, NC, 17 December 2002; Patricia Backus, interview by author, Raleigh, NC, 6 February 2003.

   According to the EPA, BCD is a "clean, inexpensive way to remediate liquids, sludge, soil and sediment contaminated with chlorinated organic compounds especially PCBs, pesticides, some herbicides and dioxins. In the BCD process contaminated soil is excavated and screened to remove debris and large particles, then crushed and mixed with sodium bicarbonate. . . . This mixture is heated in a reactor. The heat separates the halogenated compounds from the soil by evaporation. The soil left behind is removed from the reactor and can be returned to the site. The contaminated gasses, condensed into a liquid form, pass into a liquid-phase reactor. The dehalogenation reaction occurs when several chemicals including sodium hydroxide (a base) are mixed with the condensed contaminants and heated in the reactor. The resulting liquid mixture can be incinerated or treated by other technologies and recycled." EPA, *A Citizen's Guide to Chemical Dehalogenation*, April 1996, 2.
10. Eva Clayton to Jonathan Howes, 6 April 1995, Warren County File, NC Solid Waste File Room, Raleigh, NC.
11. Massenberg Kearney, interview by author, Afton, NC, 2 February 2003.
12. Joel Hirschhorn to Technical Committee of the Joint Working Group, 15 August 1996, Warren County File, NC Solid Waste File Room, Raleigh, NC.

13. Patrick A. Barnes and Joel Hirschhorn, *PCB Landfill Site Investigation Report*, BFA Associates, Tallahassee, FL, September 1997, E1. Warren County Citizen Advisory Board Files, Warrenton, NC, 2–9.
14. Ibid.
15. Ibid., 4–13.
16. Ibid.
17. Kelly, interview. "The BCD process utilized non-incineration chemical reactions to detoxify the PCBs and dioxins/furans in the contaminated materials. Chlorine atoms are chemically removed from the PCB and dioxin/furan molecules and replaced with hydrogen, rendering them non-hazardous. Detoxified soils will be replaced on-site, covered and revegetated." Michael Kelly, "Status of PCB Landfill Detoxification Warren County, NC," 26 May 1998, Warren County File, NC Solid Waste File Room, Raleigh, NC.
18. "Governor Requests $15 Million to Detoxify PCB Landfill," North Carolina Department of Environment and Natural Resources, 27 April 1998, Warren County File, NC Solid Waste File Room, Raleigh, NC.
19. Kelly, interview.
20. Laura Pulido, "Development of the 'People of Color' Identity in the Environmental Justice Movement of the Southwestern United States," *Socialist Review* 26, no. 3 (1996): 149.
21. Ken Ferruccio to Working Group members, 2 July 1997, Warren County File, NC Solid Waste File Room, Raleigh, NC.
22. Mike Kelly to Deborah and Ken Ferruccio, 5 February 1999, Warren County File, NC Solid Waste File Room, Raleigh, NC.
23. Ken Ferruccio to Wayne McDevitt, 15 June 1999, Warren County File, NC Solid Waste File Room, Raleigh, NC, 2–3.
24. Ibid., 3.
25. Jim Warren to Citizen Members and Science Advisors of the Working Group, 16 November 1996, Warren County File, NC Solid Waste File Room, Raleigh, NC.
26. Patrick Barnes to Dollie Burwell, 29 September 1995, PCB Citizen Advisory Board files, Warrenton, NC.
27. Ken Ferruccio to Dollie Burwell, 5 December 1995, Warren County File, NC Solid Waste File Room, Raleigh, NC.
28. Ken Ferruccio to Working Group, 26 December 1995, Warren County File, NC Solid Waste File Room, Raleigh, NC.
29. Warren to Citizen Members.
30. Kelly, interview.
31. Backus, interview.
32. Deborah Ferruccio, interview by author, Afton, NC, 6 February 2003.
33. Dollie Burwell and Henry Lancaster to Joel Hirschhorn, 25 March 1998, Warren County File, NC Solid Waste File Room, Raleigh, NC.
34. "Job Training Updates," *Community News Wire* 1 (August 2002): 3.
35. Joel Hirschhorn to PCB Working Group, 6 February 1997, Warren County File, NC Solid Waste File Room, Raleigh, NC.
36. Jim Warren, interview by author, Durham, NC, 3 February 2003.

CHAPTER 7: EPILOGUE

1. Beck's risk society thesis argues that class position is no longer central to understanding modernity because risk position has become the primary issue. Beck is remiss in his neglect of examining additional social locations,

including race, ethnicity, and gender. Ulrich Beck, *Risk Society: Toward a New Modernity* (Thousand Oaks, CA: Sage, 1992).

2. Center on Race, Poverty, & the Environment, California Rural Legal Assistance Foundation, "Comments on *Draft Revised Guidance for Investigating Title VI Administrative Complaints Challenging Permits* and *Draft Title VI Guidance for EPA Assistance Recipients Administering Environmental Permitting Programs*," 26 August 2000, 8, http://www.epa.gov/civilrights/docs/t6com2000_071.pdf.

3. Melanie Eversely, "Mayors Back Archer Stand on EPA Rules," *Detroit Free Press*, 23 June 1998, 5A.

4. Jennifer Dixon, "EPA Chief Hears Minority Concerns," *Detroit Free Press*, 18 July 1998, 3A.

5. *Time*, 3 August 1970, 42. http://www.sierraclub.org/environmental_justice/stories/northcarolina.asp

Index

About the Author

Eileen McGurty's work is at the nexus of inequality and environmental concerns. Her scholarship and practice center on ameliorating environmental problems in concert with the alleviation of poverty and oppression. She is currently associate chair of the graduate program in environmental sciences and policy at Johns Hopkins University and has previously taught urban planning and environmental studies at the University of Iowa and Long Island University. McGurty received a doctorate degree in urban and regional planning from the University of Illinois at Urbana-Champaign.

DATE DUE